AMERICAN INDIAN ENVIRONMENTS

▶▶▶▶▶▶▶▶▶▶ ◀◀◀◀◀◀◀◀◀◀◀

With contributions from
Kai T. Erikson
William T. Hagan
Laurence M. Hauptman
Wilbur R. Jacobs
Oren Lyons
Peter MacDonald
Calvin Martin

▶▶▶▶▶▶▶▶▶ ◀◀◀◀◀◀◀◀◀

AMERICAN INDIAN ENVIRONMENTS

Ecological Issues in Native American History

Edited by

Christopher Vecsey
and
Robert W. Venables

SYRACUSE UNIVERSITY PRESS
1980

Chapter 2 is reprinted from *Old Trails and New Directions: Papers of the Third North American Fur Trade Conference*, edited by Carol M. Judd and Arthur J. Ray, by permission of University of Toronto Press. © University of Toronto Press 1980.

Chapter 3 is © 1978 by The Pacific Coast Branch, American Historical Association. Revised from *Pacific Historical Review*, Volume XLVII, No. 1, (February 1978), pp. 1–26, by permission of the Branch.

Library of Congress Cataloging in Publication Data

Main entry under title:

American Indian environments.

    Includes bibliographical references and index.
    1. Indians of North America—Land tenure—Addresses, essays, lectures.   2. Human ecology—North America—Addresses, essays, lectures.   I. Erikson, Kai T.
II. Vecsey, Christopher T.   III. Venables, Robert W.
E98.L3A46   304.2'097   80-26458
ISBN 0-8156-2226-0
ISBN 0-8156-2227-9 (pbk.)

Manufactured in the United States of America

▶▶▶▶▶▶▶▶▶ ◀◀◀◀◀◀◀◀◀

CONTENTS

ILLUSTRATIONS

▶▶▶▶▶▶▶▶▶▶ ◀◀◀◀◀◀◀◀◀◀

CONTRIBUTORS

KAI T. ERIKSON is Professor of Sociology and American Studies at Yale University.

WILLIAM T. HAGAN is Distinguished Professor of History at the State University of New York at Fredonia.

LAURENCE M. HAUPTMAN is Associate Professor of History at the State University of New York at New Paltz.

WILBUR R. JACOBS is Professor of History at the University of California, Santa Barbara.

OREN LYONS is a chief of the Onondaga Nation, an artist, and Visiting Professor at the State University of New York at Buffalo.

PETER MACDONALD is the chairman of the Navajo Tribal Council of the Navajo Nation.

CALVIN MARTIN is Associate Professor of History at Rutgers University.

CHRISTOPHER VECSEY is Assistant Professor of History at Hobart and William Smith Colleges.

ROBERT W. VENABLES is Curator of American Indian History at the Museum of the American Indian in New York City.

▶▶▶▶▶▶▶▶▶▶ ◀◀◀◀◀◀◀◀◀◀

INTRODUCTION

CHRISTOPHER VECSEY and ROBERT W. VENABLES

N APRIL 1979, HOBART AND WILLIAM SMITH COLLEGES sponsored a two-day symposium, "American Indian Environments," in Geneva, New York, organized by Christopher Vecsey and Robert W. Venables. Indians and non-Indians convened before a large audience of students and scholars to discuss the historical and contemporary relations between native Americans and the natural world. Most of the chapters in this book derive from that symposium, although three of them were written for a panel, "Native Americans as Refugees," at the October 1979 Duquesne University History Forum in Pittsburgh.

The "environments" referred to in the title of this book are the nonhuman surroundings commonly called "nature," or more technically, "ecosystems," the inhabitable biosphere of earth, air, and water upon which all humans depend for survival. The chapters describe and analyze Indian relationships with these environments. The book examines Indians' attitudes toward their world, their subsistence upon it, and their struggles with non-Indians over possession and use of it.

In the Indians' sacred circle of creation, everything — even a stone — is equally alive and equally integrated into a balance of life. How different this perception is from that of non-Indians was demonstrated by an otherwise sensitive radio news broadcast in June 1979 over American National Public Radio. After describing the worst forest fire to sweep through an area of Ontario in eighteen years, the white reporter concluded that, fortunately, there was "no loss of life." Thousands of acres of soil, trees, and other life forms lay scorched, but the reporter and probably most of the non-Indians who made up the audience assumed that the word "life" by itself, with no qualifying term such as "animal," meant only human life, other life forms being inferior. No such separation and stratification of life forms exist in the sacred circle of the Indians' environments. The Indians' circle of life comes back upon itself, and thus any loss of life along the circle diminishes the whole. For non-Indians the straight line that is defined as progress has yet to reincorporate the unity of creation's circle perceived by many of their own ancient and medieval ancestors.

The American Indians' concept of the sacred circle expresses a physical and spiritual unity. This circle of life is interpreted according to the particular beliefs of each Indian nation but is broadly symbolic of an encompassing creation. The English verb "environ" has as its first definition in the Oxford English Dictionary: "Of things: To form a ring around, surround, encircle." While non-Indians quite willingly admit to the complexity of the circle of "things" around them, what has been left behind by the scientific, post-Renaissance non-Indian world is the universal sacredness—the living mystery—of creation's circle. One of the themes of this book is the consequence of a conflict during which most indigenous Indian nations, who saw their environments as the sacred interdependence of the Creator's will, confronted waves of post-Renaissance Europeans who saw in the environment a natural resource ordained by God for their sole benefit.

This book does not pretend to be definitive or all inclusive, but it does aim to survey the scope of Indian natural history since white contact. It focuses primarily on contrasting Indian and white attitudes toward nature, subsistence techniques, and land-based sovereignty; white removal of Indians from their land bases; and the effects of white ecological practices on the Indian population as well as on the American landscape itself. The chapters attempt to cover a broad range of time — from first contact to contemporary — and space — from the Northeast to the Southwest—as well as a broad range of specific issues and points of view.

ARCHANGEL WITH MUSKET, anonymous Indian artist, Alto Peru, early eighteenth century. Although the authors of this book deal primarily with the Indians living north of Mexico, certain themes would be as accurately applied south of the Rio Grande as north. This is strikingly demonstrated in this painting. No similar image of an archangel appears in Europe. Indeed, "paintings of angels bearing arms appear to be unique to Alto Peru," writes art historian Pal Kelemen. This painting is a dramatic synthesis from the perceptive mind of an Indian who observed the similarly clad bodyguards of the Spanish viceroy and fully understood what had brought about his people's conquest and their environment's exploitation: Christianity intent on obtaining worldly riches, armed with musket, sword, and dagger. *New Orleans Museum of Art, New Orleans, Louisiana; photograph by Robert W. Venables*

Despite the authors' multidisciplinary interests and sources, the chapters are primarily works of history. They employ ethnology, economics, law, geography, and religious studies, but all in an attempt to place in historical context the changing American Indian environmental experiences over the last five centuries. The era since white contact has been one of radical ecological alteration in North America, during which the crucial issue in Indian-white relations has been the struggle over land and natural resources. The change and the struggle continue today, and they remain relevant both to Indians and non-Indians. A large non-Indian majority now shares the Indians' environments in North America. All peoples have a responsibility to care for this vast continent. Otherwise, North America's sacred circle of life could evolve into a vicious cycle of environmental collapse.

Underlying all of these articles is the assumption that relations between Indians and the nonhuman environment, the natural world, must be considered basic to an understanding of traditional Indian life as well as the history of Indian-white contacts. The book grounds American Indian history in its material base, reminding the reader that history "takes *place.*" It exists in an environment that affects — and often effects—human events. The fundamental concerns of any people center on their ability for subsistence through interaction with the natural world, the source of existence. In this sense the book can be said to be a "materialist" history.

That is not to say that the book claims environmental determinism. To the contrary, it points out the large degree to which whites and Indians have altered the face of North America. Although the emphasis of this book might seem at first glance to be materialist, many of the chapters could more precisely be called examples of intellectual history or the history of ideas. The authors are as concerned with Indian ideas about the world, white ideas about Indian land use, and contrasting ideas about sovereignty as they are about subsistence techniques. A balance is struck between materialist and philosophical approaches to demonstrate the fullness of American Indian environmental questions.

When Europeans arrived in the Western Hemisphere, they did not find an empty continent, a virgin land, an untouched landscape. North America was already home to millions of Native Americans — some scholars say as many as twelve million north of Mexico alone — whose ancestors had arrived in the hemisphere as long as fifty thousand years ago.

In 1500 what was the Indians' influence on the environment? When whites first saw the Eastern Woodlands or the California coast near San Francisco Bay, they found numerous parklands created by

Indian burning techniques. These were not forests primeval, but rather habitats arranged by humans for the benefit of animals necessary for human subsistence — animals such as deer who foraged at the parkland peripheries. In climates which permitted horticulture whites discovered vast fields of crops: corn, beans, squash, and many other food products.

When Europeans entered the continent, Indians had already had tens of thousands of years of experience living in the North American environments. A brief account of this precontact natural history helps to place the postcontact period in perspective.

From earliest times Indians had used fire, stone tools, and other implements in order to survive and to enjoy the world. Until approximately eight thousand years ago, Indian hunters relied primarily on the killing of large animals such as mammoth, musk-ox, and long-horned bison. They used sharp-edged chert blades attached to spears, propelled with the help of atlatls. These Lithic or stone-age hunters left little trace of themselves on the terrain and apparently had minimal settlement structures. They hunted and supplemented their diet with wild vegetal matter, until the extinction of the large animals in the post-Pleistocene climate.

From this point Indians turned to a more diverse subsistence pattern referred to as Archaic efficiency. Indians adapted their stone tools to an environment which was much like our own in temperature, rainfall, and vegetation. During the Archaic period, from approximately eight thousand years ago, and up until the early nineteenth century in some parts of the continent, Indians depended upon nuts, berries, roots, and other vegetation, as well as shellfish, fish, and small game animals for their food. Archaic Indians traveled in set patterns, moving from place to place to take advantage of food sources available seasonally. They developed utensils associated with vegetal food production: manos and other milling stones necessary to prepare nuts and seeds for eating. These Indians worked with axes, adzes, gouges, and for the first time used bows and arrows. At the same time they domesticated dogs and encouraged the growth of certain edible wild plants, cultivars, by removing weeds to provide light and nutrition, and by aerating the soil with digging sticks. Because of their familiarity with cultivars—those wild plants which prosper with human aid—Indians in the warmer climes of North American began to develop cultigens—domesticated crops that require human aid in order to reproduce and grow. Under the influence of the Mexican cultures as early as fifty-five hundred years ago, American Indians in the Southwest — and then later in the Southeast—gained agricultural knowledge.

Not all North Americans entered the Formative, agricultural

Monuments on the Land, Past and Present

Past. By A.D. 1200, Cahokia was a city and religious center of some 30,000 people. Within a few centuries, it declined for reasons yet unknown. Located east across the Mississippi from St. Louis in southern Illinois, the Cahokia site today is the largest Indian archeological site north of Central Mexico. Its complex of more than one hundred religious ceremonial structures or mounds was surrounded by a log palisade, and its people traded across America. At the

stage of subsistence development. Indeed, at the time of white contact large areas of North America, particularly the Plains, Plateau, Northwest, and throughout Canada were still Archaic in almost all respects and practiced minimal or no horticulture. However, in the southern areas of the continent the fundamental shift to farming was accomplished, supporting a way of life that has continued down to the present in some areas. Sedentary villages, which had already existed in some areas during the Archaic period, became further formalized and widespread during the Formative period. Irrigation, especially in the arid Southwest, became a sophisticated process. In fact, agriculture on a large scale lay the groundwork for the growth of cities in the South-

center of this magnificent human accomplishment was—and is—a four-terrace mound more than one hundred feet high and covering fifteen acres of land. Cahokia is a stunning symbol of a series of cultures broadly called the Mound Builders whose ideas reached from the Mississippi River Valley east to the Atlantic, west into Oklahoma and Texas, and northwest into the Missouri River Valley. Across these landscapes, the mounds they built in varying sizes are constant reminders of the devotion by ancient Indian peoples to their spiritual values. *Photographs by Robert W. Venables*

east and the Southwest — urban areas with populations as large as thirty thousand, as Cahokia was in southern Illinois around A.D. 1200.

During the Formative period, Indians developed 155 species of domesticated plants used for food, tools, clothing, medicine, and other uses, but they did not domesticate large numbers of animals. Only the dog, and in some places the turkey, found a place in Indian villages. Indians possessed no draft animals, no plows, and no use of wheels in subsistence technology. Instead, hunting continued to be an important, if only secondary, means of subsistence. Animals were utilized efficiently; Indians made extensive use of each animal killed for food, clothing, tools, and shelter. Even before the development of farming,

Present. Contemporary American culture leaves behind mounds of another kind. These are the mounds of waste, not just of basic garbage but of the leftovers from industry and resource retrieval enterprises such as coal mining. These are mounds raised for profit, not piety, and they are everywhere. Examples of these new mounds lie just north of Miami, Oklahoma: the chatpiles of abandoned zinc mines. In the photograph at left they haunt the horizon along with another powerful symbol of the non-Indians' intrusion into this environment. Governments have promised clean-ups for decades, but the chatpiles remain. The photograph at right illustrates how one town has built its baseball diamond in the midst of this rubble. Although zinc pollution from the

vegetal products constituted the bulk of Indian food, even for people who are usually referred to as "hunting" people. Perhaps because of male bias in research, men's hunting activities have been overestimated in descriptions of Indian life, to the detriment of the women's contributions. It seems apparent that women's occupations — gathering and horticulture — were the mainstay of Indian subsistence throughout the Archaic period, and perhaps in the prior Lithic era, too.

At first contact with whites in 1500, Indians employed a variety

spent mines and chatpiles is already troubling some Oklahoma water authorities, the people who live among the chatpiles continue to play ball, for they have become used to the distortions around them.

There is an irony in the chatpile baseball diamond, for certain types of ball-playing were and remain traditional religious ceremonies among Indian people. Remnants of past ball games abound in the ball courts of the Southwest and are reflected in the artifacts found elsewhere in North America. Perhaps one day in the far future an archeologist will conduct a comparative study of North American ball games, mounds, value systems, and lost civilizations. *Photographs by Robert W. Venables*

of subsistence methods depending upon the possibilities offered by the local ecosystems. Pueblo farmers practiced intensive agriculture in an arid environment. Semimigratory Plains Indians hunted buffalo herds, while relying heavily on wild and some grown crops. In the Eastern Woodlands, Indians relied on farming, hunting, fishing, and gathering. In the Great Basin and Plateau regions where game was often scarce, Indians depended largely on gathered foods — nuts, berries, roots, and other vegetation — for their existence. California

Indians enjoyed a bountiful harvest of diverse food products, depending most heavily on nuts. In the Northwest Coast salmon provided the mainstay of the diet, supplemented by other flesh and fowl and wild plants. The Subarctic and Arctic areas offered little possibility for the cultivation of crops. The Eskimo represented an extreme form of subsistence, since they had practically no vegetal matter to eat at any time of the year, and their food supply derived almost totally from sea mammals, caribou, and fish.

In all these situations Indians had fitted themselves to their environmental areas, learning to adapt their culture to their local resources in order to provide themselves with life. Whether we wish to view the precontact Indians in terms of their culture areas—based on flora, fauna, climate, and terrain—or whether we wish to consider the continuities of Indian culture based on a continent with relatively few natural barriers to trade, diffusion, and transhumance, we must keep this in mind: Indians depended directly upon their environments as the sources of their life. From Pueblo farmer to Eskimo hunter, Native Americans practiced direct, participatory subsistence relations with their environments, even where extensive trade augmented their store of goods.

This brief survey of precontact environmental relations sets the stage for the subject of this book. After 1492 these environments were jarred by attempts of colonizing Europeans to ignore, to adapt, or to overwhelm them.

The first two chapters analyze the connections between material life and the life of the mind among traditional American Indians, both positing a type of subsistence spirituality as the Indian world view. Christopher Vecsey's "American Indian Environmental Religions" shows that Indian relations with the natural world, although empirical and pragmatic, transcended material considerations while remaining grounded in them. In both criticizing and affirming the image of Indians as conservationists, Vecsey makes the claim that environmental concerns constitute a foremost dimension of American Indian religions, regardless of specific ecosystem.

Vecsey draws conclusions applicable to most traditional Indians. Calvin Martin's "Subarctic Indians and Wildlife" reaches similar conclusions regarding Algonkian and Athabascan Indians of Canada, that they have perceived animals as thinking persons who behave in ways similar to humans and who enter social relations with humans. The point of contact between human and nonhuman persons is the spirituality inherent in each; humans and animals are essentially related because they share the same essence. As a result, hunting and trapping are activities supercharged with symbol and emotion. Both

authors ask the reader to keep in mind the Indians' view of the world—
a place of powerful, nonhuman persons—in order to understand more
accurately the Indian role in the fur trade and the effect of environmental change on Indian lifeways. These ideas lay the groundwork for the
chapters that follow.

Just as nature relations were crucial to understanding precontact Indian material life and history, environmental conflict has been
the central feature of Indian-white relations. Other issues over the past
five hundred years have been important, of course. However, when
we speak of the basic motif of postcontact history, it has been the
disruption and displacement of Indians from the land on which they
had lived for millennia.

To understand the whites' motivation for their actions, we
need to assess their attitudes toward the natural world as well as
toward Indians. Vecsey treats these questions in the second part of his
chapter. Wilbur R. Jacobs takes the discussion a step further in "Indians as Ecologists and Other Environmental Themes in American
Frontier History," by formulating a critique not only of white nature
concepts, but also of white nature exploitation. He refers to the white
practices of land use as "the great despoliation" and argues that white
utilization of natural resources has been characterized by its rapacity,
wastefulness, and shortsightedness. He contrasts this to the relatively
benign effects of precontact Indians on their ecosystems. He states that
even though they might not have been acting out of consciously
conservationist impulses, Indians have tended when on their own to
disrupt the environment far less than have whites.

Whites have done more than destroy Indian ecosystems. Even
more forcefully, they have dispossessed Indians, coercing them from
their tribal homelands. This process continues to this day. The quest for
energy resources, timber, and water has impelled non-Indians once
again to enter Indian lands, just as in the past non-Indians intruded on
Indian lands to seek minerals, grazing lands, or farm lands. Unlike the
past, current intrusions onto Indian lands usually leave the Indians on
the lands—the dispossession takes the form of stripping the Indians
involved of the natural resources on their land, paying them far less in
royalties than would be paid to non-Indian occupants, and then leaving the Indians with a scarred land. However, actual dispossession of
lands also continues. In 1934 the Indian land base was 2.6 percent of all
the United States lands south of Canada: 51 million acres. During the
next forty years, that land base was decreased by 1,811,010 acres,
including 488,226 acres for dams, reservoirs, and other water projects.

In "Justifying Dispossession of the Indian: The Land Utilization Argument," William T. Hagan demonstrates centuries of white

contempt for Indian land tenure. If the previous chapter by Jacobs is correct in its assessment that whites despoiled the land, there is a special irony in Hagan's observations that whites justified Indian dispossession on the grounds that Indians were not making efficient use of their lands. Since whites and Indians have differing ideas about the proper use of land, whites have perceived those differences as justifications for appropriations, and as Hagan points out, this rationale will very possibly result in future dispossessions and appropriations of Indian lands and resources. Thus the history of this issue bears directly on contemporary events.

While some reservations today are large — the Navajo nation occupies more than 24,000 square miles—most are small. Of more than 400 reservations, 2 out of 3 are smaller than the 27,000 acres of Florida's Walt Disney World. On the remnants of their once vast homelands, Indians today have a major task in maintaining rights over those remnants. Mineral and oil rights, water rights, religious and educational freedoms, and political self-determination—among many issues—center upon the Indians' abilities to control their land. This control in turn revolves around the issue of sovereignty. Sovereignty is the premise upon which today's American Indian environments are defined, maintained, or altered. Whether sovereignty rests with non-Indian authorities or with the Indians is therefore a major issue. Using the Iroquois as an example, Robert W. Venables discusses the historical background of sovereignty in "Iroquois Environments and 'We the People of the United States.'" He notes the philosophical and legal viewpoints in the clash of counterclaims by non-Indians and Indians.

The centuries of Indian dispossession have time and again created populations of displaced Native Americans who perhaps can best be described as refugees — persons alienated from their homelands under duress from outside forces. Refugee status has been the lot of almost every Indian group during the history of Indian-white contacts. Laurence M. Hauptman and Robert W. Venables describe the plight of various uprooted Indians in or from upstate New York within a refugee context. Hauptman's "Refugee Havens: The Iroquois Villages of the Eighteenth Century" describes how Indians who sought refuge within the Iroquois Confederacy and received the confederacy's political protection nevertheless suffered from starvation, disease, and extreme social disequilibrium caused by their disorientation in new surroundings. The old locales were minutely familiar, but moving to new, unfamiliar lands erased all this cultural information. For people who have lived in direct relation with their environment, whose skills are attuned to a specific location and are not transferable the way industrial skills are, such a relocation is devastating. Thus Hauptman suggests that unfamiliarity itself helped create a severe crisis of survival.

Both Hauptman and Venables stress that Indian people are not alone in the powerful intertwining of their national identity and their physical and spiritual environments. Nor are they alone as people who have lost some of that identity as a consequence of foreign domination — present generations of Irish, Cambodians, Poles, Jews, Basques, Bantus, and Palestinians are testimony to that. An understanding of the environmental sources of national and spiritual identity among Indian peoples — and how non-Indians have attempted to disrupt or destroy that identity — helps define similar world issues of nationalism and sovereignty. Venables' "Victim Versus Victim: The Irony of the New York Indians' Removal to Wisconsin" examines a complicated and often tragic aspect of refugee history: the refugees have to compete against local inhabitants for resources. He shows how the creation of refugee lands in Wisconsin caused one Indian-victim to exploit another Indian-victim. This is a situation seen more recently in the case of the Navajo and the Hopi in Arizona, where the two nations' claims to some of the same lands has led to both political and violent clashes.

In "A Report to the People of Grassy Narrows" Kai T. Erikson and Christopher Vecsey show how dispossession continues today. In describing a small community of Ojibwa in southwestern Ontario in 1979, the authors demonstrate the toxic effects of white technology on Indians. Not only do paper mills usurp Indian hunting territories, they also dump killing chemicals into Indian waters, ruining Indian subsistence and destroying Indian community life. Ironically, white culture identifies itself as superior to the Indians in part by virtue of its literacy, even as the demands of this literate public have served to devastate the Grassy Narrows Ojibwa through the effluence of a paper mill.

Erikson and Vecsey also show that the struggle between Indians and whites has not been confined to the United States. In Canada as well as the United States, Indians have been turned into refugees, alienated from their homes, confined on land bases which cannot support them, controlled by white-operated bureaucracies, and poisoned by white technology. Indian societies, already weakened by centuries of disruption, bullying, and persecution, can ill afford the impact of such poisonings as the one at Grassy Narrows, where the entire fish population upon which the Indians depend has been tainted by mercury.

The refugee model provides insight into the uprooting of Indians by centuries of white expansion. The reservations which Indians live on today are refuges for displaced Indians, with the irony that the displacer and paternalistic protector are one and the same: the white government, either in Canada or the United States. The reservations today are often unfit for subsistence, but Indians are determined to hold onto them because they are the only refuges left.

Having alienated Indians from their source of sufficiency, white society has sought to benefit doubly from the alienation. Since World War II, the United States and Canada have encouraged—some would say coerced—Indians to leave their refuges-reservations and enter cities as wage laborers. The Navajo nation today is, proportionate to its population of 160,000, the largest labor-exporting area in the continent. The Navajo and other Indians often serve in menial jobs. They lose their skills of self-sufficient subsistence in conjunction with white education while their lands are ravaged for minerals and other resources by white technology. Furthermore, Indians enter the white cash economy and spend money on needs created by an alien culture. The profits return to the white capitalist cycle. The result has been increased alienation from nature and community, and a weakened sense of sovereignty.

Urban relocation represents the latest, possibly the last, step in the historical progression of the Indians' alienation from their natural environments. Of approximately one million Indians (including mixed bloods) in the United States today, far more than half now live in urban areas. Twenty-five percent live in the Northeast, and more than 50 percent live outside the western states, according to the American Indian Policy Review Commission's 1977 report. Indians have watched their traditional ecologies and economies undermined and over-thrown. Now in the twentieth century they have been thrust into a totally new and often hostile environment in the modern industrial city. Many of these urban refuges have sought city life as an alternative to economic poverty on their reservations, while others have been moved there as part of official government programs. The economic poverty these Indians seek to escape often continues in a new form. The Indians' cultural poverty is even more devastating because the urban refugees find no refuge in a non-Indian city. Thus the long-term results of this latest removal into the "concrete prairies" could be irreparably disastrous.

Equally disastrous could be the results of recent white exploitation of energy resources on Indian reservations. It is this issue which most concerns Peter MacDonald, the Navajo Tribal Chairman, in "Navajo Natural Resources." MacDonald's hope is that Navajos and other Indian nations can lease the rights to certain natural resources, while controlling both the amount and manner of exploitation. He explains the contemporary dilemma of synthesizing practical reality with idealism. In the Navajo context this includes spiritual components which must be preserved as well as resources such as coal and uranium which non-Indians want. MacDonald's hope is that the controlled sale of these resources will bring some degree of economic stability and security to his impoverished people. The additional dilemma is that the Navajo and other Indian nations can hardly resist white demands for resources when the legal framework established by unequal treaties and unilateral laws establishes the secretary of the interior as the ultimate decision-maker on the reservation. If the Navajo and other Indians wish to control their natural resources — either in order to use them, preserve them, or make a profit from them — they must compromise in order to accommodate the Bureau of Indian Affairs which holds sway over them. This avoids bringing on the legal, economic, and possibly military wrath of the white government. As MacDonald says, the United States was willing in the past, including the recent past, to use force in order to wrest valuable land or resources from the Indians. If Indians appear too resistant to their federal overseers, withholding resources which whites crave and claim to need to support their consuming lifeways, the United States could revert to its historic use of force. Therefore, MacDonald recommends a firm, but accommodating position of bargaining in which Indians agree to supply whites with resources when they can, but at a fair price, and with guarantees of respect for the Indians' environmental concerns.

There are other issues in addition to energy resources in the Indians' struggles to secure legal rights to their traditional resources: game, fish, water, and other environmental sources of life. In the past two decades this problem has created bitter and often violent confrontations, amply described in the Indian and white media. In the Pacific Northwest and elsewhere Indians have fought — with weapons and subpoenas — for their rights to harvest salmon and other fish which were their foods in precontact days, and which were guaranteed to them in land cession treaties with the United States and Canada. Indians have initiated lawsuits to secure once again the rights of Indians to hunt, fish, and harvest their foods in order to subsist and even to prosper. The outcome of these lawsuits will do much to determine the future of Indian peoples. Without these rights Indian local economies may wither and die.

These current problems call for historical perspectives, perspectives such as those presented in this book. Each Indian nation's political, social, and spiritual concepts were and remain interdependent with a specific geographic area, not just a general love of all nature. If that specific land base is altered by non-Indians, or if the Indians themselves are removed from that specific place, the entire fabric of Indian culture is destroyed.

One who both understands and feels this with intensity is

Onondaga Iroquois Chief Oren Lyons. In "An Iroquois Perspective" Lyons shares with the reader the Onondagas' will to protect both their homeland and sovereignty. Lyons criticizes the white worldview and economy which have served to oppress Indians. He sees the preservation of the Iroquois environment as an integration of culture and land dependent upon the Iroquois' ability to assert sovereignty.

Whether the plans which MacDonald or Lyons offer can successfully maintain Indian ecosystems and sovereignty remains to be seen. Each plan is fraught with emotion and danger. And both indicate clearly to what degree Indian environments and the traditions which subsist on the environments are under siege today as a direct result of the way whites choose to live, the standards of material life which whites demand for themselves. The white American way of life threatens Indian existence, directly and indirectly, consciously and unconsciously, in the past and in the present.

To some degree Indians can protect themselves by maintaining their refuges-reservations. In this effort there are many strategies to choose from—that of Peter MacDonald and that of Oren Lyons being only two of the most articulate. Essentially the efforts, whatever course they may take, will involve maintaining and enforcing treaty rights vigorously. Indians must hold relative control over their reservation conditions. Even if Indians leave their reservations — as many must since their land base is too damaged and small to support the resident Indian population—the refuges must remain there for them to return to either periodically or permanently. The Mohawks in New York City and the Micmacs in Boston have survived in their urban environments, for example, primarily because regular visits to their reservations have reinforced their Indian identities. The reservation as refuge is always there to nurture and preserve Indian ways. After five hundred years the same premise holds true: Indians depend directly upon their land base for survival as Indians. It is still their source of life.

All of the authors point out the tragedy in the destruction of Indian traditions, past or present. Today some non-Indians—perhaps many — are beginning to recognize the value of Indian ecological perspectives for the future of the white economy and of the continent itself. Whites, blacks, orientals, and previously assimilative Indians who have listened to Indians who follow one of the many Indian traditional ways of life are impressed by the prophetic, critical message which these traditional Indians have regarding the treatment of the environment.

As outsiders looking into non-Indian cultural values, traditional Indians have the perspective of being able to criticize in a truly radical way. Their critiques of the manufacture of energy by the non-

Indians probe to the roots of the ecological issues that concerns most people today. The idea that nonhuman life forms have worth and deserve ethical considerations in their own rights challenge white conceptions. Whether or not non-Indians can accept the Indian viewpoint and learn from it, at least they can see the untenable results of their own disregard for the environment. Possibly non-Indians may even alter their own lifeways and policies because of the influence of Indian ideas, as well as the realization of the destruction their present actions bring to others not within the white cultural system.

In April 1979, when the "American Indian Environments" symposium convened, it was fitting that Leon Shenandoah, the Onondaga Iroquois who is the present "Tadodaho" of the Six Nations Iroquois Confederacy, convene the meeting with a prayer and brief address. Because the symposium met in the historic environment of the confederacy, it seemed appropriate to evoke the spiritual and political unity of the confederacy, symbolized by Tadodaho.

After his prayer, delivered in the Onondaga language, Chief Shenandoah translated and then commented on those aspects of creation for which he had expressed thanks: "mother earth," plants, trees, animals, birds, and other forms of life. "We also have the thunder which purifies the earth and washes the earth, so, therefore we must thank the Creator that we get a storm that brings the water to wash the earth." He emphasized that human beings must "thank the Creator all as one mind." Shenandoah expressed his belief that traditional Iroquois had a duty to continue to pray to the Creator to assure the perpetuation of all beings and parts of nature and to lessen the consequences of the world's current pollution. He added, "You will probably know if we fail."

AMERICAN INDIAN ENVIRONMENTS

**MAJOR INDIAN NATIONS
AND LOCATIONS
DISCUSSED IN THE TEXT**

Prepared by Robert W. Venables

Note: Hundreds of Indian nations, many of which
thrive today, are not indicated because they are not
specifically subjects in the text.

Arctic

Subarctic

Arctic

Subarctic

Arctic

Subarctic

Northwest Coast

Nez Perces

Crows

Crees

Crees

Subarctic

Arctic

Grassy Narrows Ojibwas

Lakotas (Sioux)

Black Hills

Green
Bay

Montagnais
Naskapi

Subarctic

Iroquois
Confederacy

Homelands
of
Cherokees
and Creeks

Kiowas

Kiowa-
Apaches

Eastern
Refugee
Nations
(Okla.)

Comanches

Navajos

Hopis

Zunis

Pueblos

Apaches

Aztecs

Mayas

Columbus'
Landing 1492
(San Salvador)

AMERICAN INDIAN ENVIRONMENTAL RELIGIONS

CHRISTOPHER VECSEY

> In my first contacts with Black Elk, almost all he said was phrased in terms involving animals and natural phenomena. I naively wished that he would begin to talk about religious matters, until I finally realized that he was, in fact, explaining his religion.[1]

MERICAN INDIAN ENVIRONMENTAL RELIGIONS" is concerned with both the environmental dimensions of American Indian religions, and the religious dimensions of American Indian environmental relations. Contrasting white American views of nature to those of the Indians helps establish a conceptual context for Indian-white environmental conflicts in history.

Although this chapter title acknowledges the diversity of North American Indian traditions, there is a common ground of those various tribal religions. Each generalization here is also accompanied by a specific tribal example, many of which come from the Ojibwa Indians, with whom I am most familiar.

Indian religions have both changed and persisted over the last five hundred years, as have the religions of the whites. This chapter deals with traditional, or aboriginal, American Indian environmental religions.

"Environment," as used here, refers to the nonhuman world. For the individual person, human society is environment, too, as well as climate, soil, terrain, culture, neighbors, enemies, gods, clouds, animals, and plants.[2] We are concerned here, however, with the world beyond the category of "human." American Indian classification systems differ, one from another, but all recognize a category of "human." I am speaking of matters beyond that category.

Finally, every definition of "religion" is bound to fall short, but in this chapter "religion" is the conception of, attitudes toward, and relations with the ultimate source of life.[3] This definition includes world view (conceptions or doctrines), emotion (attitudes or piety), and actions (relations or praxis). It also refers to the conceptions,

1

attitudes, and relations held by Indian individuals and shared by Indian groups.

The environmentalism of American Indian religions is not a new idea; indeed, it was first reported by the earliest white observers of Indians, and it reached its culmination as a systematic theory during the late nineteenth century. In 1871 Edward Burnett Tylor published his ideas about primitive animism, in which Indian and other tribal religions were said to be firmly rooted in their relations to nature. Tylor noted that Indians regarded the environment as living, consisting of persons who greatly determine human lives, and who could be appealed to in times of need. Tylor called such a construct "animism," because to him Indians were conceptually instilling life into a universe that was essentially inanimate. He found such conceptions and relations based on them "pitiable" and expected that they would fade away with evolutionary progress.[4]

It was Tylor's theories — with their fashionable, and then unfashionable, evolutionary biases—that faded in the twentieth century. So did the theories of his contemporaries Andrew Lang, who found North American Indian religion an institution to worship "unanimate" objects, animals, and plants; Sir James Frazer, whose *Golden Bough* posited a worldwide system of myth and religion based on nature relations; and Hartley Burr Alexander, who most thoroughly applied Tylor's ideas regarding animism to American Indians. These men's views regarding the connections between religion and ecology were reductionist and condescending; their theories and the deterministic anthropological assumptions of the turn of the century[5] saw environmental relations as the overbearing cause of all aspects of culture, including religion. These sentiments deservedly fell from public and scholarly favor; nevertheless, they all recognized the important environmental dimension in American Indian religions.[6]

I wish to examine the integration between environmental relations and religion among American Indians. I believe that they are integrated profoundly, so profoundly that I agree with ethnohistorian Harold Hickerson when he calls Indian religious expressions "the religion of nature."[7] A missionary who spent many years among the Dakota and Ojibwa once remarked that Indians worship nature; their altar and diety is the world around them.[8] And Leon Shenandoah, the Tadodaho of the Six Nations of Iroquois states emphatically: "Nature: that's our religion, our way of life." I do not wish to deny the social, psychological, historical, and purely religious dimensions of Indian religions, but I am emphasizing perhaps the most important dimension, nature.

In the following discussion I try to incorporate insights from a number of disciplines, including comparative religion, anthropology, ecology, and history. Members of each discipline tend to look at different types of sources and to frame their questions differently. Ecologists examine the day-to-day, pragmatic interrelations between humans and their ecosystems. A student of comparative religion is more likely to look at the ideal human views of nature (or geosophy), as found in myths, prayers, ceremonials, and other religious phenomena. Anthropologists attempt to understand the cultural bases of religious and environmental relations. I include ecological, religious, and anthropological data here, although the latter two predominate. I mean to use them, however, as a prologue to history, that is, to see where American Indian environmental religions influence Indian-white history. This can be useful because historians of Indian-white contacts have rarely attempted to understand Indian religions. Neither have students of Indian religions attempted to understand their historical import.

One of the most persistent and pervasive images of American Indians has been that of "natural" beings, persons who live in harmony with nature, whose identity is in congruence with the environment from whence they draw their sustenance. This image has existed since the first recorded contacts between whites and Indians, and as Robert Berkhofer, Jr. has recently pointed out, it has carried two apparently opposing connotations.[9]

On the one hand, whites have viewed American Indians as nature folk whose nobility, freedom, and spontaneity derive from their close association with the land. Although this image, normally referred to as the "noble savage" image, gained special currency in the eighteenth century with Rousseau and his compatriots, kindred spirits, and followers, it was already flourishing in the sixteenth and seventeenth centuries. Columbus, Lahontan, Las Casas, and many others held such a view. Whites who came into contact with Indians under friendly circumstances often admired their seeming oneness with the world around them. Even whites taken captive by Indians often found Indian "nature" ways alluring and refused to return to white society. To them and to the thousands of whites who ran away to live with and like Indians, Indian life represented a return to nature from which white civilization was alienated.[10]

On the other hand, the "natural" Indian in the Hobbesian tradition lives the brutal and harsh existence which is the essence of nature. Indians conjoin the savagery and unfeeling character of the physical world.[11] They are not to be emulated, as in the tradition that Rousseau epitomized. Rather, their way of life is something to be overcome, repressed, and destroyed.

Both of these traditions (which continue to today) share the common view of Indians as extensions of the environment. Both are really two sides of the same image of Indians as part of nature, and the white attitude toward Indians derives in large part from the attitude toward nature itself. The core image pictures Indians who both revere and represent the laws and substances of the environment. In the image Indians do not overly upset the natural balance and struggle of the world. They exist in the universe without appreciably changing it. Indeed, the central image is that of Indians who love the environment of which they are a part.

The image of Indians as nature lovers has held special fascination for scholars. In the first American book to propose environmental conservation, George P. Marsh argued that primitive peoples like American Indians tend to upset the balances of nature far less than civilized folk, that they understand it better and appreciate it more.[12] According to Marsh, civilized peoples neither love nor develop nature as creatively as American Indians. He paid special attention to the Indian tapping of maple sap, which milks the trees gently without hurting the organism. All humans are "disturbing agents," he said, since they use nature not only for food but also for tools, shelter, clothing, and technology; however, primitive peoples are the least harmful in this regard.

It can even be argued that the discipline of cultural ecology grew out of an appreciation of North American Indian relations with nature. From Lafitau, Montesquieu, Morgan, Marx, Engels, Steward, Wissler, Kroeber, among many others, anthropologists have formulated the idea that — at heart — culture arises from environmental relations, that is, from subsistence. The relations are both equilibrial and dialectical, containing both harmony and tension, but in either case humans shape their culture in response to environmental relations. The culture-area idea derived from observing American Indian adaptation to their physical universe.[13] Lévi-Strauss, Redfield, Diamond, and other anthropologists of philosophical bent have also argued that Indian (and other primitive) spiritual culture is also a lived response to a living, nurturing, dangerous world.

Within the ethnological discipline there has been a strong tradition of seeing Indians as nature folk. Jenks made a distinction between economic and natural people; to him, Indians represented the latter category, since they want only their immediate needs. MacLeod wrote that Algonkians and other American Indians conserve their environment because of spiritual and economic motives. They do not want divine punishments like sickness and lack of hunting success; neither do they want to deplete their sources of subsistence. Consequently, they consciously strive to upset and destroy nature as little as possible.[14] Speck best formulated the ethnological image of Indians as harmonic extensions of nature in describing the Micmacs: "The culture of these Northeastern Indians has always tied them close to nature, since originally they depended almost entirely upon the harvest of natural resources. Even today this relationship exists."[15] As much as anyone, Speck fostered the idea of Indians as lovers and conservers of nature.

Even more responsible in the twentieth century for the thorough going image of Indians as nature lovers is John Collier. His books, talks, and political policies as head of the Bureau of Indian Affairs under Franklin Roosevelt were all based on the assumption of Indians as ecologists of a mystical sort. In 1947 Collier wrote that the Indians' belief system "realizes man as a co-partner in a living universe—man and nature intimately co-operant and mutually dependent."[16] In 1962 he demonstrated this belief system in a book about the Indians of the Southwest.

Others have attempted to follow up Collier's formulation with studies of American Indian environmental attitudes and have found a deep seated Indian respect for nature. One study has documented briefly the Nez Perce conservation of nature; we are told that the Nez Perce know the land in detail, respect it, and refuse to treat it like a commodity.[17] The same is said for the various Pueblo Indians, who believe that they were born of the earth, that all natural things are alive and in harmony, that places in nature can be sacred shrines, and that such religious attitude toward nature reflects itself in Indian actions, such as apologizing to animals and plants which are killed.[18] A survey of Indian "conservation ethic" comments: "historically, the Indian has been appalled by the white man's lack of respect for other living things," because Indians truly love the world in which they live.[19] Wilcomb Washburn regards Indian intimacy with nature as the most salient characteristic that separates Indians from whites: "Virtually all Indians lived in close and intimate relationship with nature. ... The Indian relied directly upon nature for his life, and, perhaps more important, was fully conscious of that dependence. ... the Indian's mind was turned constantly toward the natural environment which was the source of life and death and of reward and punishment."[20] Wilbur R. Jacobs adds to this that whites can learn from "the Indian's historic reverence for the land."[21]

Whites are not the only ones who hold the image of Indians as nature lovers. Indians also see themselves as upholders of the environment against white onslaught. Researching American Indian religious activity in New York City, the most common statement I heard from Indians of various tribes was that Indians worship nature, whereas whites desecrate it. In a discussion with a Canadian Ojibwa chief in 1979, I heard time and again the insistent idea that one cannot understand Indians without understanding their loving relationship to the environment. And most recently a Passamoquoddy woman contrasted Indian ecological respect to the attitudes of whites who, "when they see the pine trees see only matches, toothpicks, and toilet paper."

In published sources many Indians have presented themselves and their nations as people with a land ethic which is superior in all ways to the non-Indian non-ethic which has created contemporary ecological dilemmas.[22] The two leading American Indian newspapers in this country, *Akwesasne Notes* from the east coast and *Wassaja* from the west, speak passionately of American Indian environmentalism.

Perhaps Indians have taken the image of nature lover as a way of identifying themselves as Indians. That is to say, it is "Indian" to revere nature. Doing so is a political, ontological statement. If this is true — if Indians are taking for themselves the role of contemporary prophets against an ecologically unjust society of whites — they have taken this view of themselves with a vengeance. Even if traditional Indians once had a less systematic understanding of their role in the world (which I think is not true), today many — like the Crees[23] are concerned actively, even militantly, with preserving their environment in the face of ongoing white threats.

A survey of American Indian life histories indicates that the hundreds of nineteenth- and twentieth-century biographies and autobiographies pay exceptional attention to Indian love of place and environmental harmony. Buffalo Child Long Lance, Eastman, Momaday, Nabokov, Neihardt, Standing Bear, Stands in Timber, and Whitewolf are only among the best known authors of this Indian genre. Perhaps one can say that the environmentalism in these books reflects the image of Indians which white editors and publishers wish to portray. Nevertheless, pious and loving references to the nonhuman world abound in such works, some of which have been written exclusively by Indian authors.

The two most famous Indian writers who have expressed an Indian ecologist image have been Vine Deloria, Jr. and N. Scott Momaday.[25] Each has contrasted the natural roots of American Indian spirituality to the rootlessness of white American Christianity. Each has written sincerely and devotedly of nature relations as the center of American Indian religions and lives, and they make convincing claims that Indians are more fully human than whites, because whites have repudiated an attachment to the earth. Even if we disagree with Deloria's extraneous metaphysical theories, question Momaday's poetry as a valid representative of traditional Indian ideas, and attribute both men's missionizing activism to Christian influence, we cannot but recognize that their message of an ethical practical relationship to the environment is American Indian to the core. We cannot deny that today American Indians do express an intense association with the environment that identifies them as Indians.

There exists a wider context, however, to Deloria and Momaday's works than merely Indian environmentalism. Their writings are also part of the worldwide concern about the environment which stems from recognition of the polluting effects of industrialism, but more specifically from the nuclear threat that looms over all. Today in the nuclear age whites are re-evaluating their attitudes toward nature.[26]

Especially over the past two decades Westerners have begun to perceive that one of the sources of their civilization — Christianity — might be partially to blame for the ecological disasters which whites so often engender. Many feel the Biblical dictum to subdue the environment is a foundation to such action.[27]

Many Westerners have turned to other religious traditions for alternatives to Western disenchantment from nature, e.g., to Taoism in China.[28] In this seeking process many have turned to American Indians and their image of communion with the world. Stewart L. Udall was one of the first in the surge of interest in Indian ecologies, when in 1963 he looked to Indians as exemplars who revere the "life-giving earth," who treat it well, leaving no great scars. Udall recalled Indian views of earth as mother for whom they hold emotional attachment; their feeling of placeness; their refusals to sell land. He noted that Indians and whites have always had "irreconcilable concepts of land ownership," and he found Indian concepts preferable.[29] More recently a theological historical work has charged that "the Native American religious traditions radically challenge... the Western rape of the earth and the consequent loss of the religious mystery flowing from ecological relationships."[30] Clearly Indians are viewed today as having something to offer us, something which will improve us and our world if we learn from their example.

And so today we continue to view Indians in relation to their environment. Books on American Indian religions take names like *Teachings from the American Earth* and *Touch the Earth*, indicating that Indian philosophies like the natives themselves spring from the physical universe and reflect it in an essential way.[31]

The image of Indian as spiritual ecologist filters down to education for whites, be it the antipollution television ads of Cherokee actor Iron Eyes Cody, educational publications of the National Science

Teachers Association or the National Association of Biology Teachers, or scholarly symposia.[32] (Such courses have been offered at the University of Wisconsin at Stevens Point, Hobart and William Smith Colleges, and Michigan State University.) There have been a few conferences on American Indian environmental issues, and it must be said that this is only part of a larger movement which tries to better understand American Indian environmental relations and history. It is both ironic and not coincidental that the surge of interest in Indian environmentalism coincides with the present energy shortages, because as whites turn to Indians for ecological lessons, they are also turning to Indian natural resources to fuel mechanized Western society. The white threat to Indians and their environments is as great today as in any time in history.

We cannot accept the conception of Indians as conservationists in a modern, Western sense. We must understand Indian environmental attitudes on their own terms. Similarly, we should not accept Jean Paul Sartre's opinion that primitive societies live in an exact equilibrium with nature and thus are prehistoric or nonhistoric because they have yet to establish a dialectic with the world. All humans work on the environment, changing, modifying it for human purposes. Call this harmony or disharmony, depending on one's point of view, but there exists a dialectic between all humans and their environments.[33]

More specifically, no serious scholar today thinks that Indians lived on unused soil in 1492, despite the centuries of rhetoric about "virgin land."[34] Indeed, the virgin land rhetoric may have been more of a ploy by whites to take land occupied and developed by millennia of Indians, than a description of actual conditions. American Indians influenced their environment, both as conservers and destroyers.

Since the 1930s authors have debated the question of traditional Indian conservation.[35] At the time of first white contacts, Indians practiced their own form of environmental relations in which efficiency of natural production and spiritual concern for nature maintained a creative tension. In Lithic, Archaic, and Formative aspects of American Indian subsistence, Indians combined an effective utilization of the environment with a personal participation in the world. By both exploiting and revering nature, they carried out a religious symbiosis in which both exploitation and reverence were mediated, integrated, and enhanced.

We can probably never return to an old idea that American Indian big game hunters lived a precarious existence; indeed, the wealth of large animal life made Indian subsistence, on the Plains for instance, relatively easy. One estimate of subsistence activity per day is two to four hours for primitive hunters.[36] Indian hunters, particularly buffalo hunters, are famous for their efficient use of each animal killed, and they serve as prime examples of Indian conservation of each species. Plains Indians had close to a hundred uses for each buffalo; they fashioned their food, clothing, shelter, bedding, fuel, tools, weapons, storage containers, and adornment, as well as religious paraphernalia from the buffalo. They used skin for tipis, shields, boats, coffins, and clothing; sinew for bow strings, thread, snowshoe webbing and rope; hoofs for glue; horns for spoons; gall for yellow paint; back fat for hair grease; robes for blankets; bones for needles; stomach juices for drink; even chips for fuel.

In addition to the conservation of each animal killed, Lithic Indians conserved certain members of each species of animal, sparing female or pregnant deer. We find Indian admonitions not to waste animal sources for consciously economic and religious motives to the extent that it is said, "with animals they are careful, and in general their attitudes are those which we would call conservation-minded."[37]

Indians were empirical observers of animal habits, and their hunting techniques, such as traps, were based on acute observation of animal behavior. Indeed, Indians were sharp observers of their entire surroundings, including the heavens. Their astronomical knowledge far exceeded in 1492 that of the average white person today.[38]

Indian efficiency in Archaic patterns equalled that of the Lithic hunters, producing an economically satisfying way of life. Not only were Indians resourceful with their game, but they also made use of food sources, traveling from one area to another to take advantage of whatever was in season. In the Eastern Woodlands wild turkey, partridge, pigeon, duck, geese, deer, elk, beaver, hare, rabbit, muskrat, bear, sea mammals (seals, walrus, and whales), fish (salmon, trout, shad, herring, alewives, bass, sturgeon, swordfish, shellfish, and lobster), as well as dozens of nut trees, wild berries, and other fruits like wild plums, cherries, grapes, and crabapples gave the Archaic Indians great diversity and security in a bountiful forest. In the Southwest Indians utilized practically every part of mesquite, screwbean, yucca, sotol, beargrass, agave, and other wild plants, in order to subsist in seemingly impossible dry climates. Archaic Indians' familiarity with approximately two hundred medicinal herbs was pragmatic, accurate, and vast, and a case study of Ojibwa knowledge about wild plants for food and medicine indicates a profound perception of the local flora.[39] In addition, Indians knew these plants minutely. The Tewa, for example, have forty names for different parts of each leaf.

If there was efficiency in Indian big game hunting and in the Archaic methods of gathering and hunting, there was also efficiency in the Formative development of agriculture in the New World. Indians were active modifiers of their plant life. Through centuries of experiments, hybrids, pruning, and weeding, based on a keen perception of feral flora, Indians protected and fostered species, developing them to suit human needs. Their breeding of 155 species of domesticated plants progressed through long-range planning, knowledge, and skill, as well as from security and stability of Archaic efficiency.[40] The development of corn with its sister plants beans and squash resulted from the long, scientific process of observation, hypothesis, and experiment. In the middle Rio Grande, perhaps the oldest continuous area of human habitation in America, the Indians worked their corn and other food plants so as to preserve their environment. They prevented flooding; they kept grass in the arid climate; they did not deplete wood supplies. White innovations in the same area brought about floods, erosion, and other natural disasters which seriously damaged Indian subsistence.[41]

Indians were pragmatic and efficient hunters, gatherers, farmers, and observers of their natural environment. They were skillful and resourceful in subsisting. Of course the same can be said of Old World subsistence methods. One cannot make a claim for the uniqueness of Indian efficiency. Indians possessed analytical techniques equal to any in the world, but they were not necessarily more skillful than natives of other lands. It is the claim that they were technologically backward that ignores admirable Indian adaptation to their environment with the technology they had in 1492.[42]

All people are relatively efficient in making and using tools to establish subsistence methods. The achievement of Indians lies in that their efficient utilization of nature was in 1492 only a part of their total relation with the natural world. More to the point, they established a religious association with nature that transcended but did not nullify their effective exploitation of the environment. They achieved an integration of subsistence and religious activities.

We find three types of integration between environment and religion among American Indians:

1. Primary integration, in which the religious core is molded by environmental relations. Hunting rituals in which Indian hunters tried to call in game and apologized to animals upon killing them are examples. The seasonal cycles of agricultural rituals in which planting activities are combined with prayers also illustrate primary integration. The fertilization rituals of the Pueblos or Eastern Woodland farmers were directly concerned with promoting life in humans, plants, animals, and the world at large. They were for the benefit of nature and culture alike. Salt gathering, basically an economic activity, was treated by Indians of the Southwest as a complicated, delicate ceremonial replete with taboos and spiritual significance. To a large degree, subsistence

activities to American Indians in 1492 were holy occupations, rituals which recognized the religious dimensions of promoting human life through interaction with the environment. In addition, religious rituals often served to share nature's bounty within human communities.[43]

2. Secondary integration, in which Indian social structure was molded in part by environmental interactions, and the religious structure reflected the social structure. Indian farming societies, for example, tended to have organized priesthoods because their way of subsistence allowed for, perhaps needed, a hierarchical structure of society. Hunting cultures in native North America tended more toward atomistic shamanism; the individualism of hunting carried through to an individualism of religion.[44]

3. Morphological (or symbolic) integration, in which Indian religious symbols in words, designs, and motions reflected the surrounding environment. It is well known that Indian myths contain innumerable references to natural phenomena; it could be said that they are *about* natural phenomena to a large degree. In art Indians used natural materials and shaped their designs to the contours of natural forms; furthermore, Indian art celebrated and evoked nature. Indian sacramentalism was decidedly nature oriented, whether using the symbols of tobacco, stones, trees, buffalo, or the sun to illustrate the Indians' inter-relatedness to the environment, and the environment's identity as source of life.[45]

In primary, secondary, and morphological ways American Indian religions were integrated with their environment.[46] We need to describe Indian environmental religions, however, in far greater detail, showing more precisely the integration.

In 1952 Robert Redfield published a formulation of what he called primitive world view, including American Indians in his description.[47] First, he said that primitives tend to join rather than to separate categories in the world. Second, he said that there was a sense of "participatory maintenance" between humans and non-humans, or gods and nature. Third, he said that for primitives the universe is "morally significant"; humans have duties of an ethical nature to the rest of the world. He emphasized the harmonious participation of primitives in their natural world and compared primitive and modern Western world views.

Redfield's formulation accurately portrays aspects of Indian environmental religions; however, we need to expand and clarify it. We need to see that in 1492 Indians regarded nature as their ultimate source of life; their deities represented the multifaceted aspects of the environment; their conceptions, attitudes, and relations regarding na-

THE THREE SISTERS, by Ernest Smith, Tonawanda Seneca, 1937. Corn, Squash, and Beans are the Three Sisters given as a gift to the Iroquois by a feminine spiritual force in the mother earth of a far distant past. The Iroquois were historically the major agriculturalists among their people, and their strong spiritual identity with the forces of nature around them, especially those which are feminine, continues today. *Collection of the Rochester Museum and Science Center. May not be reprinted without permission of the RMSC*

ture were both practical and mythopoeic, taxonomic and associative, loving and fearful; they conceived of themselves as both related to the world and apart from it; their universe was alive, filled with persons with consciousness and ability to suffer; their relation to these persons of the universe was ethical; they regarded their personal world as a fragile source of life requiring care as well as reverence; their major ethical issue of environmental religions was exploiting their living, natural relatives in order that humans should live; the essence of their environmental religion was a tension between exploiting and loving

their multifaceted, related, personal, conscious, fragile environment—
the ultimate source of their life. Finally, Indians conceived of their
natural source of life in specific terms connected to the particular places
where they lived.

The Nez Perce believed that they came from the earth as a child
comes from a mother. The earth was the source of human life. In
addition, "the earth is the source of all life and provides all man's
needs."[48] Like other Indians, the Nez Perce recognized their natural
roots. They conceived of themselves as deriving from the earth and
depending on it for their survival. To use a theological term, Indians
regarded nature as the ground of their being, their "unground."

The expression, "source of life," can be used as a synonym for
"God," or "first cause," or "providence." In American Indian environmental religions the environment was the source of life. In any
religion the source of life is that which humans cannot exist without; all
things come from it. In Indian world view the same was true of nature.
All material things: food, shelter, clothing, tools came from nature, and
power to use these materials also came from nature. American Indians
depended on nature for survival, and they recognized their dependence; their recognition was a conceptual aspect of their religion.

The earth consisted of living matter that preceded humans
both in time and ultimate power. The Wintu linguistic categories revealed such a conception. For them there were no words "to make" or
"to create." Humans did not create cultural materials like tools and
clothing; rather, they fashioned pre-existing nature in shapes and
combinations without influencing the essence of the matter in which
they worked. In their mythological stories there were no creation
stories; rather, they spoke of the beginning when only the world
existed. Culture heroes reshaped the primordial world, but they did
not make it. Instead, they grew out of the ground and depended on it
for all things. In Wintu thought nature preceded and continued to
precede human action. The same was true for most Indians, whose
ethnoscience was based on the belief that humans are the "product of
nature."[49]

Since the physical world was the source of Indian life, it is no
wonder that Indians conceived of their deities as aspects of nature.
Lahontan noted in 1703 that whenever something happened in nature,
whether a branch put a man's eye out, or a storm formed on the lake,
the Indians of the Northeastern forests asked who did it. They assumed that a spirit of nature was the cause.[50] In the twentieth century
an anthropologist said of the same Indians that their deities were so
closely associated with the environment that "a natural-supernatural
dichotomy has no place."[51] Nature as a unit fit the category of "source

of life," and its many aspects—Thunderers, Four Winds, Sun, Moon, Lynx, Turtle, Owl, and many others — formed a matrix upon whose collective powers the Indians depended ultimately for continued existence. Throughout native North America spirits of animals, water, light, wind, and crops filled Indian people with power and life.[52]

Guardian spirits, possibly the most common religious phenomena in the Indian world view, were almost always nature spirits, most commonly animals. Shamanistic powers came most regularly from animal spirits, giving Indians the abilities of curing, and helping provide support for subsistence activities.[53] "Owners" of animals, plants, and specific natural locations were vital links between humans and their environment. The "owners" of nature provided the Indians with foods and the abilities to utilize the natural world. The "owner" of deer, who was in fact a deer, made it possible for hunters to catch deer, or if hunters displeased the "owner," it might withhold game. The "owner" of corn gave the Indians the secrets of farming its crop in order that humans might live. The "owner" of flint revealed to Indians where the stone could be found, so that humans might fashion tools necessary for survival. In its entirety the "owner" concept was a key to understanding Indian religion, since "owners," guardian spirits, and even totems were often the same deities, all which expressed a daily intercourse with nature, as well as the deep-seated hopes and fears regarding human survival through nature relations. Sometimes each species had its separate guardian. Other times there were sky and water deities who controlled mutual halves of the environmental population. A third idea was a nature spirit who had power over all animals and/or plants.[54] Like all nature deities, the "owners" held the ability to provide or deny Indians their survival.

We can see already a seeming paradox in Indian subsistence. On the one hand, Indians were skilled hunters, gatherers, and farmers, as well as observers of their environment. On the other hand, they attributed their success at providing sustenance to nature deities. Indians expressed two different attitudes toward the world, two different modes of thinking which might be called practical and mythopoeic.

THANKING THE SPIRIT OF THE BEAR, by Ernest Smith, Tonawanda Seneca, 1938. A good hunter was one whose moral character was respectful of the spirits of the animals, enabling the coming together of the hunter and the hunted. This spiritual affinity was reaffirmed after the kill so that future hunts would continue to meet the spiritual requirements of the animals and their spirits. *Collection of the Rochester Museum and Science Center. May not be reprinted without permission of the RMSC*

Some students of Indian religions remarked on the Indians' mystical attitude toward the world, their indisposition to make distinctions between their own identity and the wholeness of the universe, their tendency to equate other entities of nature and themselves in very literal ways, by saying that humans when they put on bear masks became bears, for example. In this mythopoeic mode Indians associated almost mystically with nature, assuming an equivalence (equal value or equal worth) with other persons outside the category of "human."[55]

Others have noted the pragmatic side of tribal life. They described the scientific and "pseudo-scientific" (magical) attitudes and practices of primitives, whose desire was to get jobs done. They argued that since Indians were practical, utilitarian, and skilled, they could not also be so spiritual in their relations with the world. If Indians were practical, they could not be mythopoeic.[56]

However, it is easy to show that Indians were both practical and mythopoeic in their relations with nature. They knew the environment in impressive details, as we have seen, and they also knew the world as a connective unit whose parts — including themselves — existed only in relation to each other as a whole. Indians knew the differences between humans and animals; they were not fuzzy in their systematic thought. However, they were capable of more than systematizing. They also conceived of a world in which plants, animals, pictures, words, actions, as well as humans, storms, and sunlight had the potential of power and life. All entities in the Indian world view were potentially equivalent. A word could stand for the thing it spoke of; a human in animal skin could be the animal. There was the ability of interaction; a human could say in truth, "I *am* a deer," just as the "owner" of deer was a deer. Indians whose lives depended on corn, like the Navajo, or the Caddoan and Siouian peoples of the upper Missouri were efficient horticulturalists to be sure, but they also spoke with corn spirits and influenced corn growth with prayers as well as hoes.[57]

Indians' attitudes toward the world and their actual relations with it were flexible and full; they were both practical and mythopoeic, or as Clara Sue Kidwell has said, "In their day to day lives, Indians were empiricists and mystics. They were keen observers of nature and all of their activities centered around it."[58] Furthermore, there was a creative tension between Indian practical and mythopoeic modes which was an important ingredient of Indian environmental religions.

American Indians depended on nature for survival, and in recognizing their dependence, they expressed a range of emotions, from hope, complaint, and remorse, to fear.

Although Indians believed ultimately in the friendliness of nature, its nourishing and providing bounty, they also recognized the terrible power and wrath of natural power. Nature could both help and harm, give or withhold, create or destroy, making the difference between survival and extinction. Indians recognized the erotic and death-bringing aspects of the environment, the same reciprocal dualities that they perceived in themselves.[59]

Thus their attitude toward the world, as expressed in prayers and offerings, was twofold, or rather manifold. They both feared an environment that might withhold, and held affection for an environment that sustained.[60] As with human mothers, mother earth evoked devotion and resentment, love and guilt, and Indian religions reflected the tensions and harmonies between these emotions, sublimating their complaints into reverent rituals and myths.

Perhaps we can best see the range of Indian attitudes toward the environment in their myths. Therein we find a universe in which material precedes creation, in which humans and the entities of nature can interact. We see in Emergence and Earth Diver motifs the concept that humans arose from the earth and need to stay in contact with it in order to survive. We view the overwhelming power of nature but also the overwhelming concern that nature has for humans, the gifts of corn and other foods, the environmental pity for the distressed and punishment for the wicked.[61]

We can also see in Indian rituals, like the buffalo dance, the range of attitudes and conceptions of Indians regarding nature. Dancers dressed as buffalo actually become buffalo in the process of masking and acting like the animals. Simultaneously, the purpose of the dance is to lure the beasts in order that Indians can kill them and to thank the buffalo for giving themselves up to humans, for providing humans with continued life. The dance, and other Indian nature rituals, were polysemous expressions of a fullness of emotions and uses. The dance honors, mimics, associates with, and influences the buffalo.

In the fullness of Indian attitudes toward the environment there was an esthetic element that accompanied other responses to nature. Indians described their world in myths and speeches, in art and song, in appreciative terms. They spoke of the beauty of the earth as one would the beauty of human persons. Indian dependence on nature did not preclude esthetic satisfaction from it.[62]

Indian myths, rituals, and arts demonstrated a wide range of responses to the environment. Indian classification systems, often based on totemic signatures, both associated humans with the world and categorized the world taxonomically.

Totemic systems were also means of relating humans to the

rest of the universe; totemic organization helped Indians exploit the environment and participate in it. Zuni and Sioux clan names corresponded to directions, colors, animals, plants, and locations in the natural world that provided clan members with identity as humans, as members of a larger universe. The correspondences between humans and aspects of nature were a life-giving means of organizing and relating to a living world.[63] The institution of totem itself, including clan, tribe, individual, and village totems, was a means of joining nature and culture.[64]

Indian totemic classifications conjoined humans and nonhumans in ways that seem arbitrary and convoluted to an outsider, but upon closer examination they begin to make sense. Indeed, that was one of the functions of the totemic systems, to make sense of the connections which were thought to exist throughout the living universe. Colors, directions, seasons, species, even parts of species and humans all corresponded within the great chain of being in specific and meaningful ways. The Hopi classification system recognized a world that was "differentiated, but the differentiations are portrayed as temporal, almost accidental in nature, and are to be overcome." Hopi classification was extensively empirical; Hopis could identify almost every one of the 150 plants in their area. But the system also saw that each species of animal and plant was significant as a symbol both of humans and the environment as a whole. It is one thing to observe that Hopi totem nomenclature, "through a naming process does all it can to imitate the world around it," but it is important to see that each clan name—bear, spider, bluebird, gopher, etc.—points to a specific animal whose traits, seasonal activities, historical connections, and location all meant something to the Hopis.[65] Thus a Hopi totem clan whose totem was prominent in a certain season when certain subsistence activities were essential would be given control over the ritual calendar for that part of the year and would be responsible for promoting subsistence for its time. In their rituals the clan members would act like their totem, they would visit sites associated with their totem, their costumes would reflect totemic characteristics, and in the process the chain of being, from humans to totems to species to locations to the whole of the environment, would be integrated to a large degree.

It was necessary for Indians to assert their connections to the environment because they felt equally their separateness from it. Their myths described a world in which animals, plants, stars, and other natural phenomena converse, even intermarry, with humans. The earth is often spoken of by farming peoples as mother or grandmother. She is actually related to humans. She is fruitful, beautiful, bountiful. She bears human life. The earth as creator and womb also receives people after death; they return to their source. Yet the same myths portray communication gaps between humans and non-humans. Women who marry stars always desire to return to human intercourse. Marriages between nature spirits and humans seem fated to fail. Stories of the origin of hunting show its tragic aspect in that humans and animals become alienated; they must go their separate ways. Totemic classifications, as well as myths, rituals, and other aspects of environmental religions, reminded humans of their natural roots and of their separate identity as humans in the natural world. Indian taxonomy reflects both the Indians' systematic uses of the environment and their participation in it.

We should not think of the tension between Indian separateness and communion with nature in purely cognitive terms; neither should we see it as proof that Indians did not live in harmony with their world. (After all, harmony consists of pleasing agreement between different, separate entities.) As one ethnologist noted, "To the Ojibwa, then, all objects have life, and life is synonomous with power, which may be directed for the Indian's good or ill. ... Therefore, the Indian should treat everything he sees or touches with the respect befitting a thing that has a soul and shadow not unlike his own."[66] The same was true for all Indians. "For the old-time Indian, the world did not consist of inanimate materials to be used and of animals to be butchered and eaten. It was alive, and everything in it could help or harm him."[67] Such was a basic premise of Indian existence: the world was alive and powerful and personally significant.[68]

In saying that animals, plants, stones, clouds, celestial bodies, and other natural phenomena have life, Indians were declaring that their environment was a world of beings with souls. Tylor's theory regarding primitive animism recognized this fact. Humans and non-humans shared a basic characteristic, establishing an essential equivalence between them: they both possessed souls.[69]

Among the Ojibwas we find evidence of this belief in an animate universe throughout the historical period. Charlevoix commented that the Indians thought that the souls of animals go to the same place as souls of humans after death.[70] They thought that not only every species but every animal has a tutelary genius. In short, they believe that humans and animals are not substantially different from each other. Nineteenth-century observers remarked on the same beliefs among the Ojibwas, for instance, that "inanimate" objects and animals have souls, power, and life, or that they "believe that animals of the lowest, as well as highest class in the chain of creation, are alike endowed with reasoning powers and faculties"; in sum, birds and beasts have souls.[71]

Twentieth-century Ojibwas did not lose this belief in the personal, living quality of nature. Ojibwa linguistic categories which consider shells, stones, thunder, pipes, as well as plants and animals as animate, have persisted, and belief in metamorphosis from human to nonhuman form continues. Ojibwas still speak of bears and other animals as "relatives," "grandfathers," "brothers," and the like.[72] So much are the animals alive in the Ojibwa world view that they are said to have such religious habits as praying to the four directions.[73]

The same has been true for other Indians. Wintu hunters unlucky in the chase did not say that they were unable to kill deer; they said, "Deer don't want to die for me."[74] A Pit River Indian commented: "Everything is alive. That's what we Indians believe. White people think everything is dead."[75]

For the Indians at time of contact with whites the world was composed of living beings with souls. These living beings had consciousness and reasoning abilities to varying degrees. They had power to influence events. They had needs which humans could fulfill, and they had the ability to suffer. Like many other Indians, the Salishan speakers told stories of animals and other persons of nature who acted just like humans. They injured and they ridiculed. They were motivated like humans and could turn into humans. They competed with one another and loved one another. For the Salish, these qualities were not just the stuff of stories, since in everyday life there was metamorphosis between humans and non-humans. The moral of many of their 'stories was that the nonhuman persons of nature had the ability to suffer, and humans thus had the duty to treat them with sensitivity. They were worthy of ethical consideration. Punishment could come for mistreating an animal, just as it could for mistreating a human. Many Ojibwa myths came to the same conclusion, such as one in which a girl tried to torture a porcupine and brought down a storm of punishment on herself. Because natural entities could suffer, they were worthy of care, just as their possessing souls constituted an equivalence with humans. Nonhuman persons had souls and could suffer; therefore, they were worthy of ethical consideration.[76]

Ethics are limitations of freedom based on consideration for the welfare and feelings of others. They form a structure of morally proper action. American Indian attitudes toward the environment fit such a description. In their ethical relations with persons of nature, Indians assumed: first, that natural entities were essentially equal in value or worth to humans; second, that nonhuman persons expressed their intentions, needs, dislikes, and rights; third, that non-humans entered covenants with humans for mutual benefit; there were social contracts between humans and non-humans; and fourth, there was reciprocity in these relations between humans and non-humans.

American Indian nature ethics went beyond the proper ritual treatment of animal bones.[77] It went beyond the ceremonialism at which Indians apologized to the animals for having killed them, although this ceremony was perhaps the crucial example of Indian nature ethics.[78] Ethics included rules against boasting about hunting prowess, improper attitudes toward exploiting game and plants, and making denigrating comments about nature formations, thunder, mountains, rivers, and other earthly entities. They included the idea that humans could not kill animals at improper times, such as bears when they hibernated, or any animal when a member of the immediate family was expecting the gift of life. Indian courtesy toward nature, refusals to eat specific species at certain times, and food taboos of all kinds often have for the outsider the quality of rote or irrational compunctions, but for Indians they were part of a larger ethical matrix which took into consideration the ability of nonhuman persons to suffer.[79]

Indian ethics, especially toward animals, were also influenced by Indian fears that mistreatment of nonhuman persons would lead to a falling-out between that species and humans. Indians treated wild animals with respect because they were worthy of it, and also because, if they mistreated them, others of their species would not give themselves up for future kills. Indians often believed that animal souls returned to the "owner" of the species, reported the mistreatment, and severed relations with the hunter. The result could be disastrous.

In American Indian mythology there was a common theme that human diseases began when humans fell into dis-ease from nature, often marked by the beginning of hunting. In one widespread tradition, humans began to kill too many animals. The animals retaliated by creating diseases for humans; however, plants had pity on the Indians and offered cures.[80] Whether this tradition was aboriginal or historical makes little difference, since at heart the myth described a breakdown between humans and non-humans, in which humans sinned against animals for whom they had moral obligations, and who had the power to bring about punishments. The myth also described a system of mutual aid, in which plants aided their suffering Indians.

It is instructive in this regard to note that for the Ojibwas one of the major causes of sickness was sin, more often than not against nonhuman persons. Sin for the Ojibwas was action outside the limitations of freedom based on consideration for the welfare and feelings of others. Punishment did not necessarily fall on the immediate sinner but could visit a relative or descendant. The punishers were almost exclusively nature spirits, "owners" of animals and the like.[81]

The ethical attitudes of Indians toward their environment were based on the conception of a world of worthy persons able to suffer. Humans had the duty to minimize their sufferings. And yet these same persons, so fragile, were the ultimate sources of Indian existence. In the Indian world view humans were dependent on nature for survival; however, nature in all its aspects was not invulnerable. It could run down and needed humans to maintain its cycles with seasonal rituals. It could suffer, and thus humans had the ethical responsibility to protect and not harm it. The Indian environment was all nourishing but not indestructible. Humans could influence, offend, and please the earth (otherwise, why pray to it?). They could also treat it with care and respect, pity as well as reverence.

There was in Indian nature ethics a reciprocity akin to piety for parents. Parents bring up children; children care for old parents. For Indians the same was true for the world. The earth cared for humans and humans cared for the earth. "Land supports men and at the same time requires human care."[82] Indians entered covenants of mutuality with nature for the benefit of each. Demonstrably fertile Indian women walked through their cornfields in order to promote nature's fertility, to make crops grow, and thus to help promote human life. Ideally in Indian environmental religion, the relations between humans and non-humans was symbiotic, a harmony of equivalent persons.

The Indian ideal was harmony between humans and non-humans; however, there existed a dissonance between Indians and nature which lay at the crux of their environmental religions. We have said that Indians regarded nature as their ultimate source of existence; their very life depended on it. They regarded it with reverence and piety. They recognized its ability to suffer and treated it with ethical consideration. Nevertheless, they also realized that they were apart from nature, not in some vague way but in a manner which highlighted the first premise of their religious relation: they exploited nature in order that they should live. It was the source of their life.

The Indians' psychological bond with nature was simultaneously reverent and may have been filled with guilt.[83] Indians knew that in their personal world they were related to all its parts. Most importantly, animals were kin; they were equivalent to humans. And yet Indians had to exploit their relatives, they had to kill their animal kin in order to survive. The very world which they participated in (as source of their existence) was the world which they had to exploit (as source of their existence). In the Indians' environmental religions, "The songs and prayers were often based on the fact that they had to kill their kin, the animals, in order to survive."[84] Hunting put an essential gap, as well as an essential bond, between humans and the animal world,[85] although to a lesser extent, so did gathering and farming place a tension on human-plant relations. For the Ojibwas, "the animal has the same right to life that man has. It is necessary to use the animal for the subsistence of man, but the animal is sacrificed regretfully for this purpose."[86] As a result, Indians apologized to their killed animals; they begged the animals' pardon; they thanked them for the vital gift which animals gave, their own lives.

Indian environmental religions sought to overcome the tension between reverence and guilt toward nature; however, the method of overcoming was apologetic in a double sense. Indians apologized to the animals they killed; they begged their pardon. At the same time, Indians manipulated animals; they thanked them in order that they might kill them in the future. It was said of the Ojibwa culture hero: "While he called the birds, beasts, trees and flowers and all he saw around him his relatives and friends, yet he was always trying to outwit them and use them as servants, and would maneuver to get them to do his bidding."[87] In the same way Indians both apologized to nature and created a body of apologist (justificatory) oral literature regarding their exploitation of the environment. A large corpus of Indian myths tried to justify Indian exploitation of the natural world, including the killing of animals. Indians had the right to use corn, because the corn spirit had given the food as a gift; Indians had the right to kill animals because of a race or some accident in the primordial classification of the universe. Parts of the Ojibwa cycle of stories about their culture hero, in fact the central episodes, described his battles with the spirits of nature for the right and ability of humans to hunt and kill animals for subsistence. It was through his victory over the lords of nature that Indians became successful hunters, according to the Ojibwa story.[88]

All was not peace and good will between humans and nonhumans; there were dissonance as well as harmony in Indian-nature relations. There was even what Calvin Martin calls "a good deal of latent antagonism between the hunter and hunted — an antagonism that might erupt into overt hostility, given the proper circumstances."[89]

To say that Indians existed in harmony with nature is a half-truth. Indians were both a part of nature and apart from nature in their own world view. They utilized the environment extensively, realized the differences between human and nonhuman persons, and felt guilt for their exploitation of nature's life-giving life. Indian environmental religions were means of idealizing and attempting to attain a goal of harmony with nature,[90] for both participatory and manipulative reasons, but inherent in their religions was the understanding that they were not in fact at perfect harmony with nature.

American Indians loved nature and they exploited nature. Their environmental religions promoted both dimensions of human-nature relations. Their religions supported, apologized for, and justified subsistence activities. Their religions asserted a human alienation from nature (because nature was the Indians' economic source of life) and a human participation in nature (because nature was the Indians' spiritual source of life). Their religions recognized the lack of full human harmony with nature and sought to overcome it.

We find this attitude at the center of American Indian mythologies of both Americas, as studied by Claude Lévi-Strauss. He demonstrates that for Indians the central ontological and ethical issue was the dichotomy between nature and culture, between eaters of raw and cooked food, between naked and clothed persons. For the Indians who told these myths, their separations from nature were deeply felt problems. Indians knew they were separate from nature, their source of life, and they wished it were not so. American Indian environmental religions revealed human alienation from the source of life and revealed the means of overcoming that alienation.[91]

In order to explicate this idea further, we can look at one of the most universally accepted descriptions of religion, that of William James in *The Varieties of Religious Experience: A Study in Human Nature* (1958). James indicates that religion is not an unending state of bliss or spiritual relation. Rather, it consists of both the realization of alienation and the realization of the means to overcome that alienation. He writes in his conclusion that religion "consist of two parts: 1. An uneasiness; and 2. Its solution.   1. The uneasiness, reduced to its simplest terms, is a sense that there is *something wrong about us* as we naturally stand.   2. The solution is a sense that *we are saved from the wrongness* by making proper connection with the higher powers."[92]

We need to understand Indian religions in the same way. Indians did not exist in unending harmony with the source of their life, nature. Instead, they cared about and recognized the tensions in their relation with nature, and they tried to reckon with them, make them liveable, without doing away with the question of an ethical response to the world. Indians were uneasy about the paradox of both participating in the world and also exploiting it. Their environmental religions revealed that uneasiness and sought to resolve its tensions, not by denying either the exploitative or participatory dimensions, but rather by affirming them both simultaneously.

By pointing out the dissonance as well as the harmony between Indians and their environment does not discount the image of them as nature lovers or nature folk. Instead, their perception of alienation from nature troubled them and led them to attitudes and actions that helped unite them with the world. Their connection to the earth and separation from it were overriding concerns.

Their concern for the earth was not vague or undifferentiated. Their taxonomic systems were empirical, and their attachments were to specific places. Indians did not love the concept of nature; they loved particular locations, particular aspects of their environment. We can call their reverence and attachment to specific places "topophilia" or "geopiety."[93] Indians found their world filled with special spots where power for life was concentrated. These locales were sacred, and they desired to live close to them, where the spirits of nature most often revealed themselves. Sacred space was also the locus for tribalism, the place where human and natural kinships congrued, where humans thrived.[94] Indian sacred space was where they lived, where their myths took place, where their heroes walked and their ancestors were buried, where the nature deities were helpful, where conditions for subsistence were optimum. Sacred spaces could also be places like the Yellowstone area with its hot springs, geysers, and strange rock formations, which repelled Indians from normal use, but which were ideal spots for vision quests.[95] But whether Indians used their sacred spaces for economic or purely religious activities, they regarded them with piety and considered relation with them essential for human survival.

It was for the right and ability to continue in relation to sacred space that American Indians resisted white invaders. The crux of Indian-white relations was the struggle for land, but for Indians this struggle was far more emotion laden, far more a religious issue, than for whites, for whom it often represented simply a pecuniary interest. Land, Indians' sacred space, has been the most important issue in American Indian history. For five hundred years Indians have struggled to maintain relation to "the sources of life itself."

In the postcontact period Indians have often lost their religious grounding; they have been displaced spiritually as well as physically, or rather their spiritual and physical dislocations have been synonymous. The history of Indian-white contacts is one in which "Native Americans saw the white intruder violating the covenant with the earth, the source of all religious mystery."[97]

Understanding that Indian relations with their land and environment were essentially religious puts a new dimension on Indian-white history. It gives us a further depth of meaning, for instance, when we read that Canestego, representing the Six Nations in Philadelphia in 1742, said that he would not sell land because he considered money short lived but land "everlasting,"[98] or of a Blackfoot chief who rejected white money values with almost the same statement: "Our land is more valuable than your money. It will last forever."[99] Both Indians were expressing an idea of land as ultimate provider of life.

Smohalla, the founder of the dreamer religion, was expressing traditional Indian geopiety when he rejected the farming culture being forced upon him and his people by saying:

> You ask me to plow the ground. Shall I take a knife and tear my mother's breast? Then when I die she will not take me to her bosom to rest. You ask me to dig for stone. Shall I dig under her skin for her bones? Then when I die I cannot enter her body to be born again. You ask me to cut grass and make hay and sell it and be rich like white men. But how dare I cut off my mother's hair?[100]

Like other Indians, from the followers of the Delaware Prophet in the 1760s to the ghost dancers in the 1890s, Smohalla's dreamers were attempting to re-establish relations with an injured environment, and regain contact with lost lands.[101]

Displacement hurt Indians on all levels of environmental relation. It took them away from the herbs, plants, hunting grounds, and other places which they knew in such detail. It made Indian subsistence extremely precarious because upon removal an Indian group would have to learn a new territory, become familiar with it in pragmatic ways in order to exploit it efficiently. This took time.

Removal also meant taking Indians from places charged with meaning and emotion. Indians were dislocated from sacred space, where they had once emerged from their mother earth, where revelations occurred, where their ancestors were buried, where the powers of a living earth nurtured them. Removal was more than a political loss; it was a crisis of life itself, a religious crisis of the deepest order. When coupled with the environmental destruction brought about by white commercial technology, removal constituted a religious disaster. The source of Indian life was undergoing attack.

Finally, the realization that Indian environmental relations not only were, but also are essentially religious makes us understand more fully the meaning of the current struggle between Indians and whites for natural resources, such as the contest between Northwest Coast Indians and white commercial fishermen for the disappearing salmon. For the Indians there, fishing is more than a job, more than a right, more than a way to make a living in a money economy. It is a way of life, a relation with the source of life, a means of identity as an Indian.[102] For these Indians today, as for Indians in the past, their conceptions of, attitudes toward, and relations with nature are essentially religious.

Several objections can be raised to the preceding ideas. First, is the image of the nature loving Indians simply a white fabrication like that of the Noble Savage and other related images? The Indian documents cited seem to refute this. Yet, secondly, don't these religious documents accentuate Indian ideals and minimize Indian contradictory actions? It has been argued persuasively that religious traditions with great claims of reverence toward nature, such as Taoism, produce adherents who do not always act wisely or kindly to nature.[103]

Whereas religious materials do tend to emphasize ideals rather than other realities, the discrepancy between ideal and actual is not great enough to make us discount the ideal. Although American Indian actions have not always met their ideals, and although their ideals have not always been infallible in avoiding ecological errors, in large part there exists congruity between Indian ideals and actions.

Needless to say, there are exceptions to this, constituting a third, and most important, objection. Some have argued that American Indians, despite their land ethic, were responsible for erosion, both at Chaco Canyon and throughout the Eastern Woodlands where slash-burn farming depended on the ability of Indians to move when they depleted the soil. According to these objections,[104] Indians were not necessarily conservation minded, but rather their technology was too unsophisticated to produce a lasting damage, and their population was too low to create extended crises regarding shortage of natural resources.

One cannot argue the ecological viability of slash-burn farming, unless we put it in the context of Indian societies which purposefully limited both their population and technology. Seen in this context, the slash-burning appears relatively benign. As for erosion, obviously a land ethic does not insure infallible farming methods.

Another issue is raised regarding the extinction of large animals during the late ice age. Despite all the data on the subject, however, there is no convincing evidence that Indians were the chief or even the major contributing factors in the large animals' demise. Climate and dozens of other factors could have been just as, even more important.[105]

Even granting that Paleo-Indians did play a role in killing off the large game animals 12,000 years ago, does that in any way argue against an Indian environmental ethic in 1492? Are Indians responsible for the possible actions of their ancestors 12,000 years previous? In addition, is it not possible that Indians recalled the progressive and eventual extinction of the megafauna, and their environmental religious ideals are warnings not to repeat the exercise? Hopi myths recall the earlier Anasazi ecological errors at Chaco Canyon and warn against their repetition. Hopis recall past ecological upsets and espouse a land ethic which will better guard against such events. Looked at in this way, Hopi myths are ecological lessons well learned.[106] Neither megafauna extinction nor Pueblo Bonito erosion argue convincingly against the existence of Indian environmental religion's reality in practice.

The major objection to the assertion of an Indian environment religion comes not from distant, precontact conjectures, but rather from historical events concerning Indians. More specifically, evidence regarding Indian intransigence toward nature comes from their participation in the fur trade from the seventeenth to the nineteenth centuries.

Indian complicity in the whites' fur trade is the subject of Calvin Martin's 1978 work, *Keepers of the Game*. Martin asks how Indians could have broken their covenant with game animals, particularly beaver, in overhunting them to near extinction. He rejects the idea that Western marketplace systems caught up Indians in their web, so that Indians could not resist because they wanted white goods. Instead, he proposes that diseases, in conjunction with missionary teachings and social disequilibrium, corrupted Indian animal responsibilities. Indeed, Indians came to blame beaver and other animals for the new diseases that so demolished Indian populations for centuries, and the fur trade was in part a revenge against the disease-bearing animals.[107]

There is no doubt that diseases, along with dislocation, loss of tribal autonomy, and environmental disruption, undermined traditional Indian religions, social systems, and ecological practices through spiritual crises and loss of confidence.[108] But does Indian participation in the white fur trade rule out the thesis that Indians possessed an environmental ethic? Did Indian religious beliefs not have an effect on Indian actions in historical events?

It is unfortunate that Indian ideals regarding environment were often vitiated by white economic and religious thrusts, but weakening does not mean that ideals were nonexistent or aboriginally ineffective. They simply were not strong enough always to withstand white pressures, and it should be noted that Indians often did try to withstand the white seduction to kill animals rapaciously.[109] The Indian complicity must be seen in the context of white colonial trade in which Indians often had to sacrifice their ideals in order to survive.

Some American Indians took part in a white colonial fur trade through which enormous numbers of animals, especially beaver, were killed. But if white Christians kill inordinate numbers of human beings, do we conclude that Christians have no ethical relations with other humans? No, it is clear that Christianity and even Christians themselves hold that other humans are worthy of ethical consideration. Unfortunately, there are circumstances in which these ethical relations do not apply, or they become cancelled by events. The same can be said for the Indians in the fur trade. Events dislocated their ethical relations with the environment.

What were those events? Certain tribes had to acquire white trade items, most specifically guns, in order to maintain the precontact equilibrium among Indian nations that whites disrupted. If they did not kill beaver, other Indians would and thereby inherit the trade and gain advantage.

Through dependence on fur trade items, Indians saw their very survival at stake, and the successful hunting of beaver and other animals was their only way of staying above water. Also, white goods often preceded the trade itself and whetted Indian appetites for trade; this explains Indian eagerness to trade on first contact.

Furthermore, we must deal with the condition of identifying with the oppressor. Indians, an oppressed and exploited people, wore white clothing in order partially to share in white power that had given whites guns and other items of status. It is possible that in participating in the white fur trade Indians wanted to act like whites in order to become more like them. When seen in the context of cultural invasion, in which white missionaries insisted that Indian values were evil or infantile, it is no wonder that Indians buckled under the ideological pressure.

Furthermore, if we see Indians as part of a nascent capitalist system, we understand how they came to see animals as property, as commodities in trade, rather than as persons of nature capable of equivalence with humans. In the fur trade beaver became devalued in Indian eyes.

Indian treatment of dogs, practically the only domesticated animals in precontact America, illustrates the same point. Indians regarded dogs as property; they were domesticated. They were no longer wild, no longer free natural agents. This did not mean that Indians had no affection for their dogs, but we should note that dogs were often the objects of sacrifice and often treated cruelly. An observer commented in 1860 that Ojibwas beat their dogs if they interrupted religious ceremonies: "one is apt, at the first glance, to regard the Indians as fit subjects for the Society for preventing Cruelty to Animals."[110] These Indians regarded dogs as property, to be treated at will, either cruelly or as great objects of sacrifice. In the fur trade the Indians often fell out of relation with the beaver and came to regard them as property to be killed at will, to be treated as a commodity.

Hence the breakdown of some Indians' environmental ethics under white economic exploitation becomes more intelligible, especially in conjunction with missions and diseases.

The arguments against Indian conservation in the historical period bear questioning. One wonders when whites who are dependent on Hudson's Bay Company archives for their scholarship make a point of characterizing Indians as "a savage people ... who held the whip hand" in the fur trade as thugs who singlehandedly, it would seem, exterminated the great buffalo herds, all in vague references to Hudson's Bay Company documents.[111] One wonders when whites write publicity for the Hudson's Bay Company, posing it as scholarship when in fact its purpose is to justify the Bay's monopoly in Canada by claiming that without monopolistic control the stupid Indians would have killed all the game. It is interesting that these two whites cite almost the same quotation from Hudson's Bay Company sources, although attributed to different Company employees, each attempting to prove that "the post-contact Indian wasted game with gusto."[112] Are these whites more interested in understanding Indians (Ray's description of Indian religion is depressingly uninformed and inaccurate), or in touting the Bay Company line?

We might also ask why so many of the writers who make claims regarding Indian disrespect for nature write with such an intense disrespect for Indian people. It is one thing for a white scholar to project his western metaphysics on Indians, when he says: "A true reverence for nature, where nonhuman organisms are given a right of survival equal to that of man, has never been part of man's emotional makeup. Man shares with all other animals a basic lack of concern about his effect upon his surroundings."[113] We can only criticize such an honest error.

But at the heart of some objections to the idea of Indian love of nature is racist rhetoric and intent. Maxwell says disdainfully of the Indian: "He was wasteful and destructive, as savages usually are, and the word economy had no place in his vocabulary. ... When he had abundance, he squandered like a pirate, and when want pinched, he stood it like a stoic. The Indian is by nature an incendiary."[114] Hutchinson, writes of his "falling victim to coup-counting raiders from the 'Custer Died for Your Sins' tribe of Red Power activists" and of "being mutilated ... by their white-skinned 'Peace-Love Beads-and-Peyote allies.'" He doesn't stick to racist and political slurs but adds some sexist ones, perhaps to strengthen his case? He writes of "the Chickasaw, whose women may have invented the mini-skirt because they had good legs and knew it."[115]

Characterizing Indians as postcontact wasters of resources is

ultimately inaccurate because (1) the major example of Indian wastefulness toward animals comes from the colonialist white fur trade,
either in the north or in Florida. In these cases the impetus came
directly and cogently from white profiteers who exploited their Indian
agents far worse than the Indians exploited game. To blame the Indians
in these cases—in which their active participation in the trade determined their military and subsistence viability — is clearly a case of
blaming the victim. In doing so, white oppressors continue to deflect
accusations regarding their own rapacity by focusing on Indian culpa-
bility. And (2) except for the fur trade there is little evidence of inten-
tional Indian wastefulness. They did not, as Rich would have us
believe,[116] destroy large numbers of buffalo for their own purposes.
Indeed, the most fully researched book on the North American buffalo
finds no indication that Indians killed inordinate numbers of buffalo.
To the contrary, they often organized themselves to guard herds from
indiscriminate killing, especially during mating season. Overkill by
Indians is unfounded in the historical period outside the fur trade
context.[117]

One writer says that the "Crow once drove 700 buffalo,
roughly 350 tons of meat-on-the-hoof, over a 'jump off' in one drive,
which gave them the opportunity to do exactly what all of us do today
when times are flush, eat the best and leave the rest."[118] The author
does not say that the Crow actually *did* waste the meat, but only that—
by projecting what whites *would do* in such a case—we can guess what
Indians *might have done*. Nevertheless, if it were true that once Crow
Indians did kill too many animals, are we to conclude that Indians had
no environmental ethics? It is amazing that whites compare isolated
incidents of relatively small Indian wastefulness to the rapacity that
constitutes the white way of life. When whites killed millions upon
millions of buffalo, why do we concentrate on one case of Indian
overkill about which we know so little?

It is this last point that is perhaps the most telling in our
attempt to evaluate the extent of Indian ethics regarding nature. Indians saw themselves as both parts of nature and apart from nature.
They were not in perfect harmony with nature; there was tension in
their relationship. And yet there was a relationship that was concep-
tualized, felt, and acted upon. It is in comparison, or rather in contrast,
to white conceptions of, attitudes toward, and actions regarding the
environment that we come to see the remarkable closeness of Indians
to their land, both in ideal and practice. Through such a contrast we
observe that modern white nature contacts are subtractions from the
fullness of Indian environmental religions.

It is the opposing—one might say the conflicting—views of

nature, Indian and white, which help put the two groups into constant struggle with one another.[119] When American Indian environmental religions are contrasted to the attitudes, conceptions, and relations of whites with the same American land we realize the integrity of Indian nature religion, and we can better understand the history of Indian-white contacts.

Indians have often recognized a radical difference between their own and white nature relations, as evidenced by the following statement of a Wintu:

> The White people never cared for land or deer or bear. When we Indians kill meat, we eat it all up. When we dig roots we make little holes. When we build houses, we make little holes. When we burn grass for grasshoppers, we don't ruin things. We shake down acorns and pinenuts. We don't chop down the trees. We only use dead wood. But the White people plow up the ground, pull down the trees, kill everything. The tree says, "Don't. I am sore, Don't hurt me." But they chop it down and cut it up. The spirit of the land hates them. They blast out trees and stir it up to its depths. They saw up the trees. That hurts them. The Indians never hurt anything, but the White people destroy all. They blast rocks and scatter them on the ground. The rock says, "Don't. You are hurting me." But the White people pay no attention. . . . How can the spirit of the earth like the White man? . . . Everywhere the White man has touched it, it is sore.[120]

White and Indian values regarding nature have differed significantly over the entire history of their contact and have constituted the most common white justification for dispossessing Indians: the land use theory. Whites had the right to take Indian land, because "Whites followed the biblical injunction to 'subdue and replenish' the earth; 'the lordly savage' did not."[121] Indians were nature folk, living in communion with nature, rather than conquering it, and as nature folk they had no right to possess the American land. Furthermore, their association with nature, their identity as nature folk made them fit subjects for the same domination which whites practiced on nature itself.

Whether considering the Spanish, English, or French, we find the same lack of affection for the American environment in the early colonial period. For white Christians arriving in the sixteenth and seventeenth centuries, the American land was often a frightening wilderness, howling with wolves and evils, or a nondescript location of natural resources to be exploited for profit. French priests, Puritan divines, and Southern tobacco farmers found American nature dismal, horrible, hideous, terrible, dangerous, and devilish. It had to be transformed in order for Christians to appreciate it. On the other hand, the New World was the New Canaan, the promised land to be exploited and colonized by the Christian empire. When white Christian colonists were using the language of fear to describe America, they were also using imperial language which served for the future of white expansion. This was a land of unlimited and unused resources, virgin territory which would never run out. The best symbol for this attitude was the axe; white Americans viewed the land as something to chop down and make use of.

The discovery of the New World was concurrent with a shift in Western attitude toward nature. From the period beginning around 1492, Europeans lost a sense of geopiety. Nature to the postcontact white became landscape, or rather scenery, a backdrop to human activity. Farms overtook wilderness; cities overtook farms. The postcontact period saw a materially enriched Europe, made wealthy in great part from the exploitation of the New World's "natural resources," and a Europe become increasingly technological in conception, attitude, and action. ("Natural resources" was a term developed in the West around 1500, indicating a view of the environment as material to be exploited, existing only for its worth to humans.)[123]

There is a third type of white response to American environment: repression of affectionate instinct. It is noteworthy that the first Spanish to pass through the Grand Canyon made no comment about its beauty or unusual formations. Puritans for the first century wrote virtually no poetry describing nature. Instead, whites treated the land as a piece of property, something to be surveyed, parceled, bought, sold, argued over, stolen, and abandoned for land elsewhere.

Puritans saw the wilderness of New England as a place of sin and degeneracy; however, if they could cultivate it, turn under its natural state, reform it, and build garden villages in it, then it could become a refuge for Christian civilization. This image, the pastoral or edenic desire, permeates white American history, in which whites have seen themselves as occupying the middle ground between Indians and Europeans.[124]

In order to secure a nation of gardens, white Americans turned increasingly to technology to conquer and transform American nature into something other than itself. The identical technology was used to transform Indians into things other than themselves, through the transformation or outright destruction of their nature.

White Americans have wanted to transform the American earth without succumbing to the temptation to settle in one place. In

1774 the Royal Governor of Virginia, Lord Dunmore (who encouraged white migratory habits to foment his Indian war in that year) said:

> I have learnt from experience that the established Authority of any government in America, and the policy of Government at home, are both insufficient to restrain the Americans: and that they do and will remove as their avidity and restlessness invite them. They acquire no attachment to Place: But wandering about seems engrafted to their Nature.[125]

Perhaps because of their notorious disregard for efficient farming methods and their proclivity to deplete the soil, white Americans have failed to develop a sense of place. A nineteenth-century English traveler commented:

> There is as yet in New England and New York scarcely any such thing as local attachments—the love of a place because it is a man's own—because he has hewed it out of the wilderness, and made it what it is; or because his father did so, and he and his family have been born and brought up, and spent their happy youthful days upon it. Speaking generally, every farm from Eastport in Maine to Buffalo on Lake Erie, is for sale.[126]

In order to further our understanding white America's lack of love for nature, we should survey the history of European attitudes toward nature. The Genesis directives for humans to hold dominion over all creatures is one basis for Western arrogance toward nature.

The Christians went even further than the Hebrews and Greeks in downgrading the physical world. Early Christianity also thought of nature as inconsequential, temporary, a diversion from the real purpose of life — to serve God and seek the kingdom of God. Humans had to overcome and deny their physical nature.

One cannot attribute the entirety of Western alienation from the environment to the Christian scriptures;[127] if we look at the twelfth-century renaissance in Christian thought, we find a tradition that, if not finding nature essentially valuable, at least recognized its living and life-giving properties, as well as its connections both to God and to human existence. The sacramental system which culminated in the twelfth century used natural symbols, because nature revealed God, who made it.[128]

But the world which followed Aquinas followed Aristotle in saying that ethics excluded animals. For Aquinas, animals existed to

serve humans, and charity could not be directed to them.[129] The Black
Death of 1348 drew out resentments regarding nature, and Christians
sought further detachment from it. A new Western attitude toward
nature was evolving.[130]

Although it is always difficult to date a great shift in attitudes,
it would not be forcing the issue to say that just as Columbus was
reaching the New World, Europeans were reaching this new attitude
toward nature, losing their sense of geopiety.[131]

The American view of nature derived from this new tradition.
The Hegelian-Marxist school of Western philosophy has preserved a
respect for nature. Karl Marx wrote in 1844: "nature is (1) his direct
means of life, and (2) the material, the object, and the instrument of his
life-activity.... That man's physical and spiritual life is linked to nature
means simply that nature is linked to itself, for man is part of nature."[132] Yet even Marx saw a sharp cleavage between humans and the
rest of the natural world. His view of nature was of inorganic matter,
not living being.[133]

As an appreciative student of nature's impact on human life,
however, Marx set in motion a scholarly tradition which today finds its
heritage in the writings of Claude Lévi-Strauss and Fernand Braudel,
both who base their work on the assumption that in the universe
humans are not alone; they are part of a living universe which works its
influence on human life, as humans influence the living world.[134]
Possibly this significant sector of modern Western thought arises also
from Darwin, who showed that correspondences exist from one organism to another. In the United States, too, there is a tradition of
nature appreciation that dates to a Jeffersonian humanistic naturalistic
curiosity about the world.[135]

Within the last century a conservation movement has developed in America: from Marsh's 1864 *Man and Nature*, the first
conservationist book; through the first use of the term "ecology" in
1873, through the first use of the term "conservation" in its present
sense in 1875, when the American Forestry Association was founded;
through the back-to-nature movement of the early twentieth century
with its Boy Scouts, Campfire Girls, birdwatching, nature sermons,
and summer camps;[136] through Aldo Leopold's 1949 call for a Western
land ethic which would once again value the environment for itself;[137]
to the recent surge of ecological concern. Even so, American conser-
vationism has been based on efficiency, rather than on an idea of
obligation owed to nature.[138] The West has never recovered from its
Christian-Renaissance-commercial view of nature as something to
be exploited through scientific method and technology.

From the beginning of the modern era, Westerners have

tended to see the physical world as a source of suffering without viewing it fully as a source of existence. Contemporary atheists and Christians alike have tended to define Western civilization as effective "exploitation of the earth by man" and "protection against the forces of nature."[139] To be civilized is to be free of nature, to rise above and transcend nature, to shield oneself from nature and exploit it. For the Indians, nature is destructive and dangerous, but it is also nurturing and attractive. Indians repress and sublimate their protests against nature, turning them toward admiration of the world and its power. Most Westerners no longer have that ability.[140] Kenneth Clark, for example, claims that humans have either to admire or utilize animals, but not both simultaneously.[141]

Most Westerners believe that they live in a world in which only humans speak. The world is mute. The nonhuman environment does not speak to non-native Americans. There is no reciprocity, only silence.[142] Because the nonhuman world is devalued, because it does not speak to it, Western society persists in widespread torture and butchery of animals for the food and scientific industries far beyond the requirement for human subsistence.[143]

Racism derives in part from the devaluation of nature by Westerners. Herbert Marcuse describes the process: "The scientific method which led to the ever-more-effective domination of nature thus came to provide the pure concepts as well as the instrumentalities for the ever-more-effective domination of man by man *through* the domination of nature."[144]

American wealth has depended on expansion and therefore on the colonialization of Indians in order to gain land to sell in order to raise capital for industry, used in turn to transform nature. Since white America's wealth has come directly from the taking of Indian land, whites have been willing to espouse an ideology in which Indians have been made inanimate, just as whites have inanimated nature in order to justify exploitation of it.[145]

The sixteenth-century Spanish reformer Bartolomé de las Casas protested when he saw that his countrymen were thinking of Indians as natural resources to be exploited instead of as "rational men." Las Casas abhorred how the Spaniards treated the Indians like "pieces of wood that could be cut off trees and transported for building purpose, or like flocks of sheep or any other kind of animals that could be moved around indiscriminately."[146] Nature hatred had led directly to racism, especially toward people who were seen as nature folk, whose religions recognized and valued relations with nature.

To the white invaders Indians were a type of wild beast, totally associated with the wilderness in which they lived and in which they worshipped. The Puritans, for example, believed that the Indians' religion affirmed the satanic quality of the wilderness, just as the devilish quality of wilderness proved the evil of Indians.[147]

So closely associated with nature were the Indians and their religions that terms most commonly given to them by whites (especially missionaries) indicated their "natural" status. They were referred to as "pagans" (people of the countryside, not of the village), "heathens" (people of the wild, uninhabited places), and "savages" (people of the forests). And since they were so closely connected with nature, they had to be dominated like the rest of nature. Indians had to be transformed from their natural state, to become civilized, alienated from nature, and even destroyed if necessary.

The final series of events which assured a non-Indian domination of North America serves as an example of the ravaging of environment in order to ravage Indians. Between 1830 and 1885, especially during the last fifteen years, whites exterminated millions of buffalo. While white Americans used their technology to slaughter the animals for greed and sport, there was a simultaneous and related policy behind the killing. White military and political leaders at the time stated that destroying the buffalo would help destroy the Indians who subsisted on them, and they proposed that such a policy be pursued.[148]

The United States starved the Plains Indians into submission by exterminating their source of life, attacking them militarily in their ever-weakening position.

America under non-Indian domination continues to reflect the policies which promoted the conquest to begin with. White policy has been and continues to be a three-pronged attack on nature, nature folk, and nature religion. If non-Indian attitudes do not change, the persecution will continue.

▶▶▶▶▶▶▶▶▶ 2 ◀◀◀◀◀◀◀◀◀

SUBARCTIC INDIANS AND WILDLIFE

CALVIN MARTIN

L ONG AGO, AT THE DAWN OF CREATION "'all was man,'" the ethnologist Frederica de Laguna was told. "In myth-time all creatures appeared as human beings, speaking and living like men, yet mysteriously possessing some distinctive animal qualities or occasionally donning animal guise." This curious, unitary view of human and animal genesis prevails throughout the Canadian Subarctic. Nearly a half century ago Robert Sullivan uncovered this conviction among the Koyukon, while more recently James VanStone, describing Athapaskans in general, declared that "both men and animals. . . possessed essentially the same characteristics" when the world was new. Frank Speck, writing of the Montagnais-Naskapi of the Labrador Peninsula, remarked: "In the beginning of the world, before humans were formed, all animals existed grouped under 'tribes' of their kinds who could talk like men, and were even covered with the same protection." Because of this shared origin conjurors could declare to the game around them, "'You and I wear the same covering and have the same mind and spiritual strength,'" acknowledging that after the passage of untold generations the two were still, after all, spiritually akin.[1]

At first, then, humans and animals were identical, superimposed on each other in some nebulous human-animal form. Only subsequently did the two become differentiated, or polarized, in their outward, physical nature. "'The animals were once like the Indians and could talk as we do,'" a retired Mistassini shaman once confided in Speck. "'But some of them were overcome by others while in some animal disguise and forced to remain as such. Others assumed animal shapes so much that involuntarily they became transformed permanently.'"[2] Whatever the reasons, the change occurred: human and animal beings were no longer interchangeable, except in rare instances where certain Powerful shamans and particular animal species still seem capable of metamorphosis.[3] Under the new dispensation, "animals still remain close to men, understanding what men say, aware of their acts, and ready to bestow good or bad fortune. They are full members of man's moral universe, though living outside the human circle of his campfire light."[4]

The foregoing myth is a prerequisite to understanding the Subarctic hunter's attitude toward game resources. Its message is clear: from time immemorial there has been a fundamental equation or sympathy between human persons and animal persons—a sympathy that pervades not just the hunt itself, but all of life's experiences. Of course it would be impossible to fit this origin myth within a particular time frame; it is sufficient to know that it is the bedrock upon which virtually all modern-day Subarctic hunters construct their relationship with wildlife.

The relationship is a social one. In the words of Murray and Rosalie Wax, animals "reside in lodges, gather in council, and act according to the norms and regulations of kinship. In [American Indian folktales] . . . man and the animals are depicted as engaging in all manner of social and sociable interaction: They visit, smoke, gamble, and dance together; they exchange wisdom; they compete in games and combat; and they even marry and beget offspring." Animals and humans, despite morphological differences, remain fundamentally similar. Diamond Jenness was told by Parry Island Potawatomi (nearly indistinguishable from their Ojibwa relatives) that animals have a tripartite nature, like man's: body, soul, and shadow (the shadow functioning as the "eye" of the soul). And Julius Lips found Montagnais-Naskapi adhering to a similar principle: "the game animal is gifted with a soul similar to that of man; its reactions and social organization are imagined as similar to those of its human brethren." Earlier in this century, the ethnologist Alanson Skinner described the Eastern Cree as believing "that all animals are speaking and thinking beings, in many ways not one whit less intelligent than human beings. . . . In some cases . . . certain animals have a greater supernatural ability than the Indian. This is particularly true of the bear who is considered more intelligent and to have greater medicine powers in many ways than mankind. He walks upon his hind legs like a man, and displays manlike characteristics. In fact, some tribes regard the bear as an unfortunate man."[5]

Animals thus allegedly think and behave as humans do. The chief distinction between the two beings, animal and human, is that they live in different dimensions. The world of animals is the spirit world — the "manito world" — with the understanding that animals exist primarily as spirits who don fleshy robes from time to time for human benefit. "The fox or other animal that one kills today is not the real animal," confirmed de Laguna, "but only its fleshy clothing. The real fox himself, his spirit or shadow or soul, is alive, watching the hunter. 'His coat and dress, I get it,' explained one old man; 'his self over there,' pointing to the bushes. 'Himself, he listens, he sees. . . . That's why I take care nice, everything burn. . . . No treat right, no more kill.'" The two realms, spiritual and physical, are separate and opposite and—most important—mediated by animals. In conjunction with this, the Copper River Ahtena interviewed by de Laguna were adamant that wildlife should never be domesticated (not a universal Subarctic sentiment, incidentally): "it is taboo to keep any wild animal or bird as a pet, to tie it up or bring it into the house. . . . For though animals and men live in the same social and religious world, still each must keep a respectful distance from the other."[6] To domesticate animals evidently would destroy the integrity of this spiritual/physical relationship, with disastrous results for the devout.

Be that as it may, what is perceived here is a set of binary contrasts, or opposites (spiritual/physical), that have been effectively bridged through the goodwill of game animals. Subarctic Indians have a penchant for arranging life's experiences in terms of binary opposites; the spiritual/physical opposition is just one of many. Animals, so far as we can discern, serve as the chief reference point or transformation agent in all of the major dualities of life: spiritual/physical, male/female, outside/inside, clean/soiled, health/illness, luck-success-confidence/failure-bad luck-anxiety, Power/Powerlessness, feast-satiety-abundance/starvation-scarcity. There are undoubtedly more; these most readily come to mind. A number of the above bipolar groups are subsumed within broader, more comprehensive polarities. Nonetheless, in each case, whether dealing with superior or inferior sets of contrasts, animals appear to regulate the polar extremes.

Unlike our Western cosmology, which emphasizes the physical realm, the Subarctic Indian cosmology is principally concerned with the spiritual world. "To enter this world was to step *into*, not out of, the *real* world."[7] The crucial point is that it was often game animals who ushered the individual, usually a male, into this esoteric dimension. Animals, in short, were the prime source of Power, endowing the supplicant with the supernatural force and wisdom necessary to traffic successfully in this other realm.[8] Visitation from some guide, generally in animal guise, came at puberty during the vision quest when the youth, at the urging of his elders, went out alone and begged the "grandfathers" (in Ojibwa parlance) for their "blessings." Among those groups that did not have a guardian spirit complex, such as the Montagnais-Naskapi of the Labrador Peninsula, Power generally welled up from some inner source, one's soul-spirit, or "Great Man," as Speck was told.[9]

Whatever the source of Power, whether the inner (e.g., soul-spirit) or more common outer (animal guide) variety, its most common and acceptable use has been in subduing animal spirits in the chase. This is what Speck had in mind when he referred to hunting as a "holy occupation": animal spirits are first subdued by the hunter's spirit before the incarnate form of the beast is actually slain. In a very real sense the final bagging of the animal victim is a foregone conclusion. The hunter knows through scouting and various divinatory techniques —often scapulimancy, involving the extorting of information from an animal bone[10]—where the game awaits him on the appointed day of execution. He has been stalking the victim's spirit for perhaps days before and has managed, through the siren Power of his hunt songs and dreams, to secure its permission to be slaughtered.

Subarctic hunters thus traditionally have regarded game animals as *gifts*; in hunt dreams, the animal *surrenders* itself to be killed. This is hardly surprising among people who believe, as do the Montagnais-Naskapi, that the beaver, for example, "embodies extraordinarily high spiritual endowments. It can transform itself into other animal forms, that of geese and other birds being specifically mentioned. The beaver can disappear by penetrating the ground, by rising aloft into the air, or by diving into the depths of lake or stream, and remaining any length of time desired. In short, 'he can escape or hide himself if he wishes to, so that he can never be taken'"—except with his "amiable consent."[11]

Animals who voluntarily sacrifice themselves to the needy hunter are regarded by Mistassini Cree, at least, as "friends": "The relationship of hunters to the animals may sometimes be likened to having friends among those animals which inhabit the particular region." (One might suggest that friendship or its opposite—hostility— has always characterized the human-animal relationship throughout the Canadian Subarctic. Mutual insensibility must have been rare or nonexistent.) Indeed, this conviction formed the basis of Eastern Cree-Montagnais concepts of land tenure. Game animals, Julius Lips was repeatedly told, "were the true owners of the hunting-grounds."[12]

Descendants of these people detailed a similar belief to Adrian Tanner: within the hunting group ownership of the territory derived from the fauna, who had a cordial relationship with the hunting-group leader. "The most common use of this idea of friendship between a hunter and an animal," Tanner found, "is in stories about men who have the reputation of having killed a large number of animals of a particular species. Such a man is said to have a particular member of that species as a 'friend.' Sometimes this animal, which the man must never kill, is spoken of as being the man's 'pet.' Generally, the man who has such a reputation is already past the age of peak hunting abilities, so that while his reputation rests on past kills, the significance of his ability is that he is believed to be able to help the younger men of his group make kills of that particular species." There was always an anxious moment right after the death of such a hunting leader, when it was feared his friends would follow him to the land of the dead — a clear sign that the remaining members of the species would elude future capture by the man's survivors. "In such a case where an animal friend does stay in the group's area it is often said to be because someone else in the group has become a friend of that species."[13]

Animal persons, as friends, were to be treated courteously. "A central attitude in the conduct of hunting is that game animals are persons and that they must be respected."[14] This meant they were usually addressed by some quaint title of endearment rather than by their common name; the hunter refrained from disclosing to associates his intention to pursue a particular animal species; inwardly ecstatic relatives and friends were subdued as they greeted the returning hunter, since animal shades took a dim view of noisy celebration;[15] and the carcass was disposed of according to a procedure thought pleasing to the slain beast's spirit.

It was once common throughout the Subarctic to consume or otherwise use the entire carcass of at least certain economically and mythologically prominent species. Left-overs from the so-called eat-all feast were either burned or, more recently among the Mistassini Cree at least, wrapped up and hidden from the gaze of the animal shade. The concealed flesh would be eaten at some future time. As for the inedible remains, these were either made into useful or aesthetic objects, or decorated and prominently displayed — large-animal skulls are and were often placed in a tree so as to enjoy the view. Moreover, certain bones of most, if not all, large game species are habitually returned to their natural element (terrestrial or aquatic) where eventually they will be reclothed in flesh (at the whim of the "game boss") in order to be hunted, once more, by the Indian.[16] Hunting is thus a cycle for the game species involved, a cycle whose chief ethical principle is *courtesy* — mutual courtesy — which is a mutual obligation.

Clearly, then, animals join the physical and spiritual realms in several contexts. "The vision quest symbolically transforms the child's meat into spirit, and the hunt transforms the animal's spirit into meat," observed Robin Ridington.[17] The cooperation of animal persons is the essential catalyst in both transformation equations.

Continuing to think in structural terms, and limiting our attention strictly to the hunt, we might in sum characterize it as a spiritual/ physical transaction mediated by game persons. There are included within this umbrella transaction several minor relationships, expressed as bipolar opposites, which likewise take their cue from animals. The hunt occurs in the bush, the "outside," spiritually "clean" realm, which terms bespeak the place of animal spirits. Men, in general, are the only sex allowed to penetrate this outside space. At the other extreme, women function in the campsite, the "inside," spiritually "soiled" realm — the place of animal carcasses.[18]

It is curious that certain Ojibwa appear to equate women with game animals. Irving Hallowell noted that "the verb applied to the hunting of animals is commonly used by men when speaking of the pursuit of a girl. And this association between animal and woman appears in one of the dreams I collected. A hunter dreamed of a beautiful girl approaching him. Waking up, he interpreted this dream as meaning that an animal had been caught in one of his deadfalls. He went to the trap and, sure enough, he found a female fisher." Moreover, there is an apparent parallel between a man's prerogatives with a woman and those he enjoys with game animals. Hallowell goes on to tell of an incident wherein a woman, thought to have been made ill through the sorcery of a rebuffed suitor, retaliated by making the man more ill than she. "Her life had been threatened but she did not kill him, although she had the power to do so. This outcome is significant when considered in relation to the dominant role of men in this culture. What seems to be implied is the assumption that men have potential sexual *rights* over women that must always be respected."[19] This relationship seems roughly analogous to that of the male hunter with the game: a man may harvest animals so long as he refrains from abusing them. The hunter who violates this principle is liable to be struck down by disease — disease originating with offended game spirits. Indeed, the animal theory of disease etiology is conspicuous throughout the Subarctic. And here one discerns yet another set of binary contrasts brokered by game spirits: health and disease. Health results from a proper relationship with game; disease follows from a perverted one.[20] Likewise, an abundance of food (i.e. "'forest food,' tantamount in meaning to 'pure food'")[21] derives from an amicable relationship with game, while famine is the result of disharmony between animals and man.

Wild game flesh is loaded with symbolic significance: it is a palpable sign of animal friendship; it represents physical nourishment;

and it is medicine (prophylactic), since animal flesh is but an altered form of plant forage and "the vegetable kingdom . . . [is] the original source of medicine agency."[22] Animal flesh may also serve as a sexual metaphor. Tanner has noticed that bear and beaver carcasses are laid out in the lodge along a sexual axis: the head and foreparts face the male half of the structure, the hind parts the female half. This positioning of the animal along a gender axis is often carried over into consumption ritual, by which women are restricted to eating the hind limbs and men the forelimbs. "Eating both establishes the separate nature of men and women, and also makes possible the relationship between the two. It is the animal, which is a combination of sexual elements, which makes the establishment of sexual relations and reproduction possible." Elsewhere Tanner declares: "Bringing home an animal means for the hunter not only the end of the hunting cycle, but the start of a domestic one. . . . This reunion [of the hunter with his family] has a distinctly sexual aspect, and . . . the animal itself becomes a symbolic mediator in the starting, or re-starting, of this sexual relationship."[23]

One could explore further symbolic relationships between animals and humans. If it is true, as I believe, that animals are the linchpin holding together the paired contrasts of traditional Subarctic Indian life, then it follows that the human-animal relationship must encompass far more than just the subsistence economy. Hunting, writ large, lends meaning and inspiration to life; as a way of living it gives participants their sense of identity. A proper, cordial relationship with animals becomes vital in maintaining that sense of identity—that sense of how the world functions and how humans are to conduct themselves within this larger sphere of existence. Animals instruct human beings, at least males, in the mysteries of life; by giving heed to animals and their ways — by making themselves receptive to their counsel — hunters learn how they must behave.[24] No wonder game is typically treated with exquisite respect.

The foregoing information has been gleaned from twentieth-century ethnographic sources which describe modern Indians living more or less traditionally. We must leave to the ethnohistorian the task of determining just where matters stood between human and animal persons back through the centuries of recorded time. In particular, historians should re-evaluate what the Canadian fur trade meant for the Indians involved. If animals were as vital to the Indian sense of identity and purpose during the catastrophic years of the trade, when furbearers and other game were hunted rapaciously, how did native hunters and trappers rationalize their destructive behavior? What *was* the human-animal relationship during the height of fur trade involvement?

Why is there a tendency in this century to treat animals, once more it seems, with deference? Has there been a re-emergence of an aboriginal hunting ethic—a revival of the traditionally courteous relationship between the hunter and hunted? My reading of the evidence leads me to believe there has indeed been such a revival. I have elsewhere made the case that the hunting ethic witnessed by twentieth-century ethnographers is essentially aboriginal, although it was suspended for much of the fur trade era, for reasons which cannot be explored here.[25] Why Indians overhunted game for purposes of trade is one obvious question to be considered, given the evidence for a cordial relationship between humans and animals in this century and the suspicion (at least) that this mutually courteous arrangement has prehistoric origins.

A more fundamental yet related question is, What did the European intrusion do to the structure of the Indian world? How was the balance of life's contrasting elements affected? Thinking in today's terms and bearing in mind that animals occupy a strategic position in binding together the basic contrasts of life, what have been the social and cultural ramifications of a decline in hunting as a way of life? As traditional hunting pursuits become increasingly impracticable and other life styles take over, what is happening to these peoples' sense of identity and purpose? It strikes me that much that is distinctive about the traditional Subarctic Indian way of life hinges, as it always has, on the peculiar relationship with game animals. To undermine that rapport, either deliberately (say, by government action) or inadvertently (through subtle pressures of assimilation), is to erode a people's confidence in who they are. They were originally kinsmen to animals; that many individuals remain so even today is a powerful and, to the chauvinistic Western world, rather deflating lesson in cultural resilience.

▶▶▶▶▶▶▶▶▶ 3 ◀◀◀◀◀◀◀◀◀

INDIANS AS ECOLOGISTS AND OTHER ENVIRONMENTAL THEMES IN AMERICAN FRONTIER HISTORY

WILBUR R. JACOBS

I BELIEVE ENVIRONMENTAL THEMES, especially as they relate to the American Indian, deserve more attention in American history than they have hitherto received. Environmental history can be a window to a clearer image of the past and can offer us unique perspectives on generally accepted historical concepts of unlimited growth, frontier expansionism, and the rapid use of nonrenewable natural resources.[1]

The environmental theme goes back beyond discovery, but my analysis begins with the environmental impact of the European discovery of America, or, as it is now called, "the Columbian exchange."[2] Even at this time we have eyewitness accounts of environmental impacts. The evidence reveals that Americans and their colonial ancestors altered their natural surroundings and set in motion physical and biological processes that have had reverberating effects on the environment. Our environmental past, then, can be viewed as a history of our modification of the earth and the cumulative effects of our actions that have set new natural forces in motion.[3] With this in mind, what were the significant results of drastic changes Europeans and Americans made in the natural world of the Western Hemisphere?

Although the Columbian exchange had profound political implications, its environmental impact was also drastic. When Columbus landed on an island in the Bahamas, which he named San Salvador, the gentle Arawak Indians welcomed him warmly. They were a peaceful people who made pottery, wove cloth, and carried on a farming-fishing, handicraft life style that held little immediate interest for the admiral because they mined no gold. The Spaniards, however, were impressed with the physical beauty of the native people and the verdure of the island, "the very green trees," and the variety of delicious fruits.[4] Within little more than a century, by the time Jamestown was settled, San Salvador had experienced an environmental transformation. The Arawaks were gone; in their place were Spanish planters who had transformed the land into cotton fields worked by African slaves. By cutting down tropical vegetation and turning fertile land into one-crop agricultural fields, Spanish planters leached the soil of its nutrients. In time, swells of windblown sand filled the interior areas. Eventually the island, with its human, animal, and plant life destroyed, became virtually a desert.

Essentially the same story was repeated later on the larger island, Hispaniola. Here, likewise, the island's fertility and the large native population of skillful farmers (estimated to have developed the most productive fields in the world—cassava, beans, maize, and other crops) had been destroyed by the 1580s.[5] This destruction took place less than a century after the admiral had made the island his headquarters, divided the land among his followers, and forced Indians to work mines and fields in the land they had once called their home. Indeed, the Indians' mortality was so incredible that it called forth protests of the Spanish Dominican, Bartolomé de las Casas, who tells us that in 1552 there were only a hundred Hispaniola Indian survivors. He goes on to report that island after island had been despoiled, as he says, "totally unpeopled and destroyed." Again and again Las Casas writes that other islands were "waste and desolate," "wholly desert."[6]

Large islands like Cuba and Jamaica, Las Casas wrote, were subjected to the assault. Though Indian mortality on these islands was very high, and though tropical vegetation was altered, nature was able to fight back in later centuries. And, of course, the mainland of North America, the eastern edge of a huge shaggy continent, also felt the impact of the European invasion. The immense land mass at first gave resistance, but everywhere there was depopulation among Indian people after first contacts with Europeans.

Modern scholars now argue that Las Casas' estimates of Indian mortality were modest[7] and that there were as many as 8 million Indians on Hispaniola in 1492, some 25 million in central Mexico, and as many as 10 million people in North America, north of the Rio Grande.[8] And in the whole Western Hemisphere there were probably 100 million, possibly a larger population than in western Europe. All of these Indian people had developed subsistence patterns to support skyrocketing populations through domestication of food plants and through developing skills to harvest wild plants. They were also excel-

THE INDIAN WIDOW, by Joseph Wright of Derby, 1785. Wright's image of the widow as noble savage was painted just after Britain had lost the War of the American Revolution and, in the Treaty of Paris 1783, had turned over much of the lands of its Indian allies to the jurisdiction of the new United States. A homeland as well as a husband has been lost in battle. Compounding the impending loss of a continent, diseases accidentally introduced by Europeans and Africans set off devastating epidemics. America was indeed what historian Francis Jennings has termed not a virgin but a "widowed land." *Derby Art Gallery, Derby, England*

lent hunters and fishermen, but they had little resistance to the white man's microbes.

The disease frontier that swept across the Western Hemisphere came with the Europeans, many of them immune carriers. Smallpox, carried by an airborne virus, was undoubtedly the worst Indian killer since it returned repeatedly in epidemic waves to smother survivors of previous attacks. Other diseases, many of which we now call childhood illnesses, such as measles and chickenpox, ravaged whole Indian societies.[9]

We can round the circle of the entire Western Hemisphere appraising this first great environmental impact, though we are still just beginning to learn of its profound ramifications for the New World. One fact we must now cope with is that it caused a demographic disaster without known parallel. Although scholars may argue whether 50 million or 100 million Indians lived in the New World in 1492, they agree (except for a few stubborn Hispanics)[10] that the new data drastically change our view of what happened in early American history. We can no longer write about a peaceful occupation by English peoples of a fertile Appalachian frontier. Rather we have to deal with the displacement of millions of people, an invasion of Europeans into densely populated lands. And we must understand that the process decimated many Indians who had developed life styles to support millions of people without obliteration of the land and its resources.

After having studied a mass of evidence in the biological, physical, and social sciences, I am convinced that Indians were indeed conservators. They were America's first ecologists. Through their burning practices, their patterns of subsistence (by growing, for instance, beans and corn together to preserve the richness of the soil), by creating various hunting preserves for beaver and other animals, and by developing special religious attitudes, Indians preserved a wilderness ecological balance wheel.[11] Even the intensive farming of the Iroquois, without chemical fertilizers and pesticides, protected the ecology of the northeastern forest.[12]

Victor Shelford, in his excellent book on the ecology of North America, argues convincingly that prehistoric America was divided into a number of distinct biotic provinces. In each, Indians, as well as plants, animals, insects, and other forms of life, were integral parts of an ecological niche. Modern Americans, Shelford maintains, have altered or destroyed 98 percent of these original North American ecosystems.[13] Indian people, on the other hand, had lived within them for centuries by developing a land ethic tuned to the carrying capacity of each ecozone. Indians today know these facts, though they are couched in a different kind of language, handed down through centuries by oral recall. As one of the most recent Indian spokesmen, Vine Deloria, Jr., a Sioux, recently wrote, "The land-use philosophy of Indians is so utterly simply that it seems stupid to repeat it: man must live with other forms of life on the land and not destroy it."[14]

But let us return to the subject of historical environmental impacts. There are other environmental changes in our history that illustrate my thesis that Europeans and, later, Americans set new forces in motion which altered the face of the land. I refer, for instance, to the tidal wave of settlement that in one generation occupied most of the territories of the Louisiana Purchase and substituted domestic hoofed animals (cattle, horses, hogs, sheep, and goats) for millions of wild hoofed animals (bison, deer of various kinds, including elk, moose, antelope, and wild sheep and goats). One authority estimates that 100 million wild hoofed animals originally occupied North America, and certainly a large portion of that number were part of the organic ecological circle of the Louisiana land.[15] This environmental event that swiftly transformed the natural world of a vast area is hardly mentioned in our general histories, save an occasional word of indignation over indiscriminate slaughter of plains buffalo. The very magnitude of this environmental change, including the dispossession of the Indians, boggles the mind. Scholars like James C. Malin spent a lifetime evaluating some of the ramifications. He finally specialized in the history of plains grasses, many of which evolved from European origins. He and other investigators found hardy descendants of wild buffalo grasses growing along railroad rightaways.[16] Malin's environmental history researches have not had the recognition they deserve.[17]

To detect the themes and patterns of this environmental shift, we can turn to eyewitnesses who tell us much about how and why changes persisted. Early Virginia accounts help us to understand the gradual environmental modifications that took place in the colonial south. In particular, Robert Beverley, early eighteenth-century planter, gives us clues. The soil was so rich, Beverley tells us, that all kinds of crops flourished, but tobacco was favored from the beginning because "it promised the most immediate gain," which, in turn, caused planters to "overstock the market." His fellow Virginians, Beverley complained, "spunge upon the Blessings of a warm Sun and a fruitful soil ... gathering in the Bounties of the Earth."[18] What Beverley so clearly observed, the extraordinary exploitation of the soil by southern planters, was echoed in the writings of a series of eminent Virginians, including George Washington, Patrick Henry, and Thomas Jefferson. Washington complained that his fields were running into gullies.[19] Henry is credited with the statement, "he is the greatest patriot, *who stops the most gullies*."[20] Though the planters experimented with clover, contour planting, and other devices, soil erosion and depletion persisted. This subject is a constant theme in American agricultural history.[21]

While the farming practices in the middle colonies placed less emphasis upon cash crops which exhausted the soil, there is historical evidence of wasteful consumption everywhere in these colonies. Peter

Kalm, a Swedish scientist touring this part of colonial America in the 1750s, was surprised at the destructive habit of settlers who cleared the land, used it for crops, then for pasture, and later moved on to repeat the process in new land. Another traveler observed that in New Jersey in the 1790s there was "stupid indifference" to the land. The Americans, he said, "in order to save themselves the work of shaking or pulling off the nuts, they find it simpler to cut the tree and gather the nuts from it, as it lies on the ground."[22] Forests were regarded as "troublesome growths." A European visitor was astounded to see his landlord casually cut down "thirty two young cedars to make a hog pen."[23]

Another side of the penetration of the wilderness is given by Cadwallader Colden, colonial New York scientist and early ethnohistorian. According to Colden and other sources collaborating his statements, the entire beaver population of what is now the state of New York, then the Iroquois country, was exterminated in the 1640s as a result of the Anglo-Dutch fur traders operating out of Albany.[24] Only some thirty years after Henry Hudson had explored the wilderness river that bears his name, beaver, one of the most beneficial animals in the North American ecological balance, had become a victim of the assault on wildlife. The attack on beaver was persistent and far reaching, culminating in its extermination in many areas of the Far West. Fortunately, in recent years, this remarkable animal has reappeared in certain locations.[25]

In colonial New England there were reliable accounts of Puritan assaults upon forests, wildlife, and the soil. Carried on almost like the wars against the Indians, the war against the land resulted in cutting down the big trees, killing much of the furbearing animal population, and exhausting the light cover of topsoil.[26] As one midwestern critic alleged, New Englanders were much like their soil, intensely cultivated, but only six inches deep;[27] they left a trail of abandoned farms and old stone fences enclosing former fields and pastures.

Despite this midwestern criticism, the evidence shows that each of the New England colonies, almost from the very beginning, did have an environmental awareness which is evident in statutes providing for protection of natural resources in the immediate neighborhood of settlements. Statutes, for instance, restricted the unlimited range of livestock, especially hogs, which invaded common pastures and cornfields.[28] Streams were protected from overfishing, forests from overcutting, all of which was a part of a scheme for social control that governed the life style of entire colonies, including even rebellious Rhode Island.[29] Although some regulations were designed to prevent nearby forests from being cut so that inhabitants would not have to go great distances for firewood, we can discern here, I believe, a respect for the land. This is undoubtedly a factor which has helped to preserve much of the charm that still remains in New England today.

Jeremy Belknap, writing in 1792 of his beloved New Hampshire, goes so far as to tell us that the good life was living in harmony with nature, though he stresses a man-controlled environment. As he phrased it, "Were I to form a picture of a happy society, it would be a town consisting of a due mixture of hills, valleys, and streams of water. The land well fenced and cultivated." In his good land he sees the need for a good inn, a "practical preacher," a schoolmaster, and a "musical society," but he stresses that the society should be mostly "husbandmen." When all these elements are combined in a beautiful natural setting, one finds, he writes, a situation "most favorable to social happiness of any which the world can afford."[30]

Thomas Jefferson, of course, developed a similar agrarian theme in his Notes on Virginia. While he took great pride in the American environment, celebrating its vastness and the superior nature of its denizens to those found elsewhere (noting, for example, "that the reindeer [of the Old World] could walk under the belly of our moose"), he believed that the land should not be left to the Indians.[31] Benefits should come to the white farmers who subdue the land. He, indeed, called for immediate population growth, predicting, as did his friend Benjamin Franklin, that the American population would grow exponentially. "The present desire of America," he wrote, "is to produce rapid population by as great importation of foreigners as possible." He went so far as to assert that "our rapid multiplication will . . . cover the whole northern, if not the southern continent."[32]

In Belknap as well as in Jefferson we see clearly a pride in the American landscape as the nation expands and utilizes the bounties of nature. From the birth of the Republic, then, there was an ambivalence about appreciating and protecting nature or exploiting the land. Increasingly the evidence of eyewitnesses is that there was environmental distress, but this was seen as part of the penalty of progress as America moved west to occupy the wilderness.

Henry Schoolcraft, explorer, Indian agent, and author of a valuable survey report in 1819, is one of the many government reporters on western lands who details the environmental distress. He visited the Midwest and the Ozark Highlands during the period of early penetration of wilderness resulting from a lead mining boom. His particularized account of forty-five mines in Burton Township, Missouri, described a mining frontier that left abandoned pits everywhere in its wake as miners moved from place to place in an eager search for riches. "Unwilling to be disappointed," Schoolcraft wrote, "they fall to work and tear up the whole surrounding country." The savagery of the miners in churning up the land was almost paralleled by another group of pioneers, a society of fur hunters whom the explorer called "savage Europeans" because of their crude life style and their wanton destruction of wildlife.[33]

By the time government surveyor David Owen visited the Midwest several decades later, in 1852, swarms of emigrants from eastern American and European hives had occupied the land. Mining and fur trapping pioneers were no longer of great importance, but Owen had much to say about the assault of the lumbermen. Writing mainly on the geology of the Midwest, Owen does, however, pause to record what we now know was the disappearance of the great Wisconsin pine forests. On the Wisconsin River alone, he tells us, there were twenty-four mills running forty-five saws cutting 19.5 million board feet of lumber and 3 million board feet of shingles. The annual value of the lumber for the millowners was $123,000.[34] Mills on the other nearby rivers did four and five times as much business. Why the tremendous demand for wood? Owen says that there was an "immense consumption of building material" in cities already built. Moreover, there were numerous new towns and villages "which spring up," he says, "as if by magic, along the shores of the Mississippi and its tributaries."[35] Owen's comments help us to understand the forces behind the rapid plundering of America's midwestern timber resources.

During the westward surge of the 1850s, and in the immediately following decades, there were other government surveys, including Clarence King's *Geographical Exploration of the Fortieth Parallel*; the surveys led by Ferdinand V. Hayden after the Civil War, which were instrumental in the creation of Yellowstone National Park; and George M. Wheeler's *Report upon . . . Surveys West of the One Hundredth Meridian* of 1889.[36] They are collectively a mine of data on environmental history. The earlier Zebulon Montgomery Pike report of 1810 and the Stephen H. Long account of 1821 are excellent background reading for understanding the origins of the so-called myth of the "great American desert" of the Southwest.[37]

The Pike and Long commentaries help us to appreciate the most valuable of all the post–Civil War accounts, John Wesley Powell's *Report on the Lands of the Arid Region of the United States*.[38] This single work, acclaimed by our best scholars of conservation history, was the first study of the land to call for a scientific and environmental understanding of the West and its wilderness resources. Powell, a former professor, a one-armed veteran of the Civil War, and an explorer of the Colorado River, was concerned about the American abuse of arid lands. His *Report* of 1878 was at once a treatise and a sermon on the need to revise our western land policies which were based upon farming in the humid areas east of the Mississippi. He argued that we needed detailed maps of the arid country that identified mineral, timber, pasturage, and irrigable lands. Along with this he called for a series of land laws based on new concepts and providing for regional water planning. Eighty acres, for instance, should be sold to an irrigation farmer, but 2,500 acres were the minimum needed for a grazing operation.[39]

But Powell was battling ignorance, greed, and disinterest in conservation. In fighting speeches and published articles he elaborated on his report and also confronted a backlash of arguments. One of the strange, unscientific myths that Powell combated was the idea that "the rain follows the plow." All a farmer had to do was to plant trees in an arid area to change the climate.[40]

Powell's forceful statement on environmental abuse was but one of many eyewitness accounts which collectively helped bring about new policies and land laws. While Powell was laboring for reform as a government geologist, a contemporary of his, George Perkins Marsh, provided the first overall appraisal of what had happened to the land in America and in the world at large by the middle of the nineteenth century. Marsh, a brilliant self-made ecologist, a one-time school teacher, lawyer, businessman, and diplomat, first saw the great despoliation in miniature in his native state of Vermont where the Green Mountains, even faster than the tobacco lands of the South, had lost their topsoil.[41] After fires, timbermen, insects, and wheat farmers had done their worst, Vermonters turned their herds of sheep to denude the slopes. The resulting erosion, Marsh said, caused "deserts in summer and seas in autumn and spring."

In his book, *Man and Nature, or Physical Geography as Modified by Human Action*, Marsh showed that man's impact upon nature had become so powerful that nature could no longer heal herself. Encyclopedic in his research, probing sources in languages of antiquity as well as those of modern times, he described land abuse in the world from the time of the pollution of Rome to the 1860s. Knowledgeable in the physical and biological sciences, in engineering, in the law, and in methods of historical research, he demonstrated that the cumulative effect of all the plows and axes was ecological catastrophe in the world. He traced the violent attacks through aqueducts, reservoirs, canals, dams, diking, flooding, and the needless killing of birds, insects, reptiles, and mammals.[42] His essay, for instance, on the value of sand dunes is strikingly modern. His comment that extensive mining might alter the magnetic and electric condition of the earth's crust is still ahead of its time.[43] As Stuart Udall has noted, Marsh's book, *Man and*

Nature, was the beginning of land wisdom in this country.[44] What Marsh told us — and all other writers have had to build upon his observation — was that in nature there had been ecological balance until the arrival of man brought a serious imbalance.[45]

While Marsh's and Powell's observations were materializing into books that would, in time, help bring about an ecological consciousness in America, there were many others extolling the virtues of expansionism, land exploitation, and corralling the Indians on reservations. The most representative, and perhaps the most persuasive, of all these writers was the economist, statistician, former Indian superintendent, and one-time president of the Massachusetts Institute of Technology, Francis A. Walker.[46]

It was Walker, also a superintendent of the U.S. Census in 1870, 1880, and 1890, whose views eloquently illustrated the prevailing ideas of the day, which were based upon the social Darwinism of Herbert Spencer and other writers. Extolling the kind of men who rose "from stage to stage in intellectual, moral, and physical power,"[47] Walker at the same time praised the "genius" of Americans who had a "fire of Americanism," inventiveness, adaptability, and an ability to meet and mingle in the vast western territories which "had no history of their own." In tracing the United States' center of population as it moved westward, Walker discovered that by 1890 "the line of the frontier," that is, "a line of continuous settlement," had reached the Pacific Coast. With a burgeoning population the United States had occupied the continent from east to west. There was no longer a frontier line that could "be traced on a map."[48]

What is particularly significant about Walker, aside from his genuine popularity and influence in his own time, is the fact that he was, in effect, the creator of a frontier theory of history which, slightly modified, was later developed by Frederick Jackson Turner. Even Walker's geographical classification of land divisions, or sections, was almost exactly the same as the pattern developed by Turner when he later modified his frontier theory with his sectional hypothesis. Turner's writings and citations to Walker and his heavily lined personal copy of an address by Walker, containing seminal ideas on the frontier theory, are evidence of Walker's compelling influence in helping Turner create a theoretical scaffolding of history.[49] Thus Walker as well as Turner stressed a theory of frontier progress and growth, which in time came to mean the commercialization and conquest of nature. The land, according to this view of historical events, is generally regarded as a commodity instead of a resource because of the stress on conquistador themes of frontier expansionism.[50]

Although in his later years Turner had serious reservations about unlimited population growth and a never-ending exploitation of nonrenewable resources, this line of thought did not reach his published writings.[51] Far ahead of Turner in understanding environmental social costs was a contemporary of his, Thorstein Veblen, son of a Norwegian pioneer who had spent his early years on a farm near Portage, Wisconsin (Turner's home town), where he labored in the fields doing a man's work while still a youth.[52] Considered by some as the greatest frontier voice of his time, Veblen's stream of books and essays dissected the Spencerian theme of Anglo-Saxon elitism in America as well as the historical process of frontier development.

In analyzing America's nineteenth-century dilemma, Veblen concluded that vested interests did not bear their share of environmental costs because the "doing business" rationale of wealthy Americans caused rapid social losses for the nation at large. As an eyewitness to wasteful farming practices and to business domination of government, a situation which permitted the slaughter of buffalo and exploitation of the Indian in his time, Veblen provided a unique and penetrating assessment of what was going on in the United States. The various frontiers of "progress" — the fur trading, mining, ranching, farming, and oil drilling frontiers—Veblen understood as having produced huge social losses, almost impossible to calculate on a monetary basis.[53] As Veblen wrote: "this American plan or policy is very simply a settled practice of converting all public wealth to private gain on a plan of legalized seizure." The scheme of converting public wealth to private gain gave impetus, Veblen argued, to the growth of slavery because of the development of one-crop agriculture on a large scale fueled by forced labor. Both agricultural and real estate speculation were aspects of this progressive confiscation of natural resources. The history of frontier expansion, Veblen maintained, was marked by the seizure of specific natural resources for privileged interests. There was a kind of order to the taking: what was most easily available for quick riches went first. After the despoliation of wildlife for fur trade wealth came the taking of gold and other precious minerals followed by the confiscation of timber, iron, other metals, oil, natural gas, water power, irrigation rights, and transportation right-of-ways.[54] What was the result of such a shortsighted policy? The inevitable consequence, Veblen maintained, was the looting of the nation's nonrenewable resources to enrich the privileged few. The fur trade, Veblen said, represented this kind of exploitation and was "an unwritten chapter on the debauchery and manslaughter entailed upon the Indian population of the country." The sheer nastiness of this rotten business was such that it produced, according to Veblen, "the sclerosis of the American soul."[55]

Another perceptive witness of the ecological impact of the frontier in the late nineteenth century was John Muir, son of a Scottish pioneer and a person who, like Veblen, labored on a farm as a boy in the Portage, Wisconsin, area. Muir, a critic of the farming frontier of his youth, was an eyewitness to soil despoliation and reckless timber cutting by settlers and land speculators. He also recounted in detail the strange headhunts carried on by whole farming populations at certain times during the year when young people competed in gory contests to fill bloody bags with as many heads of small animals and birds as came within their grasp. All this mayhem, Muir recalled, was in the mistaken belief that exterminating wildlife somehow benefited the farmer.[56]

Muir, it will be remembered, went on to study at the University of Wisconsin and then to travel widely, for as his correspondence shows, he had a burning desire to study, firsthand, the forest and wildlands of the world. His travels in Asia, Alaska, Africa, Australia, South America, and most parts of North America gave him an environmental perspective that was worldwide and made him the most distinguished self-taught naturalist of his day.[57] As an eyewitness, even to the extent of following sheep migrations through the Sierras, he saw more clearly than any other American of his time what America had lost and what America needed to protect and preserve. As a persistent traveler, with an ever-present notebook that recorded his careful observations, he came to know and understand the dimensions of the cumulative impact of America's westward moving frontiers. There was no doubt in his mind that some of the most magnificent scenic wilderness areas in the world were threatened by herds of sheep and cattle, by agriculture, mining, timber cutting, dams, and other works of man. In 1889, the year when Veblen published his manifesto on wasteful consumption in America, *The Theory of the Leisure Class*, and Turner was completing his doctoral dissertation that eulogized the fur trading post as a social institution, Muir took the editor of the *Century Magazine* into the Yosemite Valley to show him the damage wrought by invading herds of sheep, the "hoofed locust."[58]

Muir, as founder of the Sierra Club and ecologist, preached with the oratory of a Hebrew prophet that it was the sacred responsibility of all Americans to prevent their land from being ravaged by the forces of greed and stupidity. Almost single-handedly he sparked the movement to preserve Yosemite as a national park, and partly as a result of his efforts, Theodore Roosevelt set aside 148 million acres as forest reserve. Summing up the environmental impact of the American frontier on the land by 1901, Muir concluded, "none of nature's landscapes are ugly so long as they are wild, but," he added, "the continent's . . . beauty is fast passing away, especially the plant part of it, the destructible and most charming of all."[59]

There are, of course, more recent witnesses of the great despoliation that refine the modern impact of society upon the land and supplement the observations of Muir, Veblen, and Marsh. For instance, in the period of the 1950s Bernard DeVoto, historian and journalist who traveled widely in the West, pinpointed what Veblen had earlier charged: private interests were the most culpable. Especially during the Dwight D. Eisenhower administration, charged DeVoto, they were exploiting the national forests' nonrenewable resources and wildlife. In probing the environmental history of the United States in a series of *Harper's* Easy Chair articles, DeVoto showed how the West had become a "plundered province" where absentee owners acted "on the simple principle: get the money out. And theirs was an economy of liquidation."[60] In an unfinished book, now among his papers at Stanford University, DeVoto described how the American West was, in large part, an arid region which had become an environmental disaster because of stupid land law legislation that ignored the good advice of John Wesley Powell. The inevitable consequence was, DeVoto wrote, a cycle of depressions, bankruptcies, and alienation of the land that caused America's dust bowl of the 1930s.[61] And DeVoto knew about arid lands because he had grown up in Ogden, Utah.

About the time that DeVoto began his environmental crusade through articles, speeches, and an unfinished book, two other conscientious objectors to land exploitation appeared upon the scene. Both had training in the sciences, both were skilled writers, and both of these remarkable men, Carl O. Sauer, a geographer, and Aldo Leopold, a forester, were astute observers, among our best historical eyewitnesses, to what was happening to the land in America and in the world at large.

Sauer, a skilled interdisciplinary researcher in the biological and social sciences and in related fields, argued that man's assault on nature in North America not only brought about the extinction of species, but also the severe restriction of other species. This was true among animals as well as plants.[62] Sauer, for example, emphasized our extreme dependence upon commercial corn which was ecologically dangerous because it increasingly reduced the range of organic evolution to only two of the species first domesticated by Indians.[63]

But it was soil destruction that Sauer called America's "dreadful problem." Loss of topsoil in many areas had reduced the United States to a deprived nation, Sauer argued. We had dissipated our land wealth. To reconstruct California soil profiles, Sauer had to go to Baja, California.[64] And in the American Southeast Sauer found that as a result of longtime erosion and wasteful agricultural practices, a new subsoil was on the surface, a red soil that could only be kept alive through heavy doses of commercial fertilizer. Such destruction, Sauer maintained, was the outgrowth of our frontier optimism that went back to the days of European freebooters. "We have not learned," he wrote, "the difference between yield and loot."[65]

Sauer's interest in environmental distress led him into brief correspondence with Aldo Leopold, forester and former hunter, who was convinced that America had to take a new look at its vanishing wilderness lands. Leopold, a Wisconsinite[66] who had studied Turner's frontier theory which alleged that primitive frontier environments helped to form our national character and democratic institutions, turned Turner upside down with the argument: "is it not a bit beside the point for us to be so solicitous about preserving [American] institutions without giving so much as a thought to preserving the environment which produced them?"[67]

In his *Sand County Almanac* of 1949 and in articles, Leopold developed the idea of "an ecological conscience," "a land ethic."[68] Inherent in this concept was the argument that even carnivors in the wilderness had a role in maintaining the environmental balance. "Just as a deer herd lives in mortal fear of wolves," Leopold wrote, "so does a mountain live in mortal fear of its deer. And perhaps with better cause, for while a buck pulled down by wolves can be replaced in two or three years, a range pulled down by too many deer may fail of replacement in as many decades."[69] Modern Americans, Leopold maintained, like the Spanish conquistadors, "were captains of an invasion," but we were not too sure of our own righteousness. Thus Leopold, forester and pioneer in wildlife management, an eyewitness to the despoliation by bulldozers, farmers, industry, government trappers, and timbermen, concluded that there was a need of a land ethic, a moral concept, in formulating policies. We must think about the land, he said, in terms of what is "ethically and esthetically right as well as what is economically expedient."[70]

Leopold wrote eloquently on this point as well as on environmental education, explaining patiently the complexities of ecological balance. There were others who followed him. One was Rachel Carson, a biologist, who in the 1950s began a book on *The Control of Nature*.[71] The title, as we know, was changed to *Silent Spring*, a graceful, articulate volume that even makes the subject of "chlorinated hydrocarbons" fascinating to the reader. She wrote eloquently about chemicals and ecology whereas her predecessors had written about chemicals and economics in the pesticide field. Carson showed that the U.S. government (in particular the Department of Agriculture) and scientists using industry research funds (especially those scientists in the universities and in the pesticide industry) had filled the country with dangerous chemical poisons without having the remotest idea of what they were doing to the environmental balance. The despoliation that resulted from foolish, unsuccessful extermination programs directed at fire ants and gypsy moths was great.[72]

One might infer, after hearing of the destructive impact of people, industry, and government, that there is not much left of America to be saved. As we know, this is certainly not the case, for America still has a reservoir of natural beauty, productive lands, and a wealth of natural resources. Yet there is no question that today the facts of life tell us that we have a national energy crisis and serious pollution problems in many areas of the country. By looking back over the highlights or themes of environmental despoliation in our history, we can, I believe, agree that there are basic environmental reasons that account, at least in part, for the severity of the problems we now face. These reasons are:

1. The competitive exploitation of furbearing animals and non-renewable natural resources greatly exceeded the extent to which this natural wealth had to be sacrificed. And further, the assault upon the land was tied closely to the dispossession of the Indians, our first ecologists.[73]

2. Pioneers from earliest times wasted natural resources, but it has been the ever increasing volume of despoliation and its cumulative effects that have brought instances of permanent environmental damage.

3. The American government has had an increasing role in the despoliation because of its links with predatory business interests and scientists, many of them associated with leading universities. In recent times we can see this trend in certain actions of such government agencies as the Department of Agriculture, the Army Corps of Engineers, and the Atomic Energy Commission.[74]

4. Population growth, as predicted by Jefferson, Franklin, and others, has culminated in an occupation of the land from sea to sea. This, with the new affluence, has brought a crowding of the land and tremendous strain upon resources and energy reserves.[75] The ambivalent attitude toward growth and conservation continues, but there is evidence that the old ideal of unlimited growth should be questioned.

5. Data from interdisciplinary research and from competent eyewitnesses show that the familiar Turnerean frontiers of first contact in the wilderness, fur trading, farming, mining, and urban settlement had reverberating environmental impacts and destructive social losses.[76] Most of these losses were unpaid at the time and later generations are therefore obliged to accept the costs in lost capital and in environmental despoliation.

We may also state that environmental history, like the "new history" of James Harvey Robinson and Charles A. Beard a generation ago, involves historical lessons and questions of morality. One of these questions is, should we have more respect for the land, even a land ethic? In short, an examination of historical environmental themes reveals a need for more emphasis upon new attitudes of Americans toward the environment. More stress could well be placed upon historical themes based upon a land ethic and respect for nature as opposed to the old conquistador interpretation. As ethnohistorical Indian literature tells us of Native American concerns for their descendants, we can also improve our sense of identification with future generations and acknowledge the fact that environmental problems in the United States usually have worldwide repercussions. We look to the past, not to discern what must be, but to understand environmental themes which help to explain origins of ecological transformations taking place in our lifetime. We may then catch a glimpse of our newly forming frontiers which forecast the environmental future of America.

What some of us may find particularly irritating in recapitulating this dismal story of white exploitation of lands taken from Indians is that the Indian whom we have often stereotyped as a savage was able to live with the land and to preserve its vitality. One reason was that many tribes moved from place to place well before the land they occupied was exhausted beyond the point of return. In fact, their touch was almost unbelievably light. A. L. Kroeber in testifying for the Indians in a court case made the point that the California Indians, living in small triblets, moved from area to area according to the seasons, fishing during winter and springtime, hunting in the fall. Whites often regarded their open brushlands as useless, but here the Indians hunted rabbits, birds, and other small animals. In the forested lands they found browsing deer, and the seashore yielded a bonanza in shell food. Though acorns were a primary food, Indians gathered a wide variety of wild food: berries, fruits, seeds, fleshy roots. Each triblet or tribe used specific fishing, hunting, or gathering territories which were regarded as theirs by themselves and by other groups; and geographical, or sacred place names were given to all major streams, rock formations, mountains, harbors, valleys, or other landmarks which were, in a sense, indications of tribal or triblet occupation of the land.

A key to our appreciation of the land ethic of these California Indian people is, of course, a more precise knowledge of their culture. But the cultural legacy of the California native people has been largely ignored by historians because they have repeated the depreciating commentaries made by original explorers, settlers, missionaries and early annalists. We are therefore indebted to the anthropologists, particularly to A. L. Kroeber and his students, and more recently to Theodora Kroeber who gave us a fascinating account of *Ishi*, for a portrait of California Indians, peaceful, intelligent, generous, who left us with a valuable, indeed, even an "intellectual" gift. For instance, a 1978 analysis of Chumash astronomy, cosmology, and rock art has been termed "an intellectual odyssey" by the Santa Barbara scholars who completed it. These writers tell us of a complex calendar explaining a land ethic and world view of the universe which was ignored by the mission padres who disciplined their wards into work cadres governed by a Christian "calendar of saints."

With the publication of the first volumes of the new *Handbook of the North American Indians* more and more is becoming widely known about our American Indian heritage, particularly in regard to native beliefs about the natural world. Articles in Volume VIII on this work are excellent ethnohistory, some of them echoing the work of ethnologists and linguists who have long understood that Indian world views can be comprehended through Indian languages as an index to culture. This point was argued some years ago by Franz Boaz in his introduction to the *Handbook of Indian Languages* and more recently by Benjamin Lee Whorf, a linguistics scholar who also trained as a chemical engineer before he turned his spotlight on the Hopi language. Whorf, whose theories have aroused controversies among linguists, nevertheless makes a strong argument for using Hopi language to understand linguistic and environmental relativity. He asserts, for instance, that Hopi thoughts about events expressed in language include both time and space.

An American Indian woman of the California Wintu people in 1925 gave us a poignant appraisal of Indian attitudes toward the land and her feelings about white despoliation of mother earth. "The white people," she wrote, "never cared for land or deer or bear. . . . The spirit of the land hates them. . . . They don't care how much the ground cries out. . . . Everywhere the white man has touched it, it is sore. . . . It looks sick."

But Indians, Kate Luckie goes on to say, make "little holes" when they dig for roots; they shake down acorns and pine nuts but don't chop down the trees. When they burn grass for grasshoppers, they "don't ruin things." White blast rocks and scatter them over the landscape. Indians don't destroy rocks, they only take small round ones for cooking. When the rock says: "Don't, you are hurting me," the whites "pay no attention."

What Kate Luckie suggests here is not so much a lament of white despoliation. There is an ethnic protest here which might be

AMERICAN PROGRESS, by John Gast, 1872, issued by George Crofutt's *Western World* in 1873. The promoters explained that "American Progress" was "Purely National in design," showing "the central and principal figure, a beautiful and charming Female ... floating Westward" with the "Star of Empire" on her forehead. She carries a book — *Common Schools* — and telegraph wires. To the right is bright civilization, but "the general tone of the picture on the left declares darkness, waste and confusion." The Indians are portrayed fleeing from Progress. They "turn their despairing faces towards, as they flee from the presence of, the wondrous vision. The 'Star' ['of Empire'] is *too much for them.*" The description goes on to claim that the twelve by sixteen inch picture has been described by a prominent art critic as *"one of the grandest conceptions of the age"* and "as richly worth $10 each." *Library of Congress*

compared to the ancient chain of being concept. She tells us that Indian people kept the land in trust, that a sacred chain relationship between plants, animals, and the land was not broken by Indian people. Whites, on the other hand, ravaged the chain, callously destroyed almost everything in nature they touched. Perhaps the great chain of being concept, which is also a part of our heritage voiced by the ancient Greeks and later men such as Thomas Jefferson, may be worth reconsidering. Certainly we have greatly disturbed the cycles of natural growth and interrupted complex food chains. And we may well have to pay the penalty for our rashness in brutalizing the land until it is, as Kate Luckie says, "sore all over." The great ecosystems nourishing the North American continent and preserved by Indian people are gone forever, but we can still protect what is left. And Indian people can help us if we will only listen and revise our attitude toward economic growth and progress.

　　And so we have come full circle, from discussions of first white intrusions into Indian homelands to a discussion of representative despoliation and the Indian legacy and land ethic. Indian-white history[77] in America is largely a story of conflict not only over possession of the land but also over land use ideals. There is evidence, from both conventional documentary material and interdisciplinary ethnohistorical sources, that these conflicts can be identified with beginnings of modern environmental history as the white frontier moved west. When traditional systems of Indian land occupation were altered by invading white societies, so began a history of reverberating environmental impacts that wrought vast ecological changes to America.

JUSTIFYING DISPOSSESSION OF THE INDIAN
The Land Utilization Argument

WILLIAM T. HAGAN

I N 1978 IN THE COURSE OF THE QUADRENNIAL LUNACY that seizes states like Texas as they go about selecting a governor, the ultimate victor, Bill Clements, asked an interesting question: "Is this area of Texas more productive, more fulfilling of God's purpose—are we playing our role of destiny with this broad expanse of Texas—than when there were five thousand Indians here eating insects?" The first Republican to be elected governor of Texas since Reconstruction did not leave us hanging. "These questions sort of answer themselves," he declared.[1]

It is not strange that Clements should have expressed such sentiments. They constitute one of the threads running throughout the history of Indian-white relations in what is now the United States. It has persisted despite the emergence of the current stereotype of the Indian as the model ecologist and conservationist as represented by Iron Eyes Cody. Cody is often seen on the TV screen viewing with glycerine-stained cheeks the pollution of the lake shore he is passing in his canoe.

From the original settlements of whites in Virginia and Massachusetts in the early seventeenth century, until the breakup of most reservations by the first decade of the twentieth, one of the justifications frequently advanced for dispossessing the Indian was the ability of whites to better utilize the land.

This is hardly a revolutionary idea. Albert Weinberg's *Manifest Destiny* published in 1935 and Roy Harvey Pearce's *The Savages of America*, which came out twenty years later, were the first to discuss the theme. Since then, others, particularly Wilcomb Washburn, Paul Prucha, and Reginald Horsman, have expanded upon it. However, all of these have restricted their discussions to the period from the first settlements through Indian removal in the 1830s. Actually, the theme runs through the rest of the nineteenth century and even into the early twentieth so long as the Indians held land which aroused the greed of their white neighbors. Under the circumstances, a review of the earlier period of some consideration of the persistence of this argument seems justified, particularly when coupled with speculation about the revival of this rationalization for dispossessing the Native American of his land.

It is not surprising that a people of the Book, such as the Puritans were, turned to the Bible to find justification for invasion and occupation. Massachusetts Bay Colony's first governor, John Winthrop, found his rationalization in Genesis 1:28:

> And God blessed them, and God said unto them, Be fruitful, and multiply, and replenish the earth, and subdue it: and have dominion over the fish of the sea and over the fowl of the air, and over every living thing that moveth upon the earth.

The Puritans and their successors in America took seriously this injunction to "Be fruitful and multiply, and replenish the earth, and subdue it." They also had no difficulty reading into this the idea that expropriation of the Indians was part of the divine plan. That it was echoed down the years even to the present can be seen in candidate Clements' confidence in being able to identify "God's purpose."

Governor Winthrop must also have been aware of Sir Thomas More's *Utopia*, with its rationalization for expropriation of underutilized land. Published a century before Winthrop attempted to justify Puritan aggression, *Utopia* held that "when any people holdeth a piece of ground void and vacant to no good or profitable use" the seizure of it by another people who would fully utilize it, even at the price of war, was right and proper.[2]

Winthrop's colleague in formulating an intellectual defense of Puritan land grabbing was that ornament of the pulpit, John Cotton. Cotton summoned up natural law to buttress divine will. He responded to Roger Williams' criticism of Puritan seizure of Indian land by arguing that the Massachusetts Bay Colony had acquired land only by purchase or by taking possession, by the "Law of Nations," of "voyd places of the country." Cotton also dismissed the idea that hunting over land gave the hunter a right to it: "We do not conceive that it is a just Title to so vast a Continent, to make no other improvement of millions of Acres in it."[3]

Although the Indians of Massachusetts subsisted principally by farming, they supplemented their crops by hunting and fishing. The Puritans were adamant in refusing to recognize Indian claims to land remote from their villages but essential to them for hunting. Such land only hunted over was classified, to use Cotton's term, "voyd places" and therefore open to settlement by whites. Nor were they reluctant to erect mill dams that interfered with the spawning patterns of fish upon which the Indians depended.[4]

The progression from occupying land described as void or waste to appropriating land actually held by Indians came quickly. In Virginia an Indian uprising against the invaders freed the English settlers of any inhibitions about seizing Indian land. With almost perceptible relief a Virginian described the new state of affairs:

> Because our hands which before were tied with gentleness and faire usage, are now set at liberty by the treacherous violence of the Savages . . . : So that we, who hitherto have had possession of no more ground than their waste. . . . may now by a right of Warre, and law of Nations, invade the Country, and destroy them who sought to destroy us.[5]

And they did so with vengeance.

By the time the United States had won its independence, the land utilization argument was a part of the conventional wisdom. It was routinely assumed that the needs of the white race were superior to those of the Native Americans because a prescribed area could support more whites than Indians. In 1774, just a year before the colonists struck the first blows for their freedom, the governor of Virginia, Lord Dunmore, had deplored their "avidity and restlessness." "They do not conceive," said Dunmore, "that Government has any right to forbid their taking possession of a Vast tract of Country, either uninhabited, or which Serves only as a Shelter for few Scattered Tribes of Indians."[6]

Incidentally, citizens of the new United States used the rationalization with equal facility against European nations. Kentuckians invoked it in 1788 in the controversy with France over our right to navigate the Mississippi River, a vital concern for Kentucky farmers needing to get their crops to market. They held that free navigation was a requirement if they were to develop the region consistent "with the immense designs of. the Deity."[7]

A people so well acquainted with the plans of the Deity would have little difficulty rationalizing the occupation of the continent westward to the Mississippi. However, although the religious argument was still regarded as our best by John Quincy Adams,[8] increased reliance was placed upon natural law. Those employing this argument depended heavily on Vattel's *The Law of Nations*. This frequently cited authority echoed More's *Utopia* and defended the seizure of land from the Indians, "erratic nations, incapable, by the smallness of their numbers" of making good use of all the land they claimed.[9]

As the white population increased in the first quarter of the nineteenth century, the pressure on Indian lands mounted in proportion. Members of Congress, territorial governors, presidents, and Supreme Court justices recited what had become a litany. A congressman from Virginia, for example, had no difficulty justifying the employment of force to dispossess the Florida Seminoles. To do otherwise, he stated, "the progress of mankind is arrested and you condemn one of the most beautiful and fertile tracts of the earth to perpetual sterility as the hunting ground of a few savages."[10]

Governor William Henry Harrison of Indiana Territory, who proved remarkably proficient at employing whatever the situation demanded to obtain treaties of cession from Indians, summed it up in one classic rhetorical question:

> Is one of the fairest portions of the globe to remain in a state of nature, the haunt of a few wretched savages, when it seems destined by the Creator to give support to a large population and to be the seat of civilization, of science, and of true religion.[11]

President Thomas Jefferson was not quite so blatant, though it was under pressure from his administration that Governor Harrison negotiated some of his most objectionable treaties. Jefferson had idealized the farmers, "the chosen people of God." Nevertheless, he was willing to try to civilize the Indians in place, encouraging them to give up their partial dependence on hunting. As a fringe benefit, this policy would satisfy those with tender consciences because as the Indian ceased hunting, they would need less land. These "waste & useless lands," as Jefferson referred to them at a conference with Creek chiefs, would then be purchased by the United States to satisfy the expanding white population.[12]

When obtaining Indian land by civilizing them in place proved too protracted a process to satisfy the impatient whites, removal west of the Mississippi, which Jefferson had considered, became the official policy. President Andrew Jackson, whose name is always associated with Indian removal, proposed it in his first annual message to Congress in 1829. A key argument in his presentation was that "it seems to me visionary to suppose that ... claims can be allowed on tracts of country on which they [Indians] have neither dwelt nor made improvements, merely because they have seen them from the mountain or passed them in the chase."[13] A year later he expanded on the same theme in justifying removal by a reference to what had been done with land already taken from the Native Americans.

> Philanthropy could not wish to see this continent restored to the condition in which it was found by our forefathers. What good man would prefer a country covered with forests and ranged by a few thousand savages to our extensive Republic, studded with cities, towns, and prosperous farms ... occupied by more than 12,000,000 happy people.[14]

The extended debate in Congress over the removal bill brought out all of the variations on the argument that whites could make better use of the land and therefore the Indians should pack up and move on. Typical was a speech by a Georgia representative. The Georgian, quoting Vattel on the law of nature, dismissed the Indian dependence on hunting as "irrational" and reminded his listeners of "the Almighty's command to his people to till the earth." It followed, he reasoned, "that the Indian claimed territories too large for the condition in which God intended men should be."[15] That the Cherokees who inspired most of this rhetoric were long past the stage of much dependence on game was ignored, as it did not fit the stereotype of the savage hunter cultivated by those who wished to supplant him.

The justices of the Supreme Court employed the same stereotype in two landmark cases. In 1823 in *Johnson* v. *M'Intosh*, John Marshall, speaking for the majority, argued among other things that the Indian title was flawed by their "character and habits." He referred to the country at the time of the European invasion as having been occupied by "fierce savages ... whose subsistence was drawn chiefly from the forest. To leave them in possession ... ," the chief justice continued, "was to leave the country a wilderness."[16]

In a concurring opinion in *Cherokee Nation* v. *Georgia* eight years later, Justice William Johnson disparaged the Cherokee claim to title by a reference to a key treaty clause referring to "their hunting grounds." "It is clear," held Justice Johnson, "that it was intended to give them no other rights over the territory than what were needed by a race of hunters." And, he concluded, "The hunter state bore within itself the promise of vacating the territory, because when game ceased, the hunter would go elsewhere to seek it."[17]

PROGRESS OF CIVILIZATION, by Thomas Crawford, 1863, United States Senate Pediment, East Front, Washington, D.C. To the left of the female figure of America, white civilization is represented by a soldier, a merchant, two youths, a schoolmaster and pupil, and a mechanic. Sheaves of wheat symbolizing fertility and an anchor, emblem of hope, are opposite what Crawford envisions as the fate of the First Americans: a grave, near which a despondent Indian chief, Indian mother, and Indian child await the inevitable advance of the white woodsman and white hunter, harbingers of white progress and Indian doom. Today some people argue that such symbolism is an inappropriate theme for the building housing the Senate of the United States, but others —for a variety of reasons—feel Crawford's nineteenth-century message is still relevant. *Library of Congress*

Removal was supposed to provide the Indians from the East sanctuaries west of the Mississippi in which they would have at least a generation in which to equip themselves with the farming skills and the modest education necessary to meet the white man on his own terms. The Indians never had the undisturbed interlude of twenty-five or thirty years to make the transition the architects of removal had envisioned. The United States could not stay the westward movement of its citizens, and within a few years the tribesmen were being pressured to abandon their new homes, or to at least submit to their reduction in size.

The familiar arguments were once again invoked but with refinements and extensions, as when Congress created a new federal territory, for example. The area might have initially a population of only a few thousand whites, but suddenly the existence of the territory unilaterally created would be used to justify the removal of the several tribes inhabiting the area, or at least the restriction of the size of their reservations. Thus a commissioner of Indian affairs argued in 1841 for the removal from Iowa Territory of Sacs, Foxes, and the Winnebagoes, who already had suffered removal from Illinois and Wisconsin:

> The citizens of the Territory have a right to expect that its growth will not long be retarded by the occupancy of so large, and valuable a tract within its limits by a people. ... whose wild and savage character renders them dangerous neighbors.[18]

In time, Iowa whites secured the removal of the tribes to whose presence they had objected. The Sacs and Foxes were shifted south to Kansas where within a few years the pattern was repeated; the Indians were retarding the progress of the state of Kansas. They and other tribes shunted west by the United States elicited little sympathy from Horace Greeley who was impressed by the magnificent corn land they occupied in Kansas. "These people must die out," the editor pontificated, "there is no help for them. God has given this earth to those who will subdue and cultivate it, and it is vain to struggle against His righteous decree."[19]

Although an argument for moving the Winnebagoes to Iowa had been that there they would become full-time farmers, that was forgotten when white settlers began to demand their land and their removal north into Minnesota. The governor of Iowa Territory, the official spokesman for its citizens, also was Iowa superintendent of Indian affairs, which guaranteed a conflict of interest which the Indian could not win. The governor maintained that because game in the area had declined the Winnebagoes no longer could make the best use of the section of Iowa they occupied, "although beautiful to behold, and unsurpassed in the advantages which it presents for agricultural pursuits."[20] The same argument was employed against the Santee Sioux in southern Minnesota. Although it was maintained on the one hand that their salvation lay in conversion to agriculture, on the other hand they should be removed from land described as "rich and fertile," and capable of being "densely settled with a prosperous and thriving white population." The excuse again advanced was that it would be of no use to the Sioux because "the game has almost all been destroyed."[21]

In situations like this it was easy — and convenient — for the white man, as it was for a commissioner of Indian affairs in 1859, to use such phrases as "redeeming a large body of lands from the incubus of the Indian title and vagrant occupancy."[22] In 1862 a secretary of the interior stated:

> The rapid progress of civilization upon this continent will not permit the lands which are required for cultivation to be surrendered to savage tribes for hunting grounds. Indeed, whatever may be the theory, the government has always demanded the removal of the Indians when their lands were required for agricultural purposes by advancing settlements.[23]

To achieve this end, the Bureau of Indian Affairs considered in the 1840s and 50s the desirability of concentrating the Indians whom it had forced to migrate west of the Mississippi. They would be grouped into two colonies, one on the headwaters of the Mississippi and the other south of Kansas.[24] But events were moving too rapidly. Before this could be achieved the United States had to deal with the tribes of the Plains and Rockies who were being pressured by miners, railroad construction crews, and settlers.

In a series of treaties in the late 1860s, the last to be negotiated before the abandonment of that procedure in 1871, the United States created a number of reservations and moved to restrict the Plains Indians to them. The nomadic buffalo hunters were dispossessed just as the eastern farming tribes had been. As one of their agents put it earlier:

> the savage, the wild hunter tribes, must give way to the white man, who requires his prairie hunting grounds for the settlement and homes of millions of human beings, where now only a few thousand of rude barbarians derive a scanty, precarious, and insufficient subsistence.[25]

As created by the treaties of 1867 and 1868, the reservations for the Plains Indians were relatively large, indeed as large as some of the smallest eastern states. However, it was never intended that the Indians should hold them intact forever. At first these reservations would be large enough for the tribesmen to support themselves partially by hunting. As they became more proficient at farming their holdings would be reduced, as a secretary of the interior phrased it, "to the dimensions required by the actual wants of an agricultural population."[26]

The Indians located on reservations by the treaties of the 1860s had an experience similar to those removed to the West twenty or thirty years earlier. No sooner were they located on their new reservations—in fact, before some of the Plains Indians had been forced to give up their nomadic life—than talk began of further cessions to be demanded of them.

The idea of concentration was again brought up. One plan in 1878 would have eliminated eleven reservations and freed an additional 17 million acres for settlement by whites.[27] Another drawn up the following year proposed to drop sixteen reservations and open 21 million acres to settlement.[28] Indian Territory (later Oklahoma) was one of the favorite subjects of this speculation as it was said to support but one Indian per square mile in the early 1870s. It was hoped to move the tribesmen of Colorado, New Mexico, and Arizona to Indian Territory.[29] Delegations of Pimas and Maricopas from Arizona were escorted to Indian Territory to inspect possible locations. However, only in a very few instances, and under the threat of force, were any tribes from outside the territory relocated there.

Although these proposed relocations of Indian population were rationalized as being in the Indians' interest, such moves were expected to incidentally provide additonal land for whites. As always, it was argued that greater utilization of the land would result. Nor were the wishes of the Creator forgotten. Trying to persuade Indians of Washington Territory to sell more land, a chairman of the Board of Indian Commissioners informed them: "The white men believe that God gave all the land for the use of all the people, and that He intends they shall cultivate it, and whenever the white people see that the lands are lying unused, they think God intends them to be cultivated."[30]

There was occasional frankness in the discussion of the problems the Indians faced in trying to retain land. For example, the commissioner of Indian affairs in 1876 stated:

> Whenever an Indian reservation has on it good land, or timber, or minerals, the cupidity of the white man is excited, and a constant struggle is inaugurated to dispossess the Indian, in which the avarice and determination of the white man usually prevails.[31]

Three years later the secretary of the interior was voicing similar sentiments:

> Many treaty reservations have turned out to be of greater value in agricultural and mineral resources than they were originally thought to be, and are now eagerly coveted by the white population. ... It is argued that the Indians cannot and will not develop these resources; that the country cannot afford to maintain large and valuable districts in a state of waste. ... This demand becomes more pressing every year, and although in many cases urged entirely without regard to abstract justice, it is a fact ... which must be taken into account in shaping an Indian policy.[32]

One area where mineral wealth had excited the "avarice and determination" of the whites was the Black Hills. The 1874 Custer expedition's confirmation of that mineral wealth led to intense pressure on the Sioux to cede the Black Hills. That the Indians might be permitted to hold the area for subsequent exploitation was never considered. Not only must the whites have the 800 square miles containing the gold fields, but also the remaining 3,000 square miles of grazing and farming land necessary to support the miners attracted to the area. A secretary of the interior in urging action on the chairman of the Senate Indian Affairs Committee maintained that the Black Hills "while of no essential value" to the Indians, retarded settlement of that portion of the public domain.[33] But he was only being realistic. Government officials dependent on the favor of the sovereign voters could not have preferred the Indian claim to the area to that of American citizens, regardless of the morality involved.

The Sioux were forced to cede the Black Hills in the aftermath of their Pyrrhic victory over Custer on the Little Big Horn. The whites were content only briefly with taking approximately one-third of the land reserved for the Sioux by their treaty of 1868. By 1882 the United States had begun a campaign to persuade the Sioux to surrender about half of what they had retained after the Black Hills cession. Seven years would pass, in the course of which several attempts were made to get the Sioux to agree to another relinquishment, before their resistance finally had been worn down sufficiently. It is interesting to note the involvement of one individual in these Sioux negotiations, Herbert Welsh.

Welsh was the driving force behind the Indian Rights Association in this period. Although the association was dedicated to defending the Indians and improving the administration of the Indian Bureau, Welsh accepted the government's premise that the time had come for the Sioux reservation to be reduced to a size more closely approximating what the Indians required for agriculture and stock raising. Welsh did insist that the Indians should be fairly compensated for the land they were asked to surrender.

Among the arguments Welsh used to rationalize his advocacy of reduction of the Sioux reservation were some familiar ones. He pointed out that the reservation was the home of only 28,000 Indians, yet it was four times the size of the state of Massachusetts.[34] His association's publications also referred to the "inevitable advance of white settlement."[35] Welsh was a man of high principles, nevertheless he showed no embarrassment in requesting a pass from a railroad, on the grounds:

> It is our aim to secure the peaceful reduction of Indian Reservations, by which vast tracts of land now lying idle and blocking the progress of railways, may be sold to white settlers, and the proceeds used for the education and civilization of the Indians.[36]

Like other Eastern reformers, Welsh assumed that the reservations contained more land than the Indians could effectively utilize, and that it would be unwise, indeed futile, to resist the government's efforts to make this surplus land available to white settlement.

Part and parcel of this attitude toward reservation reduction was the theory that the Indians' residence on reservations was, in the final anaylsis, at the whim of the government. In most cases, it was maintained, these were tracts created from land which had been sold by the Indians to the United States. This is apparent in the official policy covering the right of Indians to use timber on reservations. The Supreme Court held in 1873 that Indians could not cut and sell reservation timber unless it was incidental to clearing the land for farming. The court reasoned that standing timber was part of the realty and that the Indians had no more right in it than had any other tenant for life.[37] Not until 1889 did Congress modify this policy, and then only to legislate to permit Indians to sell or otherwise dispose of down and dead timber.[38] The right to cut live timber for the purpose of sale was still denied them.

In a similar fashion, when making allotments on reservations, the United States refused to permit Indians to select tracts rendered valuable because of deposits of minerals or stands of timber.[39] Allotments of that variety went into the public domain to be reserved for exploitation by white men. The Indian was not to be corrupted by any easy windfalls; he was to earn his right to be considered civilized at the business end of a hoe.

Although allotment of reservations and the sale of their surplus land was proceeding rapidly by the 1890s, whites still were unsatiated. Wherever Indians remained in possession of good land, or could be said to be blocking the progress of neighboring settlers, the old arguments were trotted out. This certainly was true of the reservations of the Kiowas, Comanches, and Kiowa Apaches in Indian Territory.

Although an agreement was negotiated in 1892 by which the three tribes accepted allotment and the sale of any land not needed for this purpose, eight years passed before Congress ratified the agreement. Meanwhile, settlers in surrounding areas, and those who hoped to take up residence on the surplus land, were demanding that the process be accelerated. Citizens of Wichita Falls, Texas, across the Red River from the reservation, protested that the presence of "large bodies of unoccupied lands" near the Texas border stood "like a wall of fire between Texas and her future development."[40] An Oklahoma mass meeting deplored the withholding "from the masses" of "a large and fertile body of land" capable of "supporting a dense population, making comfortable homes for thousands of homeless people."[41] A newspaper in Kansas City, a community which included many merchants with a stake in the development of Oklahoma, damned the delay in opening the reservation as "a crime against southwestern civilization."[42]

In the face of such pressure it is surprising that the opening of the reservation was delayed so long. At least a partial explanation is the fact that other whites were profiting from the reservation not being surveyed and alloted. These included Texas ranchers leasing grazing land on the reservation, one of them holding a rectangular tract twenty-five by forty miles.[43] His idea of what was good for the Indians obviously conflicted with the ideas of merchants in the small towns around the reservation who hoped to see the land rapidly populated with prospective customers.

Nor did the pressure on the Indians end with their receiving allotments. Whites who did not obtain their own farms from the breakup of the reservation now agitated for permission to lease Indian allotments or to work them as sharecroppers, and many such arrangements were permitted. At last there had developed a coincidence of Indian and white interests. The Indian was happy to have a white tenant to do the drudgery of farming and furnish the Indian the means for a modest existence. The whites were happy to have a piece of land on which they could support themselves and their families. Government officials bowed to the pressure from their white constituents and the entreaties of the Indians themselves and freely permitted such arrangements. Clearly it would have been better for the Indians to have worked their own land.

This was the situation until the 1930s, modified only by a slow but steady transfer of some allotments from Indians to whites as the trust period expired or legislation like the Dead Indian Act was implemented. During the Indian New Deal of the Roosevelt-Collier era this trend was reversed. Executive orders halted the further sale of Indian land, and tribes were encouraged to buy additional acreage. By the early 1970s Indians held approximately 50 million acres. Although this was but a small fraction of the total for the forty-eight contiguous states, two developments in particular suddenly made the Indian holdings far more valuable than they had seemed when better land for agriculture was steadily moving into the hands of whites. These two developments were the population boom in the arid Southwest which put additional pressure on a diminishing water supply, and the energy crisis which has assumed serious proportions in this decade.

Until the Winters decision by the Supreme Court in 1908, Indians seldom won when they disputed water rights with white men. The weight of the government usually came down on the side of the largest number of voters. An example is the situation of the Pimas and Maricopas as early as the 1870s. When their reservation was created it had ample water for their needs from the Gila River. But then miners began operations higher up the Gila and diverted water. As the Indians' condition worsened, the Interior Department proposed a solution. It was not to guarantee the reservation's water supply by restricting the miners' operation, rather it was proposed to persuade the Pimas and Maricopas to move to Oklahoma. They refused this solution, and instead some of them shifted to the Salt River Valley.[44]

Today, a century later, the descendants of these Pimas and Maricopas, and other Arizona Indians, are contending for water rights against a rapidly growing population of non-Indians. As elsewhere in the West the Native Americans are aligned against powerful forces. They compete for a steadily diminishing supply of a vital resource with non-Indian farmers, public utilities, miners and manufacturers, and municipalities. A bill introduced by Senator Edward M. Kennedy in 1976 to try to preserve the water rights of Indians in Arizona failed to win a single co-sponsor from among the western senators.[45] Indeed, Arizona Senator Barry Goldwater raised the spector, in the event of the passage of the bill, of the forced relocation of 4,500 of his constituents and Yuma County's becoming an economically depressed area. He also rebuked the Massachusetts senator for injecting himself into what was a western problem.[46]

As the water table in the Southwest continues to fall, and the population continues to grow, tension mounts. The Winters doctrine now looms like a dark cloud over the non-Indian constituents of Barry Goldwater and other western members of Congress. Not that it solves all the water problems of the Indian population. For example, what if several tribes draw water from the same river and their total needs exceed the potential of the river? Which Indian rights have priority in such a situation?[47] And the Winters doctrine applies not only to reservations, as a Nevada farmer recently discovered to his sorrow. He had been drawing water for irrigation purposes in such quantities as to endanger pupfish, a species found only in one National Monument set aside from the public domain. The Winters doctrine was interpreted by a federal court to apply to this situation also.[48]

Westerners, faced with the threat of reserve rights to an un-known quantity of water for both Indian reservations and federal holdings like national parks and monuments, are backing a Carter administration proposal. This is to quantify these as yet undefined rights so that the other users in the West would at least know what they might expect to have available in the future. Congressman Lloyd Meeds of Washington, whom Indians regard as personifying the white backlash, proposed a bill that would quantify Indian water rights at the highest annual level of Indian use in the last five years.[49] That is unacceptable to the Indians because it would deprive them of the possibility of supporting a larger population or engaging in more extensive irrigation projects in the future. The Indian position, simply put, is that the Winters doctrine guarantees a reservation's inhabitants as much water as they could ever need, with no ceiling other than exhaustion of the source.

The non-Indian population is not likely to accept this Indian view of matters. And they have a record of nearly four centuries of aggression to satisfy their demands on the natural resources of this continent. Certainly government officials recognize the situation for what it is, as is to be seen in a statement by Forrest J. Gerard, the assistant secretary of interior for Indian affairs. Gerard referred to the "substantial investments and the entire economies of some states" dependent on these disputed water sources. "The assertion of these *Winters* Doctrine rights poses a severe threat to these economies," said the assistant secretary. And, he concludes, "While these consid-erations are irrelevant to the tribes' rights, as a practical matter, these competing interests can not be ignored."[50]

Not surprisingly, Gerard's superior, Secretary of the Interior Cecil D. Andrus, had earlier expressed similar doubts about the ability of the government to completely uphold all Indian water claims under the Winters doctrine. Secretary Andrus observed that, "The Nation faces a conflict between the legitimate right of Indians to develop their resources and the impairment of enormous capital investments already made by non-Indians in the same water supply."[51] Given the historical record on the outcome of contests between Indian rights and non-Indian "enormous capital investments" and political clout, it is not too daring to predict that quantification will take place and limits on Indian rights to water will be imposed. A slight revision of a pertinent adage seems to be in order: "Water ordinarily flows downhill, except when it flows uphill toward money — and votes."[52]

More than water rights are at stake, as indicated earlier, now that the energy crunch has hit us. One can get a variety of statistics, but a conservative estimate would place 10 percent of the nation's coal reserves, 50 percent of its uranium deposits, and approximately 3 percent of its oil and gas reserves on land controlled by Indian tribes.

There are obvious differences among tribal members as to how to manage these resources. Some are profoundly disturbed at the prospect of destruction of range and crop land by strip mining and at the type of pollution associated with generating plants. However, it is difficult to conceive of the United States permitting such resources to lie unutilized. Other tribal members are more concerned with maximizing the return from these properties. They deplore Department of Interior leasing practices as not securing the Indians a fair return. They see in their natural resources potential jobs and income which would make it possible for their young people to remain on the reservation without undue sacrifice in living standards.

As the nation's energy crisis deepens, we can expect to see all of the variations played on the land utilization argument. However, in contrast to earlier periods, Indians are now much better equipped to defend their property.[53] Non-Indians also are more sensitive to Indian rights. The Native American Rights Fund (NARF), which tribes turn to for legal defense of their land, water, and minerals, was launched with a million dollar grant from the Ford Foundation. The government itself is helping finance the Council of Energy Resources Tribes (CERT), which sees itself as a Native American OPEC.

But one can't help, because of the historical record, feeling apprehensive about the future of the Indians' grip on their natural resources. In the 1870s and 1880s one of the arguments advanced for the Indians selling more land to the whites was that in this fashion the Indians would become less of a drain on the United States treasury.[54] Tribes are likely to encounter comparable arguments today if they seek recognition of tribal sovereignty and try to withhold resources from development, while at the same time insisting upon the continuance of multimillion dollar subsidies. In this era of belt tightening they are unlikely to have it both ways.

And the land utilization argument is still with us, as a case even now in the courts illustrates. It involves nearly 3,000 acres whose ownership has been brought into question by the meanderings of the Missouri River. The Omaha Tribe claims the land, but so do white farmers who insist that the tract had been utilized until they occupied it. As one of the whites declared: "It was land that was worthless and people cleared it and developed it and started farming it."[55] That is an argument John Winthrop, Benjamin Harrison, and Andrew Jackson could have understood, and which we will be hearing more of in the future.

IROQUOIS ENVIRONMENTS and
"WE THE PEOPLE OF THE UNITED STATES"

Gemeinschaft and Gesellshaft in the Apposition of Iroquois, Federal, and New York State Sovereignties

ROBERT W. VENABLES

PEOPLE AND LAND: the stakes in Iroquois affairs are basic and obvious elements in human society. Those Iroquois who follow the traditions of their ancestors perceive people and land as spiritually and politically integrated—as major components of American Indian environments. The Iroquois' right to determine what human activities occur in their environment is their sovereignty. This sovereignty, the Iroquois believe, is based on moral precepts revealed during their history by leaders who were inspired by the Creator (God). But Iroquois sovereignty is continually being challenged by the white-dominated governments and institutions which surround the Iroquois. This non-Indian challenge is based on the claim that non-Indians have sovereignty over the Iroquois.

Whether the Iroquois or the non-Indians successfully implement their sovereignty will determine the future of lands claimed or still possessed by the Iroquois. This will in turn be both a cause and an effect of whose culture predominantly shapes Iroquois society—in the education of new generations, for example. A resolution of the issue of sovereignty will determine the physical reality of the Iroquois environment and how that environment is perceived. Thus sovereignty is a major topic of discussion among Iroquois who are concerned about their environment.

The primary contenders for sovereignty in Iroquois affairs are the Iroquois confederation of Six Nations and two non-Indian federations: the United States and Canada. The Iroquois confederation is made up of the Mohawks, the Oneidas, the Tuscaroras, the Onondagas, the Cayugas, and the Senecas. The people refer to themselves collectively as the Houdenosaunee: "their house is extended" or the People of the Longhouse. Sovereignty in Houdenosaunee—Iroquois— affairs is not simply an issue of Indians versus non-Indians, however, because of the internal debates going on within each political structure. Individual Iroquois viewpoints range from those held by traditional people who follow the Iroquois religion as reformed by the prophet Handsome Lake (ca. 1735–1815) to those of assimilationist, Christian Indians. The traditional Iroquois believe that the survival of their culture is tied to their land and their ability to control that land through an exertion of sovereignty. Thus culture, land, and sovereignty are interrelated. Among non-Indians, there are those who support (to varying degrees) the rights of the traditional Iroquois to maintain their cultural and political separateness. At the other end of the spectrum among non-Indians, there are those who wish to see the Iroquois —and all Indians—placed into the so-called American mainstream or melting pot.

Within the Iroquois Confederacy the debate is primarily carried on at the Six Nations council when it convenes at Onondaga, near Syracuse, New York; at the Six Nations' territory at Grand River, Ontario; and within each of the Six Nations themselves — Mohawk, Oneida, Tuscarora, Onondaga, Cayuga, and Seneca—in each of their many locations in North America. Within the United States the debate primarily involves the governments which have the most contact with Iroquois people: the federal government, the state of New York, the state of Wisconsin, and the state of Oklahoma. Within Canada, the federal government has to contend primarily with the provincial governments of Quebec and Ontario. Although these political units of Iroquois and non-Iroquois peoples are all engaged in debates as to the nature of sovereignty as it relates to Iroquois affairs, the concept itself admits only a single ultimate authority. Thus Jeremy Bentham's 1782 definition—written during the era of the American Revolution, which literally set the boundaries of the issue—notes that a sovereign is "any person or assemblage of persons to whose will a whole political community are (no matter on what account) supposed to be in a disposition to pay obedience: and that in preference to the will of any other person."[1]

The roots of the conflicting claims lie in part within the medieval traditions of the Iroquois and the European pasts. All contending powers can base their claims to sovereignty on selected historical facts and political logic evolved during the past five centuries.

Although there have been continuing struggles to create a single sovereign power in Iroquois history at least since the sixteenth century, an actual sovereign authority has never emerged from within the confederacy structure. Rather, each of the nations of the Iroquois Confederacy has maintained its individual sovereignty while contributing its power and influence to the confederacy. Sovereignty has not been successfully imposed from outside the confederacy by rival powers, red and white. Thus the absence of a sovereign authority in Iroquois affairs is due primarily to the confederate rather than federal nature of the Six Nations and to the contentions among non-Indian governments such as the United States federal government and the New York state government. The multifaceted apposition is not likely to abate in the near future.

One method by which the points of view in Iroquois affairs can be analyzed is to apply an interpretation of human perception and social behavior proposed in 1887 by the German sociologist Ferdinand Tönnies. Tönnies suggested that all human societies have within them two major impulses: one toward what he termed Gemeinschaft and the other toward what he called Gesellschaft. The two concepts might be contrasted as follows:

GEMEINSCHAFT	GESELLSCHAFT
Moral bonds	Legal contracts
Common interest	Self-interests
Symbols	Definitions
Reciprocity	Profit
Community	Society

It is important to stress that both Gemeinschaft and Gesellschaft exist simultaneously within any one given society — no single impulse is ever exclusive. Tönnies suggested that this dualism coexists in differing proportions. By identifying which impulse is dominant in any one society, that society's *raison d'etre* may be more clearly understood. Specific characteristics of any given society are shaped by the interaction of Gemeinschaft and Gesellschaft even as they then determine which of the two impulses will be primary.

Tönnies suggested that human societies are in the process of evolving from social organizations emphasizing life within Gemeinschaft toward social organizations emphasizing life within Gesellschaft. The evolution always remains dualistic. The evolution is not predetermined or inevitable but is caused by human perceptions, decisions, and inventions which shape the religious, social, political, economic, and other aspects of a society. Tönnies believed that his two concepts, Gemeinschaft and Gesellschaft, were only theoretical explanations and had to take into account many modifying details within each society being analyzed.

Tönnies perceived that societies primarily in Gemeinschaft and societies primarily in Gesellschaft are both basically positive, comfortable, and good for people living in them as full citizens. Both, Tönnies explained, involve

> an aggregate of human beings [in] which ... the individuals live and dwell together peacefully. However, in the Gemeinschaft they remain essentially united in spite of all separating factors, whereas in the Gesellschaft they are essentially separated in spite of all uniting factors.

While Gemeinschaft emphasizes interdependence, Gesellschaft gives rise to an alienated individual living in the midst of other alienated individuals. Consequently, in Gesellschaft

> we find no actions that can be derived from an a priori and necessarily existing unity; no actions, therefore, which manifest the will and the spirit of the unity even if performed by the individual. ... everybody is by himself and isolated, and there exists a condition of tension against all others. Their spheres of activity and power are sharply separated, so that everybody refuses to everyone else contact with and admittance to his sphere; i.e., intrusions are regarded as hostile acts. ... nobody wants to grant and produce anything from another individual, nor will he be inclined to give ungrudgingly to another individual, if it be not in exchange for a gift or labor equivalent that he considers at least equal to what he has given. It is even necessary that it be more desirable to him than what he could have kept himself; because he will be moved to give away a good only for the sake of receiving something that seems better to him.[3]

Tönnies stated that an emphasis on Gesellschaft can grow to dominate a society which in the past had emphasized Gemeinschaft. Specifically, he believed that the postmedieval Europeans (and their American descendants) were evolving toward a greater emphasis on Gesellschaft. Tönnies was primarily interested in the history of western civilization, and hence he did not apply his ideas to American Indian history. However, he did refer broadly to American Indians north of the Rio Grande as people whose communities emphasized Gemeinschaft.[4]

According to Tönnies, Gemeinschaft coalesces people in relationships based on "mysterious understanding" — moral bonds —

while Gesellschaft coalesces people through "contractual relations" or legal contracts. In Gesellschaft what is legal is perceived as right. Each human group—for example, each family, village, or nation—combines Gemeinschaft and Gesellschaft in different degrees. The relative proportions of Gemeinschaft and Gesellschaft determine the means by which each group of "human beings are in unison with each other and in agreement about their rights and obligations." Tönnies theoretical framework can be used to place Indians and non-Indians into a dualistic perspective which is useful in understanding a complicated history in which the Indians and the non-Indians often perceived each other as acting irrationally—that is, outside the framework of their own perceptions in Gemeinschaft or in Gesellschaft. Specific details and circumstances such as politics, geography, economics, technology, religion, and social order can be analyzed to suggest how the participants perceived the proportions of Gemeinschaft and Gesellschaft, and what the consequences of these perceptions were.[5]

Indian emphasis on Gemeinschaft was never static, either before or after European contact. The degree of Gemeinschaft also varied according to the individual Indian nation involved. An emphasis on Gemeinschaft might be affected by changes in commercial networks, for example. However, relative to the white societies with which Indians dealt in any given era, Indian populations north of the Rio Grande emphasize Gemeinschaft.

Gemeinschaft and Gesellschaft seem especially useful in helping to understand what treaties and laws meant to Indians (whose societies emphasized Gemeinschaft, moral bonds) and, what treaties and laws meant to whites (whose postmedieval society, according to Tönnies, increasingly emphasized Gesellschaft, legal contracts, with each passing decade). For example, specific application of the Gemeinschaft concepts to Indian land claims and other suits may help to clarify further the legal premise that "treaties with the Indians must be interpreted as they would have understood them," expressed by Justice Thurgood Marshall in the majority opinion of the 1970 Supreme Court decision *Choctaw Nation* v. *Oklahoma*.[6] This premise is a significant if unconscious attempt to define legally, within Gesellschaft, a concept in Gemeinschaft because it stresses that the Indians' understanding (in Gemeinschaft) was not attuned to the Western culture's legalisms in Gesellschaft. The premise has a long history, dating to the Supreme Court of Chief Justice John Marshall in the 1832 decision, *Worcester* v. *Georgia*, a case specifically involving the Cherokees but legally applicable to Indian affairs in general.

Chief Justice John Marshall and the Supreme Court of 1832 convened at a time when the Revolutionary generation which had

The manner of their attire and
painting them selues when
they goe to their generall
huntings or at theire
Solemne feasts.

made the first treaties for the United States was passing from the scene. Before that generation's complete disappearance, however, it was vital that the court clarify the context of the treaty-making process. In Article III of the 1785 Treaty of Hopewell, the Cherokees were recorded "under the protection of the United States of America, and of no other sovereign whosoever." Article IV defined "the boundary line allotted to the Cherokees." Legally, the word "allotted" meant that all Cherokee lands were actually held in fee simple by the United States as the sovereign power, and that the lands defined as the Cherokees' reservation were technically lands provided *by* the United States for the Cherokees. Did the Cherokees, Marshall inquired, understand the legal complexity implied in the word "allotted"? Marshall noted:

> Is it reasonable to suppose, that the Indians, who could not write, and most probably could not read, who certainly were not critical judges of our language, should distinguish the word "allotted" from the words "marked out." The actual subject of contract was the dividing line between the two nations, and their attention may very well be supposed to have been confined to that subject. When, in fact, they were ceding lands to the United States, and describing the extent of their cession, it may very well be supposed that they might not understand the term employed, as indicating that, instead of granting, they were receiving lands. If the term would admit of no other signification, which is not conceded, its being misunderstood is so apparent, results so necessarily from the whole transaction; that it must, we think, be taken in the sense in which it was most obviously used.[7]

The "sense" to which Marshall refers is what would be understood in Gemeinschaft as opposed to that which would be legally defined in Gesellschaft. This has a specific application to Iroquois affairs, for the 1785 Treaty of Hopewell with the Cherokees and the 1788–1789 New York State treaties with the Onondagas, Oneidas, and Cayugas have comparable legal maneuvers. The New York treaties,

INDIAN OF NORTH CAROLINA, by John White, 1585. The Englishman White, governor of the Roanoke colony in 1587, has portrayed "the manner of their attire and painting them selves when they goe to their generall huntings, or at theire Solemne Feasts." This may be one of two possible depictions of the chief of the Roanokes, Wingina, who was assassinated by the English in 1586. *The British Museum*

written by the whites, stipulated that these Iroquois had ceded all their lands *to* New York and had received reservations, in return, *from* the state. Thus New York has claimed and continues to claim that the lands of the Onondagas, Oneidas, and Cayugas were, legally, reserved *to* the Indians by the state, and not reserved *by* these Indians to themselves.[8] However, it is likely that if Marshall's premise is applied to the Iroquois as it was applied to the Cherokee, present-day courts may redefine the Iroquois' status as land owners, and a Gemeinschaft definition of the treaties — "as they would have understood them" — will replace the legal complexity of Gesellschaft.

The Gemeinschaft-oriented premise of *Worcester* v. *Georgia* is further demonstrated by Justice John McLean's concurring opinion which put the sense of treaties in a broad context.

> The language used in treaties with the Indians should never be construed to their prejudice. If words be made use of which are susceptible of a more extended meaning than their plain import, as connected with the tenor of the treaty, they should be considered as used only in the latter sense. ... How the words of the treaty were understood by this unlettered people, rather than their critical meaning, should form the rule of construction.[9]

By distinguishing between the words "understood" and words defined by "their critical meaning," McLean was reflecting a perception of what would be in Tönnies' terms the difference between Gemeinschaft and Gesellschaft.

THE TRUE PICTURE OF ONE PICTE, by John White, about 1590. White cooperated with Theodore de Bry of Frankfort in illustrating de Bry's 1590 edition of Thomas Hariot's *A briefe and true report of the new found land of Virginia* (originally published in 1588). White added three female and two male portrayals of ancient Picts, "to showe how that the Inhabitants of the great Bretannie have bin in times past as sauvage as those of Virginia."

In observing the various Indian peoples from Mexico's highest civilization to the provincial cultures of the East coast of what is now the United States, many Europeans were conscious that the Indians were representative of the various stages of civilization which the Europeans had themselves experienced or were experiencing. It was a conscious understanding of a chronology which might be termed as progressing from an emphasis on Gemeinschaft to one of Gesellschaft. *Private collection; photograph by Robert W. Venables*

The premise of *Worcester* v. *Georgia* was further defined in *Jones* v. *Meehan* (1899), in which Justice Horace Gray stated:

> In construing any treaty between the United States and an Indian tribe, it must always... be borne in mind that the negotiations for the treaty are conducted on the part of the United States, an enlightened and powerful nation, by representatives skilled in diplomacy, masters of a written language, understanding the modes and forms of creating the various technical estates known to their law, and assisted by an interpreter employed by themselves; that the treaty is drawn up by them and in their own language; that the Indians, on the other hand, are a weak and dependent people, who have no written language and are wholly unfamiliar with all the forms of legal expression, and whose only knowledge of the terms in which the treaty is framed is that imparted to them by the interpreter employed by the United States; and that the treaty must therefore be construed, not according to the technical meaning of its words to learned lawyers, but in the sense in which they would naturally be understood by the Indians.[10]

The court's reference to the Indians' "sense ... naturally ... understood" is what can be termed an idea in Gemeinschaft. It is clearly set off against what might be called Gesellschaft: "the various technical estates known to their [white] law" and treaties couched in "the technical meaning of its words."

In 1905, in *United States* v. *Winans*, the premise was again presented by the Supreme Court, as Justice Joseph McKenna declared: "we will construe a treaty with the Indians as 'that unlettered people' understood it. . . . How the treaty in question was understood may be gathered from the circumstances."[11]

This same court case provided an important definition of the Indians' "reserved rights," a doctrine especially important in Iroquois sovereignty issues. *United States* v. *Winans* involved the Yakima Indians in the state of Washington. The Yakimas had signed a treaty in 1859 with the United States which stated that the Yakimas had ceded all their lands to the United States. However, there were "reserved from the lands . . . ceded" a reservation for the Yakimas. Hunting and fishing rights were guaranteed on the ceded lands as well as on the reservation. This treaty is similar to the 1788–1789 New York State treaties with the Onondagas, Oneidas, and Cayugas, the terms of which state that these three nations ceded all their lands to the state and received sections of lands — their reservations — back from the state. By these treaties the Indians also had hunting and fishing rights throughout the ceded territories as well as on their reservations. Were these rights granted *to* the Indians, or reserved *by* the Indians to themselves? The "reserved rights" definition in *United States* v. *Winans* chose to interpret such issues not in what might be defined as a Gesellschaft, limited, legal context but in what might be called the Gemeinschaft context—what the sense of the treaty meant to the Indians: "the treaty was not a grant of rights to the Indians, but a grant of right from them, —a reservation of those [rights] not granted."[12]

From *United States* v. *Winans* has grown the concept in Indian law that any sovereign rights such as hunting and fishing which were not granted away by the Indians are retained by the Indians. In this context *United States* v. *Winans* may also supplement a Gemeinschaft interpretation of Iroquois land cessions which will ultimately be based on the majority opinion in *Worcester* v. *Georgia* (1832) written by Chief Justice John Marshall. Thus the Iroquois will be perceived as believing they were reserving to themselves the lands of their reservations, and that they had not granted away all of their lands so that they could then receive a portion of those lands back from the whites.

John Marshall had also remarked, in the 1831 decision *Cherokee Nation* v. *Georgia*, that "the condition of the Indians in relation to the United States is perhaps unlike that of any other two people in existence. . . . the relation of the Indians to the United States is marked by peculiar and cardinal distinctions which exist no where else."[13] While Marshall may have exaggerated the uniqueness of Indian-United States relations, he perceived an association which Tönnies might have termed as one dominated by Gemeinschaft with one dominated by Gesellschaft.

In *Cherokee Nation* v. *Georgia* Marshall chose to define the Indians' role in this relationship as that of "domestic dependent nations." This term is an attempt to recognize in legal terms — in Gesellschaft — what is the Gemeinschaft moral responsibility of the United States toward the Indians, as well as recognizing the Gemeinschaft context of the Indian nations themselves.

> It may well be doubted whether those tribes which reside within the acknowledged boundaries of the United States can, with strict accuracy, be denominated foreign nations. They may, more correctly, perhaps, be denominated domestic dependent nations. They occupy a territory to which we assert a title independent of their will. . . . they are in a state of pupilage. Their relation to the United States resembles that of a ward to his guardian.

> They look to our government for protection; rely upon its kindness and power. . . . They and their country are considered by foreign

nations, as well as by ourselves, as being so completely under the sovereignty and dominion of the United States, that any attempt to acquire their lands, or to form a political connexion with them, would be considered by all as an invasion of our territory, and an act of hostility.[14]

Marshall's definitions of Indian-United States relations on this and other occasions have created more questions than clarifications. Nearly a century and a half later, Supreme Court Justice William H. Renquist stated in *United States* v. *Mazurie* (1975) that "Indian tribes are unique aggregations possessing attributes of sovereignty over both their members and their territories."[15] Rehnquist's opinion involves a contradiction, however. Attributes of sovereignty cannot be divided up among competing or even complementary political entities. All attributes of sovereignty must reside in the sovereign power—otherwise, the sovereign power is not sovereign. If the word "sovereignty" is to avoid becoming meaningless or newspeak, its exact definition must be consistently utilized. Theoretically, there can be no partial, limited, or residual sovereignty any more than there can be "partial death" or "partial pregnancy." Yet Rehnquist is hardly alone. In describing Indian rights, the term sovereignty has been modified to "limited sovereignty" by such eminent legal scholars as Felix S. Cohen in his 1942 *Handbook of Federal Indian Law*.[16] As if the semantics of the word were not complex enough, the issue of sovereignty is even more intricate.

To define even half a century of the issue of sovereignty would take a tome of gargantuan proportions—another like Thomas Hobbe's *Leviathan*, favorite reading of none other than Ferdinand Tönnies. The brief attempt which follows therefore concentrates on the issues raised in the claims of sovereignty by the Six Nations of the Iroquois, the state of New York, and the federal government of the United States.[17] This tripartite apposition demonstrates the major issues involved in the question of sovereignty in Iroquois affairs and in Indian affairs in general. It also exemplifies the confusion and frequent tragedy of ongoing relations between the Indians, perceiving communication and social order primarily within Gemeinschaft, and whites, perceiving communication and social order primarily within Gesellschaft.

Do Indian leaders, state officials, or federal authorities possess the ultimate legal responsibility—the sovereignty—to direct American Indian communities? Who has sovereignty will determine the future of

American Indian environments: controls, for example, over education, government, mineral rights, and land usage in the territories of
Indian nations. The debate over sovereignty involves each Indian
nation in a different set of historic circumstances. The debate can be
better understood by keeping in mind, along with many other possible
explanations, the concepts of Gemeinschaft and Gesellschaft.

As in the premise that "treaties with the Indians must be
interpreted as they would have understood them," the Supreme
Court's *Worcester* v. *Georgia* decision provides a significant precedent in
the ongoing debate over sovereignty. Chief Justice John Marshall reviewed in that case his court's understanding of sovereignty as it
related to Native Americans.

> The general law of European sovereigns, respecting their claims in
> America, limited the intercourse of Indians, in a great degree, to the
> particular potentate whose ultimate right of domain was acknowl-
> edged by the others. ... the strong hand of [white] government was
> interposed to restrain the disorderly and licentious from intrusions
> into their country, from encroachments on their lands, and from those
> acts of violence which were often attended by reciprocal murder. The
> Indians perceived in this protection only what was beneficial to them-
> selves —an engagement to punish aggressions on them. It involved,
> practically, no claim to their lands, no dominion over their persons. It
> merely bound the nation to the British crown, as a dependent ally,
> claiming the protection of a powerful friend and neighbour, and
> receiving the advantages of that protection, without involving a sur-
> render of their national character. ...

> From the commencement of our [United States] government, con-
> gress has passed acts to regulate trade and intercourse with the
> Indians; which treat them as nations, respect their rights, and man-
> ifest a firm purpose to afford that protection which treaties stipulate.
> All these acts ... manifestly consider the several Indian nations as
> distinct political communities, having territorial boundaries, within
> which their authority is exclusive, and having a right to all the lands
> within those boundaries, which is not only acknowedged, but
> guaranteed by the United States.[18]

Most of the evidence which is available for a historical analysis
of sovereignty in Indian affairs is the product of non-Indians. Chief
Justice John Marshall acknowledged in *Worcester* v. *Georgia* (1832) the
ethnocentricity of the legal definitions used in Indian affairs and in-

sisted that if these white-generated concepts were to be valid, whites
would have to apply them equally.

> The words "treaty" and "nation" are words of our own language,
> selected in our diplomatic and legislative proceedings, by ourselves,
> having each a definite and well-understood meaning. We have
> applied them to Indians, as we have applied them to the other nations
> of the earth. They are applied to all in the same sense.[19]

While "nation" and "treaty" may have been "well under-
stood,"[20] the concept of sovereignty was not as readily defined because
the concept was — and still is — evolving, within both Indian and
non-Indian societies. At the moment of initial contact between the
Indian peoples and the various European nations, Indians were faced
with challenging issues within their own cultures. In the Southwest
the Pueblo people were still redefining their relationship with a land
that had suffered a severe drought from 1276 to 1299, forcing a contrac-
tion of populations and the deterioration of the ancient traditions of the
Pueblos' forebears, the Anasazi. The Pueblos were also attempting to
cope with the challenges of Southern Athapascan invaders who were
evolving toward the Navajo and Apache nations of today. Concepts of
sovereignty in the Southwest were in the sixteenth century as diverse
as the communities of the Pueblo people were numerous, compounded by frequent conflict with the Southern Athapascans.[21] East of
the Mississippi Indian nations were struggling with a cultural and
physical environment altered by the collapse of the various sophisticated cultures broadly labeled "the mound builders."[22] Both east and
west of the Mississippi, Native American religous perceptions of the
role of humans within the context of the whole of nature differed but
had (and continue to have) one singular similarity: with specific variations of detail, Indian peoples believed that they were part of an
interrelated structure of living things in which creatures, including
humans, attempted to maintain a balance with, rather than a domi-
nance over, the others.[23] They did not share the belief held by most of
the Europeans they eventually encountered, who adhered to a
Judaic-Christian concept which might be labeled "the Genesis complex." The perspective of the Genesis complex was that humans were
at the top of an ecological pyramid of living things, a structure in which
the Creator, or God, had granted them the right to dominion over
nature and other creatures. Thus the Genesis complex of dominion
was a divinely ordained right of sovereignty.
    The Europeans, like the Indians, were at the times of initial
contact (that is, until about 1650), also facing challenges to their political

and social orders. Between 1300 and 1650, just as Indian peoples were adapting to changing circumstances in the Western Hemisphere, the Europeans were evolving from the feudal Middle Ages into a Renaissance and, after 1517, into a sweeping Reformation. The nature of the medieval governments which were slowly being transformed by the Renaissance and the Reformation were, in general, based on consent and on limitations: the monarch ruled by the consent of the feudal lords, the church, and the corporate towns which formed checks on the monarchy. Although the monarchies during the late Middle Ages and the Renaissance consolidated their powers and were able to weaken the checks of the older feudal institutions, the power of these institutions was not eliminated. Furthermore, new institutions in administration arose which were staffed by powerful, wealthy individuals, including leaders of commerce. Although these individuals served in new administrative posts created by royal authority, they nevertheless became new checks on the monarchies. Thus the medieval concept of limited centralized power responsible to checks and balances was altered and redefined during the late Middle Ages and the Renaissance, but it was not abandoned.[24] Within this European context of limited power, it is significant that the first modern, detailed definition of sovereignty did not emerge until 1576 when the Frenchman Jean Bodin published *Les Six Livres de la République*, titled in its 1606 English edition *The Six Books of a Commonwealth*. Bodin proposed a sovereign authority to supersede the highly complex and confusing values of feudal checks and balances so as to achieve a greater social order. Bodin defined sovereignty in the eighth chapter of his first book: "Soveraigntie is the most high, absolute, and perpetuall power over the citisens and subjects in a Commonweale. . . .that is to say, The greatest power to command. . . . not limited either in power, charge, or time certaine."[25]

Bodin believed that the exercise of sovereignty was best achieved through a single human, a monarch, whose sovereignty over a lifetime would be undiminished. In the seventeenth century the English philosopher John Locke and others would shift the justification for sovereign power away from a single person and toward a legislative body. But the concept of sovereignty as Bodin described it would remain a keystone of European political theory.[26]

Because the European transition from the medieval to the modern was coincidental with a comparable transition among American Indians, Europeans and Native Americans confronted each other while their respective continents were already convulsed with changes. In northeastern North America one of the Native American reactions to these circumstances of change redefined the political na-

ture of the state. One Indian redefinition of sovereignty was as significant as Jean Bodin's was to Europe, and it preceded Bodin's by many
years—perhaps even by centuries. It was the message of the Iroquois
Peacemaker, Deganawidah, who gave to the Iroquois people in
present-day New York the authority of the Good Tidings of Peace and
Power. The Great Law, as it is also known, sought an end to intra-
Iroquois warfare through a confederation in which the member states
renounced warfare against each other ("Peace") in order to concentrate
on a defense ("Power") against other Indian nations who threatened to
overwhelm them. The Iroquois Confederacy evolved from this message of the Peacemaker and initially consisted of the Mohawks, the
Oneidas, the Onondagas, the Cayugas, and the Senecas — the Five
Nations—but incorporated a sixth nation, the Tuscaroras, about 1722,
to be represented in the grand council by the Oneidas.[27]

A major principle of the League of the Iroquois is its perpetuation of authority. Today, as in the past, Iroquois people stress this
political continuum. Like the Iroquois, Jean Bodin and subsequent
white philosophers also stressed the perpetual power of a state as an
attribute of sovereignty. Thus the Iroquois and the Europeans had the
continuum concept in common. Because both Iroquois and Europeans
shared this belief, each stressed that a change in the actual per-
sonalities running each government caused by the deaths of prominent leaders would not and did not change the purpose or resolve of
the state. But the Europeans and the Iroquois differed in what constituted their absolute sovereignties. For the Europeans, absolute authority was enforced by legal sanctions imposed, by force if necessary,
downward from a pinnacle of power. To Europeans, sovereignty was a
means to an end. For the Iroquois, no centralized authority could
rightly exist as a means or by its own accord. Instead, absolute authority was (and is) sought within the context of consensus.[28] Therefore,
Iroquois sovereignty was (and is) inherent not in the means but in its
end, its result. Because of the difference between the concepts of
European and Iroquois sovereignties, conflict resolution has often
been manifest in a common human alternative: force.

Warfare, however, was not the primary alternative used by
either the Iroquois or the Europeans in their quest to secure
sovereignty. The primary method was acculturation, beginning with
an emphasis on a common political system. During the creation of their
confederacy's empire during the seventeenth and eighteenth centuries, the Iroquois brought subject nations under the jurisdiction of
the confederacy's political teachings as defined broadly in the Good
Tidings of Peace and Power. This acculturation process reached its
ultimate end when many individuals from among the subjected

peoples were adopted directly into one of the confederacy nations. Adopted individuals (such as many Mahicans) became as Iroquois as the Iroquois and occasionally reached positions of leadership. In fact, it is possible that a reason the political teachings of the confederacy were recited at the beginning of most council meetings was because the league's political lessons had to be constantly introduced or reinforced to new members. The Europeans' acculturation process in North America was more intense, largely because of the Europeans' ever-expanding population, but it was a variation on the same theme.[29]

Since neither Europeans nor Iroquois could enforce their sovereignty without the acceptance of their cultures by the subjugated peoples; and because their cultures preceded the new political organizations by centuries, both the Europeans and the Iroquois buttressed their claims with medieval concepts, that is, with ideas which preceded the current systems of political order. Thus the Iroquois could tell the Hurons in 1656: "Thou knowest, thou huron, that formerly we comprised but one Cabin and one country. I know not by what accident we became separated. It is time to unite again."[30] Religious traditions similar to those of the Mound Builders helped give continuity to culture even as the new political order grew stronger. Two and a half centuries ago the European and the Iroquoian peoples momentarily shared, on terms of equality, a medieval concept which linked them conceptually as well as politically. This was the Chain of Friendship which both sides, during the decades immediately prior to and after 1700, strove to keep polished. This Chain of Friendship or covenant was a concept not unlike the medieval chain of being, in which parts of the universe were linked and interdependent, and although the medieval and the Iroquois chains have distinct differences as well as a common element, both are also concepts in Gemeinschaft. The Chain of Friendship, however, soon deteriorated into a ritual manipulated by the whites as a method to invoke favors and thus obtain Indian lands as gifts from their red friends.[31]

With the European concept of sovereignty still in its formative stages, the whites relied heavily on another part of their medieval heritage, feudal vassalage. The Spanish utilized this feudal concept by claiming that the papacy, as the temporal representative of God, had given them dominion over Indian lands in the Western Hemisphere. Thus the 1512 Requirement warned Indians that rebellions would not be perceived as wars between equal states, but rather as wars by the Spanish against "vassals who do not obey and refuse to receive their lord and resist and contradict him."[32]

Since the Protestant English could not claim rights by papal authority, they were quick to obtain a temporal liege pledge from

Indian leaders. Under feudal law once these Indian leaders swore that the English monarch was their liege or sovereign, they not only owed the crown their personal loyalty, they—probably without realizing the implications—also turned over jurisdiction of all their peoples' lands to the English sovereign. This feudal concept of vassalage had as a premise that order depended upon one rule of law, and that this single rule of law could only be enforced if all territories over which it was enforced were part of a single political entity, the sovereignty of the monarch (and, for the English after 1688, the sovereignty of the state through Parliament). Thus in 1587 the English colonists at Roanoke, North Carolina, crowned an Indian named Manteo as lord of Roanoke and Dasemunkepeuc.[33] At Jamestown in Virginia, the English crowned Powhatan in 1608.[34] And in 1622 the English contentedly reported that the Wampanoag leader Massasoit encouraged the English to keep out the French, because New England was "King JAMES his Countrey, and he [Massasoit] also was King JAMES his man."[35] It was probably the imposition of this feudal concept of vassalage upon Native American societies which gave rise to the whites' references to Indian leaders as "kings." In feudal order one king could be the vassal of another, more powerful king. Thus the Wampanoag leader King Philip, for example, was viewed by the English during the 1670s within the English legal structure as king over the local Indians and vassal to the king of England because in 1622 his father, Massasoit, had commended himself to James I as James's "man" or vassal. When Philip went to war with the English, he did so as a rebellious vassal from the whites' point of view and not as the leader of an independent people. After his death in battle, Philip's head was exhibited on a pole in Plymouth:[36] a grisly but traditional public proclamation among the English of what would befall a traitor to the realm on either side of the Atlantic.

        The use of the medieval concept of feudal vassalage to establish sovereignty is at the core of the struggle between the Iroquois, the state of New York, and the federal government of the United States. In 1783 England used various treaties with the Iroquois and the English-French treaties of Utrecht (1713) and of Paris (1763) in which the English claimed jurisdiction over Iroquois lands as the premise for turning over this domain to the newly formed United States.[37] The upstart revolutionaries then imposed a series of treaties in which feudal vassalage was put in eighteenth century terms: in the Second Treaty of Fort Stanwix, 1784, the first article states that "The United States of American give peace to the Senecas, Mohawks, Onondagas and Cayugas, and *receive them into their protection*" (emphasis added).[38] But then the state of New York claimed the right to impose a similar concept of feudal vassalage in 1788 and 1789 when it made three separate treaties with three of the Six Nations: with the Onondagas (September 12, 1788, at Fort Stanwix), the Oneidas (September 22, 1788, at Fort Stanwix), and the Cayugas (February 25, 1789, at Albany). All three of these treaties had identical first articles: that each of these Iroquois people "do cede and grant all their lands to the people of the State of New York forever." Then each treaty stipulated that New York returned a part of these "ceded lands" to the Onondagas, the Oneidas, or the Cayugas.[39] The United States-negotiated Second Treaty of Fort Stanwix 1784, is contradicted by the three New York-negotiated treaties of 1788–1789 because the Onondagas, Oneidas, and Cayugas were forced to accept two different non-Indian sovereignties. If the United States in 1784, at that time governed under the Articles of Confederation, claimed sovereignty over the Iroquois, how could the state of New York claim sovereignty? Moreover, if two conflicting powers—New York and the federal government of the United States—both claimed sovereignty, can either claim to sovereignty be valid when by the whites' own definitions sovereignty is exclusive and cannot be shared?

Further complicating these questions is a viewpoint held by many Iroquois today that they themselves have never ceased to be a sovereign people. The whites base their claims of sovereignty over the Iroquois specifically to the Treaty of Utrecht in 1713 in which the French acknowledge that the Iroquois are within the jurisdiction of the English. While the Iroquois were occassionally allies of the English, the Iroquois did not see this alliance as vassalage. In 1684, for example, Onondaga and Cayuga chiefs noted that "they have put themselves and their lands under the Protection of the King." That this was not within the white context of vassalage is clarified by these same chiefs: "That being a free people uniting themselves to the English, it may be in their power to give their land to what Sachim [the French or English kings] they please."[40] Only an English translation of this 1684 Iroquois proposal survives. Why was the term "sachem" used in referring to the monarchs of Europe? Sachem is a Narragansett Algonquin word meaning leader or chief, a word which was widely used by the English. Did the Iroquois use the word, or did the interpreter? In any case, a sachem does not have the sovereign power possessed by a European monarch. It seems evident that the Iroquois perceived European monarchs from an Iroquois frame of reference and thus misperceived the sovereignty claimed by these monarchs. The term "sachem" best expressed their meaning, whether the word was used by the Iroquois or by the translator. There are many examples of "the white man's Indian"[41] — perceptions of Indians by whites within a white frame of reference. Here is an important example of the Indians' white man.

What the Onondaga and Cayuga spokesmen were proposing in 1684 was similar to the political relationship within the Iroquois Confederacy in which the member states could only create a confederacy policy by consensus. Except for the use of force, there was no internal method such as a legal hierarchy to enforce their confederation's covenant. Since the Iroquois' perspective was this confederation of consensus among independent though allied nations, it is unlikely that the Iroquois would have knowingly agreed to become vassals of the English crown. Finally, the Iroquois' alliance with the English, which the English chose to interpret as that of a forest vassal to a European sovereign, was in any case dependent upon the ability of the English to comply with the other terms of the Iroquois' covenant. In 1684 and indeed in subsequent alliance conferences, these terms always included aid against the French and controls over white expansion. Neither the London government nor their American-based representatives were ever to fulfill both of these pledges. Although the French were finally defeated in Canada in 1763, the American Revolution broke out in 1775 with the British still unable to control white settlement. Given the failure of the British to comply with the basic terms of the covenant, it is perhaps understandable why the British commander-in-chief for North America, General Thomas Gage, wrote such a frank letter to Sir William Johnson on October 7, 1772, regarding debates in London over whether the Iroquois were subjects of the king:

> As for the Six Nations having acknowledged themselves Subjects of the English [as was contended in London] that I conclude must be a very gross Mistake and am well satisfied were they [the Iroquois] told so, they would not be well pleased. I know I would not venture to treat them as Subjects ... I believe they would on such an attempt, very soon resolve to cut our Throats.[42]

After the American Revolution the Iroquois maintained that the British had no right to give the United States jurisdiction over their domain in the 1783 Treaty of Paris. Gage's letter would seem to support the Iroquois' position. The Iroquois also protested that the United States could not claim jurisdiction by right of conquest, because, as the Mohawk leader Kanonraron (Aaron Hill) noted in 1784: "We are free, and independent, and at present under no influence."[43] In fact, most Iroquois lands were indeed unoccupied by white troops and were clearly under Iroquois control.

The whites, on the other hand, emphasized that in 1779 a Patriot army under General John Sullivan had successfully invaded and devastated forty Iroquois towns. Even though the army had not remained in Iroquois country as an occupying force, Sullivan's expedition and the overall victory in the war with the British and their Iroquois allies were used by the whites as justifications that they were entitled to jurisdiction over Iroquois lands under the Treaty of Paris. For the whites the primary debate over sovereignty was between state and national white governments and not between whites and Indians. New York noted that its claim to preemption over Iroquois lands had colonial precedents, although this right had always been contested by other colonies such as Massachusetts. Furthermore, the Iroquois themselves had frequently met in conference with New York officials and proclaimed that their lands were under the protection of the governor of the colony, whom the Iroquois referred to as Corlaer. New York noted that its legal rights preceded those of the national government, because the state constitution took effect in 1777 whereas the Articles of Confederation, the first plan of government for the United States, were not ratified until 1781. An explanation if not a solution, to the conflicting claims lies in an understanding of the historical context in the years immediately following the American Revolution.[44]

Appropriately, an examination of the non-Indian viewpoint can begin with quotes from two of the founding fathers. On November 15, 1784, James Monroe wrote to James Madison. Madison had attended the peace council at Fort Stanwix in New York. In discussing the negotiations between the Iroquois and the representatives of both the United States and the state of New York in what would become known as the Second Treaty of Fort Stanwix, Monroe wrote:

> The questions wh. appear to me to arise upon the subjects *of variance* are 1. whether these *Indians* are to be consider'd as members of the State of *N. York*, or whether the living simply within the bounds of a State, in the exclusion only of an European power, while they acknowlidge no obidience to its laws but hold a country over which they do not extend, nor enjoy the protection nor any of the rights of citizenship within it, is a situation wh. will even in the most qualified sense, admit their being held as members of a State? 2. whether on the other hand this is not a description of those whose manag'ment is committed by the confideration to the U.S. in Congress assembled? In either event the land held by these *Indians*, having never been ceded either by *N. York* or *Massachusetts* belongs not to the *U. States*; the only point then in wh. *N. York* can be reprehensible is, for preceding by a particular [state treaty], the general *Treaty*. This must be attributed to a suspicion that there exists in *Congress* a design to injure her. The transaction will necessarily come before us, but will it not be most expedient in the present state of our affaris to form no decision

thereon? I know no advantages to be deriv'd from one. If the general *treaty* had been obstructed the injury sustain'd in that instance is now without remedy. A decision either way, will neither restore the time we have lost nor remove the impressions wh. this *variance* hath made with the *Indians* & in the *Court of G. Britain* respecting us. If the right *of Congress* hath been contraven'd shall we not derive greater injury by urging it to the reprehension of *New York* who holds herself aggriev'd in other respects than by suffering our sense of that delinquency to lay dormant? Our purchases [that is, land purchases by the United States] must be made without her bounds & those *Indians* whose alliance we seek inhabit a country to which she hath no claim.[45]

On November 27, Madison replied:

As far as N.Y. may claim a right of treating with Indians for the purchase of lands within her limits, she has the confederation on her side; as far as she may have exerted that right in contravention of the Genl. Treaty, or even unconfidentially with the Comisrs. of Congs. she has violated both duty & decorum. The foederal articles give Congs. the exclusive right of *managing all affairs* with the Indians *not members* of any State, under a proviso, that the *Legislative authority*, of the State within its own limits be not violated. By Indian[s] not members of a State, must be meant those, I conceive who do not live within the body of the Society, or whose Persons or property form no objects of its laws. In the case of Indians of this description the only restraint on Congress is imposed by the *Legislative authority* of the State. If this proviso be taken in its full latitude, it must destroy the authority of Congress altogether, since no act of Congs. within the limits of a State can be conceived which will not in some way or other encroach upon the authority [of the] States. In order then to give some meaning to both parts of the sentence, as a known rule of interpretation requires, we must restrain this proviso to some particular view of the parties. What was this view? My answer is that it was to save to the States their right of preemption of lands from the Indians. My reasons are 1. That this was the principal right formerly exerted by the Colonies with regard to the Indians. 2. that it was a right asserted by the laws as well as the proceedings of all of them, and therefore being most familiar, wd. be most likely to be in contemplation of the Parties; 3. that being of most consequence to the States individually, and least inconsistent with the general powers of Congress, it was most likely to be made a ground of Compromise. 4. it has been always said that the proviso came from the Virga. Delegates, who wd naturally be most vigilant over the territorial rights of their Constituents. But whatever may be the true boundary between the authority of Congs. & that of N.Y. or however indiscreet the latter may have been, I join entirely with you in thinking that temperance on the part of the former will be the wisest policy.[46]

Madison's analysis, which tries to give credit to both the national and the state points of view, distinguishes what may be termed the Gemeinschaft from the Gesellschaft. Madison acknowledges the legal constrictions of Gesellschaft but then notes that these legal definitions need to be seen in the context—the sense—in which they were made: in the Gemeinschaft relationship between the national and state governments. Unable to resolve the community of the states and nation in Gemeinschaft with the legality of Gesellschaft, Madison joins Monroe in suggesting that the issue not be pressed. Since the conflicts of Gemeinschaft and Gesellschaft within the white society could not be easily resolved, it is no wonder that the Gemeinschaft and Gesellschaft of Indian-white relations has also proven to be so complex.

The question of sovereignty so adroitly avoided by two of the founding fathers survives to this day. Within the non-Indian society it is basically the issue of states' rights versus national authority. It was an issue for non-Indians in America long before the Revolution. A major theme in white American history is the struggle between centralized authority and those diverse political units which were colonies and, after 1783, states. The American Revolution and the American Civil War are the two primary examples of this struggle between what might be termed centralized classical order and decentralized baroque order. The federal government of the United States after 1789 inherited the problems of wielding classical, centralized order from the clearly baroque structure of the Articles of Confederation and from the imperial governments of England. The various states carried on the tradition of individual colonial rights and extended it into the twentieth century with the issue of states' rights.

In this struggle of centripetal and centrifugal forces, Indian affairs have been a significant focus though only one of the many major issues involving these contrary perspectives. In 1643 the New England Confederation of four colonies—Massachusetts Bay, Plymouth, Connecticut, and New Haven—noted the possibilities of future warfare with the Indians and of becoming involved in the ongoing Puritan civil war then being fought in England. Thus declaring that even "the justest wars may be of dangerous consequence," the four colonies agreed not to participate in any war "without the consent and agreement" of at least six of the eight commissioners, two from each colony.[47] From 1685 until 1688, England's King James II attempted unsuccessfully to impose a centralized authority over Massachusetts, Plymouth, New Hampshire, Rhode Island, and Connecticut, adding in 1688 New York and New Jersey, and planning to include Pennsylvania and perhaps even Maryland when he was deposed in England's Glorious Revolution.[48] In 1697 William Penn proposed a plan of union which would have confederated Massachusetts, Connecticut, Rhode Island, New York, New Jersey, Pennsylvania, Maryland, Virginia, and Carolina.[49] Benjamin Franklin's hope for a union of colonists was premised on a need to coordinate Indian affairs and was seen by Franklin partly within the context of an already-existing confederacy, that of the Iroquois, for on March 20, 1751, he wrote to James Parker that

> It would be a very strange Thing, if six Nations of ignorant Savages [Franklin's opinion of the Iroquois] should be capable of forming a Scheme for such an Union, and be able to excute it in such a Manner, as that it has subsisted Ages, and appears indissoluble; and yet that a like Union should be impracticable for ten or a Dozen English Colonies, to whom it is more necessary, and must be more advantageous; and who cannot be supposed to want an equal Understanding of their Interests.[50]

Yet despite a catchy slogan—"Join or Die"[51]—invented by Franklin and the 1754 Albany Congress which met in an attempt to form such a confederacy, Franklin was absolutely wrong. A satisfactory union — under the Constitution — was not formed until 1789, after an experiment with the Articles of Confederation during and after the American Revolution. Even after 1789 the United States was not able to determine and consistently enforce a delegation of authority in Indian affairs. The pre-Revolutionary rights of individual colonies became post-Revolutionary states' rights.

For more than two hundred years, the contending sovereignties of New York State and the United States remain an issue. In 1775, after the Revolution erupted in Massachusetts that April, Patriot representatives in the Second Continental Congress at Philadelphia enacted during July a centralized Indian policy even though, at the time, reconciliation with Britain and not independence was anticipated as the likely outcome of the conflict. Congress appointed commissioners of the Indian affairs for the northern and middle colonies on July 13, 1775, and for the southern colonies on July 19, 1775. Congressional policy called for treaties with Indian nations in which the Indians would declare their neutrality, for Congress declared to the Indians that "We don't wish you to take up the hatchet against the king's troops. We desire you to . . . keep the hatchet buried deep."[52]

New York's claim that its 1777 constitution and its provision for jurisdiction in New York Indian affairs precedes any centralized authority by a Congress of the United States is challenged by the July 1775 events in Philadelphia. In fact, New York did not establish claims of sovereignty even with regard to other *states* until 1786. At Hartford, Connecticut, on December 16,1786, New York finally wrested from the state of Massachusetts the statement that, except for 230,400 acres for its own use,

> The Commonwealth of Massachusetts doth hereby cede, grant, release and confirm to the State of New York, forever, all the claim, right and title, which the Commonwealth of Massachusetts hath to the government, *sovereignty* [emphasis added], and jurisdiction of the lands and territories so claimed by the State of New York.[53]

With Massachusetts' claims put aside, only three claims of sovereignty remained: those of the Iroquois, of the centralized government, and of New York State. A review of the historical circumstances following the Revolution reveals how New York State and federal authorities contested for sovereignty in Iroquois affairs. In the fall of 1784, delegates from the New York government met with the Iroquois to make peace at Fort Stanwix. The New York delegation was to be followed by representatives of the United States government (under the Articles of Confederation). Prior to the start of actual negotiations with the New York delegation, the Mohawk Iroquois war leader Joseph Brant remarked that the upcoming negotiations with two separate political entities, New York and Congress, was a concern: "Here lies some Difficulty in our Minds, that there should be two separate Bodies to manage these Affairs, for this does not agree with our ancient Customs."[54] The determination of the New York negotiators to proceed was not deterred. No land transfer was authorized, but the Iroquois representatives said such a transfer would be considered. The New York delegation and the Iroquois agreed, however, that any land sales would be authorized by the state.[55] Then the New York delegates were replaced by United States negotiators (together with a delegation from Pennsylvania which agreed to negotiate under the authority of the United States). An epidemic of disease was reported raging in the Iroquois settlements near Niagara. Brant had already left Fort Stanwix to return to the stricken Iroquois, hoping that the United States negotiations might be postponed until the spring. Despite — or perhaps because of — the fact that the Iroquois could hardly put forth their strongest front, the whites proceeded. In the Second Treaty of Fort Stanwix, October 22, 1784, the United States delegates proclaimed their country's sovereignty over the Iroquois, forced the cession of some Iroquois lands, and made the Iroquois surrender all claims to jurisdiction over their confederacy's empire[56] to the west of the present boundary of Pennsylvania. The Pennsylvania delegates then acquired all of northwestern Pennsylvania from the Iroquois.[57] These were the negotiations which elicited the exchange quoted earlier between James Monroe and James Madison.

Thereafter, the issue of sovereignty in Iroquois affairs was bandied by events and trends which would, from a white point of view, alternately support claims of New York and then of United States authority. Problems of sovereignty within the Iroquois Confederacy were also manifest, for just as the American Revolution had been a civil war within the English community, so the struggle had also been a civil war among the Six Nations of Iroquois. The Iroquois reaffirmed the cohesiveness of their confederacy through a ritual of amnesty at Fort Stanwix in 1784 prior to their negotiations with the United States. As recorded by a white eyewitness,

> we were witnesses of the reconciliation of the Oneidas with their [Iroquois] enemies. Although both dwelt, for several days, near the fort, and in spite of the cessation of hostilities, communication had not been reestablished between them. The "Great Grasshopper" [an Oneida leader]... followed by five other savages... went to the cabins of the Senecas. They walked stiffly, and stopped from time to time. The chief of the Senecas came out and went to receive them at some distance. They sat on the grass and compliments were exchanged by the two chiefs. They smoked the pipe of peace and separated. The next day the visit was returned by the Senecas to the Oneidas with... the same formalities.[58]

The forces of local jurisdiction among each of the Six Nations, however, remained as they had been prior to the American Revolution, a potent balance—and always a potential detriment—to confederacy authority. Thus in 1788 and 1789 New York took the opportunity to make separate treaties with the Onondagas, the Oneidas, and the Cayugas,[59] an opportunity made all the more favorable to New York by the fact that its own central government, Congress, was making the transition from a national government under the Articles of Confederation to one under the new federal Constitution. The outgoing confederated United States government made one final effort to assert a national authority in Iroquois affairs, however. Even as New York was negotiating separately with individual Iroquois nations rather than with the entire confederacy, the United States under the Articles made the Treaty of Fort Harmar in Ohio on January 9, 1789, with some Iroquois representatives. This treaty recognized the political entity of the "Six Nations" as a confederacy rather than as six separate nations as New York was doing. The treaty also stated that "the United States of America confirm to the Six Nations" their lands in what is now central and western New York: the United States would "relinquish and quit claim to the same and every part thereof, excepting only six miles square round the fort of Oswego."[60] The treaty was ignored by the state of New York.

The new federal government under the Constitution took office in March and April 1789. New York's demonstration of states' rights were finally countered in 1790 when Congress passed a Trade and Intercourse Act denying states' rights in Indian affairs:

> no sale of lands made by any Indians, or any nation or tribe of Indians within the Unites States, shall be valid to any person or persons, or to any state, whether having the right of pre-emption to such lands or not, unless the same shall be made and duly executed at some public treaty, held under the authority of the United States.[61]

But in 1793 Congress admitted in its next Trade and Intercourse Act that the states did have certain rights. Although land cessions still had to be federally authorized, the act also stated that

> nothing in this act shall be construed to prevent any trade or intercourse with Indians living on lands surrounded by settlements of the citizens of the United States, and being within the jurisdiction of any of the individual states.[62]

To indicate the confusion generated by this passage, as recently as 1972 a United States assistant attorney general argued that the above "is the first of a series of provisions which indicates that Congress chose to deal differently with Indians in the settled Eastern states than with Indians still in the wild frontier country to the West."[63]

Then, in 1794, the United States federal government made a treaty at Canandaigua, New York, with the Six Nations. It was a treaty vital to the United States, for it was made specifically to court Iroquois favor and keep the Iroquois from joining a frontier Indian coalition in Ohio at war with the United States. Had the Iroquois joined that coalition and gone into battle, the relatively new United States' experiment in independence might have been abruptly altered, even terminated—a possibility all the more likely because the Ohio Indians were being encouraged by the British. From the Iroquois' point of view, the treaty was made in order to secure their remaining lands and define their diplomatic relationship with the federal government. The treaty recognized treaties already made with the state of New York. In the wording of these 1788–1789 New York treaties, legally in Gesellschaft, the Onondagas, Oneidas, and Cayugas had ceded all their lands to the state and received back from the state specific, limited reservations. The treaty also implies, legally in Gesellschaft, that the Iroquois living south of Canada were within the sovereign jurisdiction of the United States. The treaty stipulates, for example, that the annuities promised in the treaty will be distributed only to Iroquois residing "within the boundaries of the United States." The annuities would not be distributed to Iroquois who were living in Canada (where many had resided for over a century and where others had fled after the Revolution). Another implication of sovereignty is the stipulation that only the people of the United States (not, for instance, the British in Canada) have the right to purchase Iroquois lands south of Canada, should the Iroquois ever decide voluntarily to sell them. This implies United States sovereignty, for if the Iroquois were sovereign, they could sell to whom they pleased. However, the 1794 Canandaigua treaty notes that the Iroquois' reservations were "their [the Iroquois'] property" and that the reservations "belong" to the Iroquois. The treaty also states— twice—that the United States would not "claim" any of the reservation lands "nor disturb them [the Iroquois]. . . in the free use and enjoyment thereof."[64]

How did the Iroquois — in Gemeinschaft — understand the terms of this 1794 treaty when it was translated from English? Certainly, a potential for confusion and misunderstanding is present over what is clearly stated in the treaty—the reservation lands "belong" to the Iroquois and the United States will not "claim" them. Confusion and misunderstanding is also likely over what is implied in the complex legal structure of the treaty which would make the United States sovereign.

There is strong evidence that the Iroquois believed that the 1794 treaty guaranteed their rights as a free and independent people. It is found within the Gai'-wiio', the religious teachings of the Seneca prophet Handsome Lake. Handsome Lake had fought against the United States during the American Revolution. He was probably present at the 1794 negotiations at Canandaigua. His spiritual and moral teachings among his people between 1800 and his death in 1815 did much to insure the survival of those Iroquois who did not wish to convert to Christianity, for Handsome Lake's lessons inspired many Iroquois to rise above the social and economic depression which was part of the legacy of the post-Revolutionary period. Within one of the lessons which he taught is an insight into the Iroquois' perspective on the 1794 treaty. That treaty had been the diplomatic keystone of President George Washington's Indian policy. Handsome Lake told his followers how four spiritual messengers had revealed how the Creator, God, had provided Washington (who died in 1799) with a comfortable home in the afterlife because Washington had treated the Iroquois with justice during his administration. The four spiritual messengers had aided Handsome Lake in interpreting a vision of "a house suspended in the air and on the porch with a railing about it a man was walking and with him was a penny dog [a dog which loyally follows its master]. Now moreover the man was a white man."

> Then the messengers said, "Truly you have seen. It is said that the man is the first and oldest president of the United States. Now he enjoys himself and he is the only white man so near the new world of our Creator. Now it is said that there was once a time when the Thirteen Fires and the King were in trouble. The Thirteen Fires were victorious and this man won the victory from the king. Said the king, "You have overpowered me, so now I release everything that was in my control, even these Iroquois who were my helpers. It rests with you what shall be done with them. Let them be to you a thing for a sacrifice." Then said the president, "I shall let them live and go back to the places that are theirs for they are an independent people." So it is said. Now this man did a great work. He has ordered things that we may enjoy ourselves, as long as the sun shines and the waters run.[65]

The era of the American Revolution has been telescoped in this vision, but the meaning is clear: Washington did "a great work" which "ordered things"—in the Trade and Intercourse Acts of 1790 and 1793 and in the 1794 Treaty of Canandaigua, for example — so that the Iroquois would remain what Washington himself, in this vision, had called them: "an independent people."

From the Iroquois' point of view, both in 1794 and in the present, one of the most important aspects of the Canandaigua treaty was that it was meant to reverse New York State policy of dealing with each of the Six Nations as individual political units rather than acknowledging the political status of the whole confederacy. The treaty acknowledged the political viability of the Iroquois Confederacy—the Six Natons — as a representative of all of the member nations, while nevertheless noting that the individual nations might act on their own behalf as well. This dual acknowledgment was in keeping with the "confederated" context of the Iroquois' *own* perceptions of their Six Nations. It is an ironic, even cynical, acknowledgment by the United States, however, because at the same time the United States is outwardly recognizing the confederacy's viability, the United States is implying in the treaty's legal labyrinth that the United States is sovereign.

One sovereignty is clear in the 1794 treaty. A federal supremacy over state authority is stipulated — New York State is not even mentioned.

> Lest the firm peace and friendship now established should be interrupted by the misconduct of individuals, the United States and Six Nations agree, that for injuries done by individuals on either side, no private revenge or retaliation shall take place; but, instead thereof, complaint shall be made by the party injured, to the other: By the Six Nations or any of them, to the President of the United States, or the Superintendent by him appointed: and by the Superintendent, or other person appointed by the President, to the principal chiefs of the Six Nations, or of the nation to which the offender belongs: and such prudent measures shall then be pursued as shall be necessary to preserve our peace and friendship unbroken; until the legislature (or great council) of the United States shall make other equitable provision for the purpose.[66]

This provision was meant to reinforce the federal sovereignty defined in the Trade and Intercourse Acts of 1790 and 1793. On June 29, 1795, Secretary of War Timothy Pickering (who, before becoming secretary, had negotiated the 1794 treaty), instructed the federal government's Indian agent to the Iroquois Confederacy, Israel Chapin, Jr., not to countenance New York State's negotiation of treaties with any of the Iroquois nations without federal authority, because such action would violate the Trade and Intercourse Act of 1793:

> The Attorney General of the Unites States has given his opinion that the reservations of those tribes [Oneida, Onondaga and Cayuga] within the State of New York form no exception to the General Law: but whenever [land is] purchased, the bargains must be made at a treaty held under the authority of the United States.[67]

Despite this federal assertion, New York in 1795 made an illegal land cession treaty with the Oneidas—the state acted without federal authority. On the grounds that New York State had acted illegally, the Oneidas eventually obtained access to a federal court — in 1975. The court found in favor of the Oneidas in 1977, but appeals will probably continue until the mid-1980s or longer. Since the state of New York dealt with other Iroquois nations within the confederacy in much the same way — illegally, as defined by the 1790 or 1793 Trade and Intercourse Acts and subsequent legislation—negotiations and court cases demanding reparations are or will be undertaken by other Iroquois nations during the rest of the twentieth century.[68]

Given the obvious conflict of sovereignties, definitions of federal and state authorities became dependent upon the political persuasions and interpretations of the whites in power. Land cession treaties continued to require federal supervision whether carried out by federal or state authorities, but states, including New York, ensured that their rights would be protected by placing states' rights supporters in Congress and in the executive. During the first half of the nineteenth century states including New York, with federal approval, acquired lands from Indians in treaties. They also encouraged and then forced Indians within their borders to remove to areas to the west. The removal of most of the Oneidas and a portion of the other Iroquois from New York after 1815,[69] as well as the land cessions made by each of the Six Nations to New York betwen 1785 and 1846,[70] occurred because the federal government permitted New York to negotiate with each of the various nations separately rather than through the confederacy's grand council which represented all six nations in confederation. Furthermore, representatives of each of the individual Iroquois nations accepted the premise of separate, tribal negotiations rather than negotiation through the confederacy's council, thereby stressing a sovereignty for each nation. Thus the Iroquois communities were as involved in the issue of states' rights versus centralized authority as were the states of the United States. Separate sovereignty for each of the Six Nations reached its most extreme assertion on December 5, 1848, when Senecas on the Cattaraugus and Allegheny reservations in New York carried out a coup d'etat against the traditional chiefs who were both part of the confederacy structure and leaders of the Seneca nation proper. Many of these traditional chiefs stood accused by their own people of accepting white bribes and selling off Seneca lands. The revolutionary Senecas, with the encouragement of white reformers, elected a president, a clerk, a treasurer, and other officials under a constitution which, among its many ideas borrowed from the whites, disenfranchised the women who in traditional Iroquois politics had wielded considerable political power. The new Seneca constitution and government was recognized by the state of New York and the United States in 1849.[71]

The emphasis on states' rights, in which the federal government turned over its powers to the states, reached its full force during the administration of Andrew Jackson. He included in his first annual message statements and a rhetorical question regarding New York's rights in Indian affairs because he was confident that New York's successful assertion of control of its Indian population — when required, with federal compliance — was an example he could use in justifying the exertion of states' rights by Georgia against the Cherokee Indians who were surrounded by that state. That Jackson also believed that Indian sovereignty did not exist is evident. Jackson, referring to Georgia, asserted:

> There is no constitutional, conventional, or legal provision which allows them less power over the Indians within their borders than is possessed by Maine or New York. Would the people of Maine permit the Penobscot tribe to erect an independent government within their State? And unless they did would it not be the duty of the General Government to support them in resisting such a measure? Would the people of New York permit each remnant of the Six Nations within her borders to declare itself an independent people under the protection of the United States [that is, under federal authority]?[72]

Despite presidents' proclamations, however, the issue of state versus federal sovereignty persisted. Because federal and state authorities cooperated in treaty making, the issue of sovereignty became focused on states's rights to police power and to legislation such as taxation. In 1856 the Supreme Court in *Fellows* v. *Blacksmith* struck a blow for federal authority over New York State's Indian affairs and then in 1858, in *New York* ex rel. *Cutler* v. *Dibble* struck a blow for New York State's right to control Indian affairs. But in 1866 in *The New York Indians*, federal sovereignty was delineated.[73] In each of these cases specific areas of sovereignty were being defined, but their broader tendencies alternately encouraged New York State and the federal authorities with evidence supporting their own contentions of sovereignty.

In 1887 Congress passed the General Allotment Act (Dawes Act), which was intended to break up the communal land holdings of Indian nations across the country by redistributing the lands among individual Indians and non-Indians so that private enterprise would be encouraged. Because of preemptive land claims by the Ogden Land Company, the act specifically exempted "the reservations of the Seneca Nation of New York Indians in the State of New York" but did not mention in any context the other New York Iroquois.[74] To assert state authority and to establish the groundwork for allotment (never actually accomplished), the New York legislature in 1888 authorized the

"Special Committee to Investigate the 'Indian Problem' of the State of New York."[75] The report of this committee is known as the Whipple Report, after its chairman, J. S. Whipple. Under Whipple's leadership the committee took as its premise that New York State, not the federal government or the Iroquois, possessed sovereignty in Indian affairs. Furthermore, Whipple clearly set out to prove in his committee's investigation that the Iroquois were debased and relatively few in number. A proof of these conditions, he believed, would further justify a New York takeover of reservation affairs. In fact, Supreme Court Justice John McLean had noted in his concurring opinion in *Worcester* v. *Georgia* (1832):

> Is there no end to the exercise of . . . power over Indians within the limits of a state, by the general government? The answer is, that, in its nature, it must be limited by circumstances.

> If a tribe of Indians shall become so degraded or reduced in numbers, as to lose the power of self-government, the protection of the local [that is, state] law, of necessity, must be extended over them.[76]

During the committee's hearings which formed the basis for its foregone conclusion, chairman Whipple was careful to lead witnesses when necessary toward the reaffirmation of state sovereignty which the committee wanted to hear. Thus while the committee interviewed the chancellor of Syracuse University, C. N. Sims, about the nearby Onondaga Iroquois, the following exchange took place between member B. H. Davis, Sims, and Whipple. It demonstrates the willful direction of the inquiry:

> [Davis to Sims:] . . . what do you say as to the power of the State, in view of the existence of treaties, to control this particular reservation? A. [from Sims] On the letter of the law I don't think the State has a right; I think there has arisen a condition of things in which the nation has ceased to be a nation; I think it is not a nation for justice, not a nation for progress, for the making of roads and educating the children, and for the protection of its citizens against each other; I don't think it punishes crime nor restrains crime, and, therefore, I think the nation has ceased to exist as a nation.

> Q. [Davis to Sims:] What about the existence of any police power upon the reservation? A. There is none at all.

By Mr. WHIPPLE:

> Q. The question was more particularly as to the rights of our national government and of the State of New York in relation to this particular reservation? A. [by Sims:] I should say that there is a condition of things which nations must recognize from time to time when that which calls itself a nation ceases to be a nation, in fact is dead; here is a dead nation; it is not in the condition of a nation, and I am not sure but the letter of the law would justify the State interposing and administering.

> Q. You think they should be treated as wards rather than as nations? A. I think so.[77]

Additional testimony (including some by Onondagas), however, indicates that the Onondaga nation was viable as a political entity. The following statement was made, for example, by Sims:

> I think they [the Onondagas] are very positive in their opposition to anything that looks toward a destruction of the traditions of the tribe, and the destruction of the perpetuity of the tribe; I think they will oppose anything; the more thoughtful, at least, who are loyal in their Indian notions.

But Whipple always returned to what he wanted to hear and thus addressed the chancellor a third time:

By Mr. WHIPPLE:

> Q. The question I was trying to get at, chancellor, I think you did not quite understand me, I wanted to know if you could tell me if our national government had control of these Indians, in your judgment, or the State of New York? A. O, I think the State of New York.[78]

In 1903 the Supreme Court set an ominous precedent in *Lone Wolf* v. *Hitchcock* which affirmed federal sovereignty and denied any contention of sovereignty by an Indian nation. The court declared, in a case involving the Kiowa-Comanche reservation in Oklahoma, that Congress had the unilateral power "to abrogate the provisions of an Indian treaty."[79] By its affirmation of federal authority, the decision also challenged the claims by any state that a state could have

sovereignty over Indians. Justice Edward D. White in his majority
opinion quoted *United States* v. *Kagama* (1885):

> These Indian tribes *are* the wards of the nation. They are communities
> *dependent* on the United States. ... They owe no allegiance to the
> [individual] States, and receive from them no protection. Because of
> the local ill feeling, the people of the States where they are found are
> often their deadliest enemies. From their very weakness and
> helplessness, so largely due to the course of dealing of the Federal
> government with them and the treaties in which it has been prom-
> ised, there arises the duty of protection, and with it the power. This
> has always been recognized by the Executive and by Congress, and by
> this court, whenever the question has arisen.[80]

In 1917, when the United States entered the First World War,
the Iroquois were encouraged by the Seneca pan-Indian leader Arthur
C. Parker to take a unique opportunity to assert sovereignty: they
declared war against Germany.[81] In 1920 in *United States* v. *Boylan*, a
federal court of appeals affirmed federal authority in Indian affairs and
as a result the Oneida Iroquois recovered thirty-two acres of land—the
basis of the present-day New York Oneida reservation.[82] As a result of
the Boylan case, the New York legislature established the "New York
State Indians Commission,"chaired by Edward A. Everett, whose
commission made its report in 1922. The report was not what the state
legislators wished to hear, and so they did not publish it. Given the bias
of the Whipple Report of 1888 which maintained state sovereignty in
Indian affairs, it is easy to see why the Everett Report was suppressed
by the state legislature. The report, a 399-page manuscript, ended with
the statement by Everett:

> I further find that the said Indians of the State of New York, as a
> nation, are still the owners of the fee simple title to the territory ceded
> to them by the treaty of 1784, unless divested of the same by an
> instrument of equal force and effect as the said treaty of 1784.[83]

In this statement, Everett advocated the validity of 1784 medieval and
feudallike return of ceded lands to a vassal client, but he also concluded that only a new treaty between federal and Iroquois authorities
could alter prior treaty obligations. Yet in 1871 Congress had abolished
the possibility of making any further treaties with any Indians:

> hereafter no Indian nation or tribe within the territory of the United
> States shall be acknowledged or recognized as an independent na-

tion, tribe, or power with whom the United States may contract by treaty: *Provided, further,* That nothing herein contained shall be construed to invalidate or impair the obligation of any treaty heretofore lawfully made and ratified with any such Indian nation or tribe.[84]

Thus Everett was maintaining that Indian lands were secure from state interference — including the possibility that they might be allotted in the manner advocated by the federal Allotment Act of 1887.[85]

When Everett attempted to bring his viewpoints into federal court, the subsequent *Deere* v. *St. Lawrence River Power Co.* (1929) weakened federal authority. The court declared that federal courts had no jurisdiction in an "ejectment" action.[86]

In 1930, when Congress proposed to cede to New York state civil and criminal jurisdiction over the Indians of New York, the Indians protested and the bill (Snell bill, H.R. 9720) was not passed.[87] Then in 1942 a federal district court declared in *United States* v. *Forness*, a case involving the Senecas' leases on their reservation lands, that

> The Indians are not subject to state laws and the process of its courts. ... This proposition has long since and many times been decided by the Supreme Court of the United States and by the court of last resort in the State of New York.

The court added that "state law does not apply to the Indians except so far as the United States has given its consent."[88] Challenged by these declarations, New York State sought and secured the assent of Congress for authority over Indians in criminal cases in 1948, and in civil cases in 1950 under the condition, agreed to by both state and federal officials, that the federal government retained ultimate sovereignty in Indian affairs.[89] But in 1960 the Supreme Court affirmed federal authority over state authority in *Federal Power Commission* v. *Tuscarora Indian Nation*.[90]

Ultimate federal sovereignty was asserted in 1974 by the Supreme Court in *Oneida Indian Nation of New York et al.* v. *County of Oneida, New York, et. al.* which declared that the Oneida Iroquois could press their land claims in federal rather than in state court. In the decision written by Justice Byron R. White, however, the court noted:

> This is not to ignore the obvious fact that New York had legitimate and far-reaching connections with its Indian tribes antedating the Constitution and that the State has continued to play a substantial role with respect to the Indians in that State.

He then referred to the issue of sovereignty over the past two centuries:

> There has been recurring tension between federal and state law; state authorities have not easily accepted the notion that federal law and federal courts must be deemed the controlling considerations in dealing with the Indians. *Fellows* v. *Blacksmith, The New York Indians, United States* v. *Forness*, and the *Tuscarora* litigation are sufficient evidence that the reach and exclusivity of federal law with respect to reservation lands and reservation Indians did not go unchallenged; and it may be that they are tu some extent challenged here.

Justice White then concluded: "But this only underlines the legal reality that the controversy alleged in the complaint may well depend on what the reach and impact of the federal law will prove to be in this case."[91] In fact, the case which then went into federal court during November 1975 — *The Oneida Indian Nation . . . v. The County of Oneida, New York, and the County of Madison, New York, Defendants and Third-Party Plaintiffs*, v. *The State of New York, Third Party Defendant*, is, after an initial finding in favor of the Oneidas in 1977, still on its way up the judicial ladder of appeals. Thus in the summer of 1980 the test of sovereignties between the federal government and the state of New York goes on. The situation could be further complicated should Congress, especially in reaction to the lobbying efforts of the anti-Indian sovereignty organization, The Interstate Congress of Equal Rights and Responsibilities, declare that as the sovereign in Indian affairs it chooses to delegate its responsibilities to the states. Such a maneuver was manifest in the February 1980 Congressional bill (H.R. 6631) "To provide for the settlement of the land claims of the Cayuga Indian Nation in the State of New York, and for other purposes." This bill would, as reparation for past land frauds, grant to the Cayugas land which, by Congressional authority, would be under state rather than federal law.[92]

To traditional Iroquois the very debate between state and federal authorities over sovereignty permits them to conclude logically that no ultimate non-Indian sovereignty has ever existed. Because the United States was not able to exert sovereignty upon its own structure during the centuries of contention between centralized and decentralized authorities, the case may be made by the Iroquois that non-Indian sovereignty does not exist.

The Iroquois could first claim that their political situation is unique. Although they are a people surrounded by a larger nation, each people has negotiated with the other through treaties, diplomatically, as separate nations. But to confront non-Indian governments which claim sovereignty over them, the Iroquois could make their case utilizing evidence from the non-Indians' point of view to demonstrate that non-Indian-defined sovereignty can exist only if it is imposed upon its own citizens and only if it is imposed equally upon both its own citizens and any new populations over which, through conquest, it claims sovereignty. Such a contention could begin with the philosopher Thomas Hobbes. In 1651 he published *Leviathan, Or the Matter, Form, and Power of a Commonwealth Ecclesiasticall and Civil*.

Hobbes favored sovereignty enforced through a monarchy but noted that sovereign power could be asserted in other forms as well: "an Assembly of All that will come together, then it is a DEMOCRACY, or Popular Commonwealth: when an Assembly of a Part [of society] onely, then it is called an ARISTOCRACY." He further noted that the dominion of a country was acquired by the sovereign power either from the indigenous people or by conquest. Hobbes first noted what the defeated population's responsibilities were after any peace negotiation:

> It is not ... the Victory, that giveth the right of Dominion over the Vanquished, but his own Covenant. Nor is he obliged because he is Conquered; that is to say, beaten, and taken, or put to flight; but because he commeth in, and Submitteth to the Victor.[93]

But Hobbes then notes that the sovereign power must dispense the law equally to the people who have voluntarily subjected themselves to a national dominion and to the people who have been conquered:

> to demand of one Nation more than of the other, from the title of Conquest, as being a Conquered Nation, is an act of ignorance of the Rights of Soveraignty. For the Soveraign is absolute over both alike; or else there is no Soveraignty at all; and so every man may Lawfully protect himselfe, if he can, with his own sword, which is the condition of war.[94]

The latter circumstance is precisely what the American Patriots did when they followed the advice of one of their own philosophers, Thomas Jefferson, in 1776: "That whenever any Form of Government becomes destructive of these ends, it is the Right of the People to alter or to abolish it."[95] For the Iroquois to contend Jefferson's right to independence, however, the Iroquois would have to resort to force just as the Patriots did in the colonial revolt against England's George III. In fact, force is not just a means to achieve sovereignty. Once sovereignty is achieved, force remains a powerful component. It is the exertion of force, or the potential for its exertion, which is the realistic, nontheoretical aspect of sovereignty. Sir Henry Sumner Maine noted in 1875 that most theories of sovereignty include the concept of force, not just order, and that the two are linked.[96] There is no doubt, realistically, that the United States has a potentially greater physical force when compared with the Iroquois. But even within precedents accepted by non-Indians, a dilemma arises again as to what is the nature of the relationship between a small nation and a larger nation within whose boundaries the smaller nation exists. John Marshall defined the problem within a non-Indian context: "A weak state, in order to provide for its safety, may place itself under the protection of one more powerful, without stripping itself of a right of government, and ceasing to be a state."[97]

Perhaps an examination of Marshall's idea is best made in comparative terms, for two centuries prior to Marshall's explanation the Iroquois had begun a process of expansion which evolved into an empire. This empire incorporated subordinate Indian nations such as the Delawares and the Shawnees within the protection and rule of the laws of the confederacy. During the eighteenth century, these subjugated nations made claims against Iroquois sovereignty not unlike those later brought by the Iroquois against the United States.[98] What was an inherent premise of the Iroquois definitions of sovereignty in these circumstances was later shared by non-Indian governments. This was the goal of avoiding any internal dissension which would weaken the major political structure. Such dissension could be generated by subjugated areas.

The Iroquois also knew how difficult it was to maintain sovereignty over nations it had defeated in war. Under the laws of the Iroquois Confederacy, the Delaware Algonquins, for example, were subordinate to their Iroquois conquerors. In 1742 the Iroquois supported a Pennsylvania claim of Delaware land to demonstrate to the Delawares that they were in fact subordinate to the confederacy. In 1758 the Iroquois outlined a strategy by which the Delawares would have to give up some of their own lands and move in among the Iroquois so that the confederacy's homeland would remain intact, on the premise that without united action between subordinate Delaware and superior Iroquois, the whites would divide each and eventually move in on all their lands. In 1774, when the Iroquois found some of the Delawares fighting white frontiersmen without the permission of the confederacy, the Iroquois leadership was hard put to decide whether it was better to help the Delawares stop white frontier expansion or whether the Delawares should be allowed to be defeated by the whites as a lesson on what would befall a nation which tried to go its independent way apart from the desires of the Iroquois Confederacy. The Iroquois chose the latter. The Delawares are but one example of many Indian nations who chafed under Iroquois sovereignty but learned that if they moved independently the consequences—usually defeat at the hands of white frontiersmen, as occurred to the Delawares and Shawnees in 1774 — were worse than continued subordination to the Iroquois.[99]

The Iroquois Confederacy made every attempt to secure its goals, which were premised on maintaining sufficient power to counter the ever-expanding number of white colonists on its borders. This often meant that consolidation of subordinate Indian populations —such as the Delawares after 1758—was desirable lest Iroquois power be too widely dispersed. For example, in 1768 the Delawares and the Shawnees found that the Iroquois had granted jurisdiction to some of their lands to the English at the First Treaty of Fort Stanwix so that the Iroquois homeland would remain intact. Although the confederacy thus funneled off white frontiersmen toward the Iroquois' own frontier, the Iroquois did bring into their own territories any Delawares or other tribes who agreed with them that consolidation was the best policy — other Delawares could fend for themselves at their own peril.[100]

English policy encouraged this resettlement of refugee Indians on Six Nations' lands because it permitted whites to move onto the lands of weakened tribes without the risks which might lead to a costly war. Coincidentally, it seemed to offer a humane alternative in that refugee Indians were placed beyond the danger of white assault. In this sense, the Iroquois domain was an eighteenth century "Indian Territory" — just as Oklahoma would become a century later. The mutual convenient congruence of Iroquois and English policies is exemplified in a speech given by a Six Nations spokesman, Teyawarunte, to Sir William Johnson at Johnson Hall in December 1766:

> We now desire your attention on behalf of our Children the Nanticoks, Canoys, and Delawares who have lately requested of us to lay their desires before you, and begged our Interest on this occasion. — First that as their People who yet remain near the Sea Side, are in a very poor Situation, and desire to come & settle among the rest [of the other Algonquins in their nations] on the Six Nations' Land, we request, to this end, you will grant them Passports, as you have done to the Tuscaroras, and others formerly.[101]

The Iroquois sought "passports" for the refugees so that these refugees could safely travel through British-controlled areas. What the word "passports" was before it was translated into English is not known. It is possible that the term "passports" refers only to safe conduct passes. However, the Iroquois spokesman's use of a term which in eighteenth century English was translated as "passports"[102] is an indication of how the Iroquois considered themselves and the refugee Indians — "our Children" — as separate nations from the British.

The historical basis for Iroquois sovereignty exists within the ideals of the Good Tidings of Peace and Power as defined long ago by the league's founders, but the proof of sovereignty is evident in reality. In their theories of sovereignty, the Iroquois and the whites both perceive a simultaneous existence of force and order, but the Iroquois maintain that force ("Power") had to exist before order ("Peace") could exist. The United States, on the other hand, was founded on principles such as those of John Locke who defined the existence of a natural order which provided an impetus to subsequent events. While events might challenge that order the premise never ceased to exist. In this sense, Locke had secularized through the laws of nature the absolute order claimed earlier by popes and divine right monarchies.[103]

The early years of the United States found a white population believing itself to be the representative of an order which never ceased, even when challenged successfully for a short duration, while the Iroquois had demonstrated through their own relations with subordinate tribes that they defined sovereignty only as it could be practiced and enforced. Such enforcement rested not on theory but on the real ability of the contending sovereign power to back up claims with physical reality.

Thus the definition of a sovereign order in the postmedieval era has been as elusive for Europeans and their American descendants as a clearly defined feudal order was to their medieval ancestors. Subsequent to the eighteenth century, non-Indian Americans discovered that problems of sovereignty are only relatively more recent, not less elusive, than problems of feudal order. Nearly two hundred years after the end of the Revolution, the issue is still not resolved between state and federal authorities. If sovereignty cannot be agreed to by the non-Indians, does it exist? Again, many Iroquois would say it does not, and that the confusion of the non-Indians over a definition of sovereignty has by default affirmed the sovereignty of the Iroquois peoples.

In response to this, state and federal government officials claim that their continuing attempts to resolve precisely how the state and how the federal government have jurisdiction over Iroquois people is a discussion with a common context: that whatever the nature of the final definition of sovereignty, the Iroquois do not have a claim to it, having lost it in the aftermath of the American Revolution. Such a claim is based on one of Supreme Court Chief Justice John Marshall's statements regarding the Iroquois—an ironic circumstance, since other statements by Marshall can be used to defend Iroquois rights. Nevertheless, in 1831 Marshall had noted that:

> Treaties were made with some tribes by the state of New York, under a then unsettled construction of the [Articles of] confederation, by which they ceded all their lands to that state, taking back a limited grant to themselves, in which they admit their dependence.

Referring then to Indian nations in general, Marshall noted that: "They may, more correctly . . . be denominated domestic dependent nations. They occupy a territory to which we [the United States] assert a title independent of their will."[104]

Yet during the 1970s, Onondagas have successfully left the United States, traveled to Europe and elsewhere, and reentered the United States, traveling back and forth across the United States to the Onondaga reservation with passports issued by the Six Nations and without United States passports. For example, in 1977 a delegation of Six Nations representatives traveled to Geneva, Switzerland, to attend the Conference on Human Rights sponsored by the Non-Governmental Organizations (NGO). They did not use any U.S. passports.[105]

At Onondaga the determination to practice sovereignty has an impressive record, one that is fitting for what is the capital of the confederacy. In 1888, for example, the Whipple Report noted that among the Onondagas the traditional government of chiefs continued, and that the majority of Onondagas practiced a traditional, not a Christian, religion. In fact, the Whipple Report noted that if one of the chiefs of the council became a Christian, he was removed from office.[106] While the state and federal authorities debated sovereignty, the Iroquois persisted, keeping their own society together with a continuum of tradition. Members of other Iroquois nations, especially Oneidas, moved to Onondaga during the nineteenth century so that they could continue to live a traditional rather than a Christian life as non-Indians, and their culture pressed over most of the Iroquois lands in New York. Thus the spirit expressed by an Oneida, Joseph Johnson, on the Onondaga reservation to the Everett Commission in 1920 is

maintained by the Onondaga council and the larger council of the Six
Nations today:

> I live in the same land that my father and forefathers were born in and
> possessed thousands of years ago. . . . I say we Indians in the State of
> New York, as long as we have treaties with the State and the United
> States Government, we are a separate government surrounded by
> the United States. The Indians made their own laws right on this res-
> ervation.[107]

Johnson then brought up an important observation on how he
perceived the pressures of the United States both to keep Onondaga
apart from the influence of foreign nations, most probably Canada. He
also expressed his viewpoint on how the United States kept foreign
powers — probably Canada again — from exerting their influence
among the Iroquois on the Onondaga reservation by making an anal-
ogy to the United States' Monroe Doctrine: Onondaga was in
Johnson's view within the United States' sphere of influence, not
unlike Latin America: "We had treaties and the United States had the
Monroe Doctrine working with this reservation, the same as the countries surrounding the United States had." In this context, according to
Johnson, the Iroquois were still sovereign. He then berated the commission about all the "papers which run back to the seventeen hundreds stacked up in Albany [many, it should be noted, destroyed in a
1911 fire] and Washington which they might have brought and shown
some light on the subject."[108] When a commission member, Assem-
blyman De Hart H. Ames, interjected, "But some of the Indians tell me
these papers are not correct," Johnson was quick to retort: "How do
they expect us to have the correct papers, if you have not?"[109]

When the commissioners discovered that Johnson was an
Oneida, whose people were supposed to be heard the next day, Everett
requested that only Onondagas speak at the moment, to keep the daily
record straight as to which nation's representatives were speaking. To
that suggestion, Chief Chapman Skenandoah, another Oneida, spoke:

> It looks as if you are trying to separate the tribes. It looks like some
> foreign country coming and trying to separate the states of Pennsyl-
> vania and New York and make them ask for themselves. We are a
> league of nations, like you are today with Uncle Sam as boss and
> when the South tried to get away we had a civil war.[110]

After a discussion of local issues with Onondaga representatives, the Everett Commisson adjourned until the following day when

the Oneidas came forward again, this time on the day appointed to them. Chief Chapman Skenandoah raised a point which, like the points raised the previous day, is contemporary; it suggests that the whites' preconception of the Indians differed from the reality the whites encountered:

> I would first like to have your Commission look at this as when the white man first came here; when he first came here what did he imagine in his thoughts? [The white man imagined:] There is a legal status there. When he came no doubt he was surprised to see a human being like himself.[111]

The Oneida Chief Chapman Skenandoah expressed an insight into the whites' preconception by referring to the whites' initial view of Indians as "a legal status." The whites initially did stress a Gesellschaft legalism in their dealings with Indian people, defining what these people meant in the structure of empire so that colonialism could be legally justified and defended. Whites subsequently found it all too easy to believe that what was legal—for example, as defined in treaties written in their own complex terms—was also just or moral. The letter of the law, Gesellschaft, was put ahead of the spirit, Gemeinschaft.

Nineteenth century legal scholar Sir Henry Sumner Maine pointed out the problem caused when two different cultures came into contact and conflict by referring to Julius Caesar's observations of Celtic people in Europe, a perspective which might be applied to non-Indians observing Indian peoples, or vice-versa:

> The mistake, so far as there was error, I conceive to have been an effect of mental distance. It had the imperfections of the view obtained by looking on the Gangetic plains from the slopes of the Himalayas. The impression made is not incorrect, but an immensity of detail is lost to the observer, and a surface varied by countless small elevations looks perfectly flat.[112]

It is probable that Iroquois people were living in a greater degree of Gemeinschaft that were non-Indians in America during the seventeenth and eighteenth centuries. Within the context of Gemeinschaft, the Iroquois were in their own perspective a nation which had sovereignty and a viable political, social, economic, and religious order. To Benjamin Franklin, who was less in Gemeinschaft, the Iroquois were "six Nations of ignorant Savages."[113] During the last two centuries, the Gemeinschaft and Gesellschaft differences between Iroquois and non-Iroquois peoples have narrowed, but the different perceptions do continue.

If sovereignty is defined within a Gemeinschaft context by traditional Iroquois of any era, the needs and desires of all peoples within a given set of boundaries will be perceived to be interdependent and supportive. If at the same time it is apparent to these Iroquois that United States citizens and governments view Indians as "others" who — despite treaties of friendship — can be exploited by the "us," it is understandable why these Iroquois could feel that the Americans were not practicing sovereignty. The Good Tidings of Peace and Power are perceived primarily in Gemeinschaft; the United States Constitution is conceived primarily in Gesellschaft. Thus it is even possible to have two simultaneous sovereignties, one perceived and defined in Gemeinschaft and the other in Gesellschaft. There is a broad human potential for ego, cruelty, greed, perfidy, and violence, whether humans are living within a society which is primarily in Gemeinschaft or within a society stressing Gesellschaft. Thus human failings were compounded by the misperceptions of the Indian and non-Indian societies. Each society could ethnocentrically view the other as irrational and even evil. Because attempts at bridging the cultures were always begun from a single rather than a dualistic premise, even the best attempts were ethnocentric.

The "wampum issue,"[114] as it has become known, is the most striking example of the contrast of societies in Gemeinschaft and Gesellschaft — and also an example of the clash of sovereignties. Twenty-six wampum belts are presently in the possession of the state of New York. Some belts have been exhibited in Albany since 1898, while others arrived during the next three decades. The traditional government of the Six Nations at Onondaga want the belts returned for use in religious and political ceremonies. The leaders of this government maintain that the belts were acquired — or at least continue to be held — in underhanded ways. From the non-Indian point of view, the belts are in the museum legally — in Gesellschaft. From the chiefs' point of view, the belts are not where they should be — in Gemeinschaft. It is a conflict of perspectives, sovereignties, and priorities. It is a clash of objective, scientific preservation advocated by some anthropologists and museum directors, versus subjective, religious utilization.

In Iroquois affairs, and broadly in all Indian affairs, there is not likely to be a single sovereign power recognized, voluntarily or otherwise, by all people involved, at least in the foreseeable future. It seems possible, however, that a pluralistic order based on two compatible though different definitions of sovereignty, one in Gemeinschaft, the other in Gesellschaft, could evolve.[115] Such an order would be dependent upon all peoples accepting their historic differences through an understanding of broad sociological explanations such as Gemeinschaft and Gesellschaft and through a specific understanding of the complex historical events which resulted in unique treaty relationships. A pluralistic order of separate but interlocking responsibilities would result in a political dualism which would not be entirely new. For example, in the relationship of church and state under the Constitution, the United States already permits separate, different, but compatible domestic sovereignties.

If the United States, in the courts, the Congress, and/or the executive, determines to define Indian affairs primarily as a legal question — in Gesellschaft — Indian nations may find their sovereignties legally denied. If the institutions of the United States determine to view Indian affairs primarily as moral obligations — in Gemeinschaft—Indians may find their sovereignties recognized, and may also obtain compensation for past wrongs.

It is possible that the United States and the various Indian nations will recognize each other's different sovereignties: that a traditional Indian sovereignty is primarily in Gemeinschaft, while the United States' sovereignty is primarily in Gesellschaft. On the other hand, sovereignty both internationally and domestically, may be an obsolete concept:[116] it has demonstated an inability to exist without a resort to force (such as economic sanctions or massive armed intervention, increasingly perceived by all concerned as too costly in moral as well as material terms). In international affairs, especially in business and commerce,[117] it is increasingly clear that in an interdependent world a single nation cannot exert absolute sovereignty. Domestically in the United States, there is increasing evidence — in the manifestations of states' rights, sunbelt politics, affirmative action, special interests, and Indian affairs, to list a few—that there exists an interdependence of peoples of all races whose rights are protected by different and often apparently conflicting institutions, laws, treaties, and constitutional guarantees. This complexity and interdependence is neither a sign of weakness nor a sign of strength for anyone concerned, but claims of sovereignty cannot ultimately secure the rights of all concerned. Negotiation and compromise between equals, not between sovereign and subordinate, is required. Claims of preference or precedence should be redefined so that the rights of individuals and individual groups are perceived dualistically, mutually, and simultaneously with the necessity to achieve a composite order without which no individual can survive in peace. The only alternative is for one group to secure and use the institutions of coercion: if order cannot perpetuate itself it must be imposed by force. A redefinition of Indian affairs may provide an initial step toward a pluralistic revision of domestic politics. If Chief Justice John Marshall's nineteenth century definition of Indian nations as "domestic dependent nations" can be transcended, a recognition may evolve that all political units — federal, state, local, and Indian — represent interdependent American peoples. Each of these peoples have specific and separate rights in Gesellschaft, but all share the same continental environment in Gemeinschaft.

▶▶▶▶▶▶▶▶▶ 6 ◀◀◀◀◀◀◀◀◀

REFUGEE HAVENS
The Iroquois Villages of the Eighteenth Century

LAURENCE M. HAUPTMAN

> Brother, you recommended to us the Six Nations, last fall, to consider the distressed situation of the Montauk Indians who, being surrounded by the white people of Long Island, were in a fair way of being dispossessed of all their lands by them, on which they had requested that we would afford them a piece of land in our country to which they might retire, and live peaceably hereafter. We have taken your desire into consideration, and agreed to fix them at Canawaroghere. We are glad the opportunity of serving them in this respect, and shall with pleasure take them under our protection in the same manner as fond parents do their children and hope they may prove deserving of it.
>
> Iroquois Confederacy Chiefs to Sir William Johnson
> July 9, 1774

⬛ N THE LAST THREE AND A HALF DECADES numerous studies have appeared focusing upon refugees and their problems of adjustment to new environments. According to one United Nation's report, 45 million people were displaced from their homelands between 1945 and 1967, including Jewish survivors of the Holocaust, Palestinian Arabs, Cuban, Hungarian, and Tibetan political exiles as well as religious sects fleeing the partition of the Indian Subcontinent.[1] In the 1970s the worldwide problem of refugees has steadily increased with large scale out-migrations of East Indians from Africa, of Ibo tribesmen from Nigeria during the Biafran War and, most recently and tragically, by the "boat people" from Indochina.

Social scientists have begun to understand the impact of refugee status on personality, individuals, families, groups, tribes, and institutions.[2] In a recent article in the *American Journal of Psychiatry*, Richard Harding and John Looney summarized the findings of these studies.

Since World War II refugees have been studied by numerous authors who have noted their increased incidence of mental disorders. Psychological problems for refugees increase when the period between immigration and definitive resettlement is protracted or when the group cohesiveness is interrupted. The first several years after migration are particularly stressful, with problems being accentuated when refugees are culturally and racially dissimilar to the indigenous population. Successful adaptation in the host country has, in some cases, been unconsciously sabotaged by failure to learn the new language. Refugees isolated because of a language barrier developed increased insecurity and anxiety comparable to the feelings of isolation and mistrust experienced by individuals with increasing deafness. Such feelings of isolation may be at least a partial cause of the paranoid reactions so frequently noted in the literature on refugees. Other reasons suggested for the increased incidence of mental illness among refugees are 1) decreased social status, 2) loss of individuality incurred by becoming part of a mass refugee group, and 3) the actual stress of the experience of flight.[3]

Historians have generally not treated American Indians as refugee populations, except in some notable studies specifically dealing with Indian Territory.[4] Yet from earliest colonial times many tribes were dispersed from ancestral homelands in the manner of present-day refugees. It may even be suggested that at least some of the American Indians who migrated to urban centers under a government policy of relocation in the post–World War II period experienced many of the same problems of adaptation as did refugees from abroad.[5]

The colonial records are filled with instances of American Indians seeking refuge with kindred or more powerful nations. The most frequently documented instances are the refugee havens under Iroquois Confederacy aegis along the Upper Susquehanna River Valley and the environs south and west of the Mohawk Valley. In the eighteenth century alone the Catskill, Conoy, Esopus, Housatonic, Mahican, Miami, Mohegan, Montauk, Nanticoke, Narrangansett, Sapony, Shawnee, Susquehannock, Tuscarora, and Wappinger fled to Indian towns in this region. From approximately 1714 to 1785, consolidated remnant populations often referred to in the historical literature as Brothertown, Long Island, New England, River, and Stockbridge Indians found their way to the roots of the "Great Tree of Peace," the metaphor for Iroquois Confederacy protection and suzerainty. These settlements of displaced Indians of the Eastern Woodlands included Oquaga (Onaquaga and numerous other spellings), Otsiningo (Chenango), the two most important towns, as well as Brothertown, Chemung, Chugnuts, New Stockbridge, Owego, Tioga, and Unadilla.[6] This process of resettlement was not without trauma and social disintegration as reflected in the increased use of alcohol, violent behavior, and even perhaps apathy leading to starvation.

European colonial expansion and resulting Indian land dispossession and wars were the major reasons for the establishment of the refugee communities along the Upper Susquehanna and in other parts of Iroquoia. Moreover, epidemics weakened and depopulated large numbers of coastal Algonkian and Iroquois Indians from New England to North Carolina leading to tribal consolidation and outmigration.[7] This process of dispersal was further accentuated by the depletion of fur sources causing Mahicans and other Hudson River tribes to journey far west as early as the 1660s.[8]

The appearance of these scattered populations in Iroquoia was not a haphazard occurrence nor a sudden development of the eighteenth century. These unfortunate victims of colonial expansion were initially used to create a defense perimeter against French aggression from the north or west, a planned arrangement that served the needs of English colonial as well as Iroquois authorities. As early as the 1670s, the dispersed Indian survivors of the bloody King Philip's War resettled twenty miles northeast of Albany along the Hoosic River near present day Schaghticoke at the invitation of Governor Andros. Perhaps one thousand Indian refugees made their way to Schaghticoke, an Indian refugee haven largely under Iroquois influence until its abandonment during the French and Indian War. This pattern of resettlement based upon the defense needs of both the Iroquois and the English was subsequently employed along the Upper Susquehanna.[9]

From the beginnings of the eighteenth century, homeless Indian populations began settling at Oquaga, formerly Susquehannock Indian hunting territory, and at other Iroquois-dominated areas of the Upper Susquehanna. By 1714 Tuscaroras, victims of colonial expansion in the Carolinas, had taken shelter among their Iroquois brethren in the north. Perhaps as many as 500 Tuscarora families resettled in this area over a ninety-year period.[10] Within a decade remnants of Hudson Valley tribes also made their way to the area around present day Binghamton, New York.[11] Soon these earlier migrants were joined by the Shawnee, Nanticoke, Conoy, Miami, and Tutelo, all fleeing from white persecution in the South.[12] One prominent Iroquois Confederacy leader, in addressing the colonial governor of Pennsylvania, explained the reasons for the resettlement: "The People of Maryland do not treat the Indians [Conoys and Nanticokes] as you and others do, for they make slaves of them and sell their children for money."[13]

The era of the French and Indian War gave impetus to this resettlement process. In September 1753, even before the formal outbreak of hostilities, more Nanticokes from Maryland had been relocated to the Upper Susquehanna by English colonial authorities.[14] Ten years later Johnson counted 200 warriors of the Nanticoke, Conoy, Saponey, and Tutelo nations in this area. By February 1756, Mahicans, Shawnees, and Tuscaroras were in the majority at Oquaga.[15]

Despite the diverse representation of Indian nations, this concentration of population was a systematic and planned effort on the part of English and Iroquois officials. As early as 1755, Johnson had suggested that Hudson River tribesmen move from the "back settlement where they might be taken for enemies and destroyed" to the protection of the towns. In the same year English colonists murdered nine apparently friendly Indians at Walden, New York, including three women and two children.[16] Paranoic fears and suspicions about Indians living in close proximity to colonial settlements prompted Johnson's removal and resettlement policy. Johnson was to pinpoint the reasons further, indicating that Mahicans, who had been dispersed throughout the colonies of New York and New Jersey, had "from some misunderstandings" begun "to be troublesome and dangerous."[17]

On March 10, 1756, an incident occurred at Kingston, New York, which contributed directly to Johnson's removal of the River Indians and other tribes. A party of English entered a wigwam in search of the murderers of some of their neighbors. Fearing for their lives, the Indians resisted their efforts, killing several of the Englishmen and making their escape. Subsequently, Colonel Johannes Hardenbergh and several others wrote to Johnson asking him what to do with the "40 or 50 of the same Nation [Esopus] of Indians" that remained in that city. Johnson then approached the Mohawks about his dilemma. Three days later the Mohawks accepted responsibility for these unfortunate victims of war and agreed to go to Esopus country to persuade the River Indians to relocate at the Mohawk's "lower castle" in the Schoharie. Johnson thanked the Mohawks, promised to supply them with provisions and an interpreter en route, and assuaged any fears by affirming that he would support and clothe the River Indians until they could provide for themselves.[18] Upon the arrival at Fort Johnson in April, May, and July 1756, Johnson assured the River tribesmen that their Mohawk "Uncles" would protect them as long as the Indians behaved themselves, were sober and industrious, and were faithful to the king of England by fighting the French.[19] Behind Johnson's intentions appeared to be the strengthening of his Mohawk allies. His correspondence clearly indicates his motives to build his British-allied Indian forces in the already intensifying French and Indian War.[20]

Johnson carefully carried out this and subsequent removals, especially to the Susquehanna. In a letter to the magistrates at Fishkill, he insisted upon smooth, orderly, and law-abiding removals. A total of 196 River tribesmen reached Fort Johnson by July 1756. Johnson outfitted them with clothes, paint, and ammunition and assigned them to lands at Otsiningo.[21]

The settlement of the Upper Susquehanna continued even beyond the end of the French and Indian War. On May 5, 1764, Tuscaroras came before Johnson on behalf of their friends the Esopus asking him to assist in bringing more Esopus to Otsiningo. Four years later, another sizeable migration of Catskill and Esopus Indians was well under way.[22]

Johnson was not the only individual urging a resettlement policy. Missionaries urged their Indian parishioners to seek refuge in Iroquoia. New England and Long Island Indians were encouraged in this endeavor by Reverends Samuel Kirkland, Gideon Hawley, and Eleazar Wheelock and by Indian missionaries David Fowler, Joseph Johnson and Samson Occom. From the late 1760s onward, the Iroquois, at the urging of colonial authorities and missionaries, began to grant these "praying Indians" permission to settle in their territory. These Brothertown Indians from the towns of Charlestown, Groton, Stonington, Niantic, Farmington, Mohegan, and Montauk included remnant populations of Narrangansetts, Pequots, Mohegans, and Montauks. Led by Occam, Johnson, and Fowler, these Indians secured a promise of a ten-mile tract, later expanded, from the Oneidas in October 1773. One year later the Oneidas formally deeded this land to these Indians since the Brothertown has been "reduced (in New England and Long Island) to such small pittances of land that they could no longer remain there." These Indians, except for those intermarried with blacks, were granted communal lands and full liberty of hunting with the exception of the beaver trade.[23]

Ironically, these refugees arrived in Iroquoia in 1775, a most inopportune time to seek a better life. The retaliatory campaign against Iroquois settlements made by American Generals John Sullivan and James Clinton in 1779 laid waste and burned Chugnut, Chemung, Oquaga, Tioga, and Unadilla to the ground, while the Indians at the other towns of the Upper Susquehanna were virtually faced with slow starvation during the prolonged fighting of the American Revolution.[24] Nevertheless, once hostilities ended, the migrations of weakened Eastern tribes to the Upper Susquehanna resumed.[25] As early as March

1784, Kirkland made reference to large-scale Oneida preparations for the expected sizeable migrations of Stockbridge, Mohegan, and Narrangansett.[26] By 1788, as a result of the collapse of the notable mission experiment at Stockbridge, Massachusetts, 420 of these "praying Indians" had migrated to this region.[27]

Being caught in the middle of the American Revolution was only one of the many problems faced by Indian refugees along the Upper Susquehanna. The Tuscarora, a conquered people from the Virginia-North Carolina Tidewater, found themselves in the second decade of the eighteenth century dependent upon the generosity of their Iroquois brethren. As a consequence of a devastating war (1711–1713), resulting cultural trauma, land loss, and depopulation, these Indians were forced to accept a subordinate position in the Iroquois League structure that has, according to David Landy, affected not only their political role but also their psychological outlook right up to the present day. As disorganized homeless exiles knocking at the door of the great alliance, they became a "relatively powerless, denigrated member of the Iroquois League." Landy has described them as a "mendicant cousin who shuffles with self-consciousness and embarrassment into the peripheral shadows of the Council fires."[28] Although escaping complete annihilation in the south by migrating, the Tuscarora among the Iroquois were never to achieve their former independent status and powerful national standing as had existed in the Tidewater.[29]

Refugee status not only had a long-lasting impact on personality and intergroup relations but also produced dysfunctional states leading to violent behavior. As early as 1737, trader Conrad Weiser in his journal described Otsiningo as "this miserable place, where more murders occur than in any other nation."[30] Disorderliness caused by alcohol appears to be the major factor in the rise of aggressive behavior. Weiser was told by the Indians at Otsiningo that "rum will kill us and leave the land clear for the Europeans without strife and purchase."[31] In June 1753, the Reverend Gideon Hawley, on his way to Oquaga, described the results of the activities of one George Winedecker, a nefarious rum trader, sailing from Otsego Lake to the Indian towns of the Upper Susquehanna.

> This night we went to sleep with some apprehensions. We were awoke by the howling of the Indians over their dead. The whole village was agitated. We arose very early in the morning. We soon saw

the Indian women and their children skulking in the adjacent bushes, for fear of intoxicated Indians, who were drinking deeper. The women were secreting guns, hatchets, and every deadly or danger- ous weapon, that murder or harm might not be the consequence.[32]

By the time Hawley had reached Oquaga and slept overnight, Winedecker's cargo had made "many of the worse for the rum that came with us." The New England missionary soon found himself threatened by some of the inebriated Indians there.[33]

Despite the richness of the region as a major agricultural cen- ter, the Indians of the Upper Susquehanna were frequently faced with starvation. During the French and Indian War and the American Revo- lution, the lack of adequate food supplies reached crisis proportion. Sir William Johnson was beseiged by requests for corn during the period of heaviest fighting against the French.[34] In 1756 Oneidas, Mohawks, and Tuscaroras appealed to "Brother Warraghiyagey" (Johnson, doer of great things) for the recently arrived River Indians who were "naked and destitute of everything."[35]

Yet starvation is also indicated along the Upper Susquehanna during years of relative peace. Weiser's journal in 1737 reveals that a majority of the Indians at Otsiningo were surviving "for more than a month on the juice of the sugar-tree."[36] Weiser's party of traders reluctantly gave some of their provisions to the Indians while the rest was stolen while they were sleeping. One shaman blamed the food crisis on alcohol and by overtrapping by employees in the fur trade.[37] Even after the end of the French and Indian War, the lack of food in the region is also evident in Johnson's correspondence and Kirkland's journals.[38] Almost four years after the Battle of Johnstown, the last battle of the American Revolution in New York, Kirkland described the food shortages.

> I want exceedingly now and then to take a dish of tea with you — or have something more nourishing than potatoes and squash soup — I was obliged on my arrival to pass eight and forty hours on two small meals — but I can now take a tolerable dinner (that is whenever I eat one) upon a dish of boiled potatoes and milk — or an ear of corn — Meat, is very scarce among us at this season, I have not eaten any but twice since in these parts — but thro' divine mercy I enjoy health.[39]

Starvation during relatively pacific periods can be explained in several ways. First, there could have occurred a series of severe climatic changes and/or severe famines that reduced food supply. Secondly, epidemics, which were frequent but sporadic, could have caused the inability to cultivate Indian fields. Thirdly, although unlikely, the population could have swelled to the point that food supplies were inadequate. Fourthly, the Indians of these communities could have largely abandoned agriculture for employment in the European fur trade. When the game ran out, their position as employees ended and poverty and starvation ensued. Fifthly, the change of life styles from semisedentary existence to fixed Indian communities may have led to disaster. When the lands around the towns gave out, possibly because of overutilization and poor conservation techniques, a food problem developed.

All these explanations, except for the climatic change and epidemic theories, do not take into account the sporadic, impermanent, nature of the famines. As late as the American Revolution, this region was the breadbasket of Iroquoia, a fact that prompted Generals Clinton and Sullivan to torch the area. It may be suggested that a sixth reason was the dysfunctional setting of the Indian communities of the Upper Susquehanna. As a consequence of being uprooted from their homelands, these displaced human beings at times exhibited apathetic behavior leading to a sense of hopelessness, and with it an ignoring of their cultivation. Giving up on life, they soon were faced with starvation. This sense of near-suicidal behavior has been recently interpreted to exist at Jamestown Colony during the "starving time" during the winter of 1609. Karen Ordahl Kupperman concluded that the "colonists unwillingness to help themselves, their surrender to melancholy, resulted from the complex interaction of environmental and psychological factors."[40]

Although the historical parallel is cross-cultural, the Indians along the Upper Susquehanna were faced with problems ranging from being forcibly uprooted from their ancestral lands to being caught in the crossfires of wars — the French and Indian and American Revolutionary wars — conflicts not of their choosing. The horrible circumstances that these refugee populations faced are indeed parallel in degree to any suffering at Jamestown Colony![41]

In the medical literature on stress, American Indians taken from tribal ancestral lands and put onto reservations within close proximity of their homelands have been shown to suffer long-lasting

Bridging Two Cultures

East. BOTH SIDES OF THE RIVER (Ee-Tow-O-Kaum), Stockbridge (Mohe-gan), painted by George Catlin in 1831 or 1836, probably at Green Bay, Wisconsin, after many of the Stockbridges, Oneida Iroquois, Brothertowns, and Munsees had been removed there from New York. Catlin called this chief of the Stockbridges "a very shrewd and intelligent man, and a professed, and I think sincere Christian." Typical of the Christian Indian leaders who out-maneuvered the Menominees in their land dealings at Green Bay, "Both Sides of the River" is also representative of those Indians who took refuge among the Iroquois during the eighteenth century and then discovered during the re-moval era of the nineteenth century that it was difficult to try to function on both sides of white Christian-Indian context of Native American history. *The National Collection of Fine Arts, Smithsonian Institution; Gift of Mrs. Sarah Harrison*

WOHAW

West. By Wohaw, Kiowa, January 1877. The Indian refugee trauma moved west with United States expansion. Beginning in 1875, Wohaw (born 1855) was held at Fort Marion, Florida, as a prisoner of war after giving up hope of resisting white expansion on the Plains. In prison, Wohaw was persuaded (re-educated) to pledge that he would forsake his traditional Kiowa ways and take up the ways of the whites. He recorded his pledge to do so in this work. He turns from the buffalo, the tepee, and the uncultivated Plains toward the cow, the cultivated field, and a frame house or schoolhouse. (Wohaw means "beef" or "beef animal.") The sacred breath of both buffalo and beef, of both cultures, are blown toward him, and he offers both the symbol of respect, the sacred pipe. Thus he acknowledges his pride in his past but looks toward a new pride. Mother earth, the sun, the moon, and a meteor or comet witness his pledge. Returning to his people in Oklahoma in 1878, Wohaw went to school, served as an Indian policeman, and enlisted in an all-Indian unit of the United States Cavalry (Troop L, Seventh Regiment). In 1895 he gave up trying to adopt white ways but was never able to rekindle entirely his past culture. His people's lands were allotted. Wohaw died in 1924. *Missouri Historical Society, St. Louis, Missouri* and permanent disabilities. In one study social disorganization was precipitated by the changes leading to an increase in mortality from tuberculosis.[42] Employing this framework, refugee Indian populations in Iroquois-dominated villages along the Upper Susquehanna faced the trauma caused by displacement from their original lands by also manifesting patterns of societal disintegration as reflected in heavy use of alcohol, violent behavior, and perhaps even apathy leading to starvation.

Nonetheless, the trauma of refugee status and the poor conditions of life in refugee camps may obscure other aspects of being uprooted. For example, the stresses of becoming a refugee may be substantially less than the anxiety caused by remaining in a homeland (e.g., Lebanon, Northern Ireland). All of the relocated tribes along the Upper Susquehanna faced insurmountable pressures that made their migrations to Iroquoia an acceptable alternative, and, in some instances, one that was beneficial to them. In February 1764, the Esopus Indians at Otsiningo indicated to Johnson that they were "happily seated" and even offered the remaining fifty-six-square-mile tract of their former lands to the Mohawk Baronet.[43] Moreover, in August 1770, the Nanticokes requested "a passport and letters to the Governor of North Carolina" to return to their homeland in order to bring the remainder of their people north and to "dispose of some land they yet have there."[44] The constant addition of new tribes to the "Great Tree" in the eighteenth century through peaceful overtures further suggests that Iroquoia was a viable, and perhaps a less stressful, alternative to remnant tribes of the Eastern Woodlands.[45] Furthermore, several of these peoples such as the Stockbridge and Munsee Delaware (e.g., Esopus) retained their Iroquois surroundings to the point that they continue to be recognized as tribes on their own Wisconsin[46] reservation today. In addition, some elements of the culture, language, and separate identity of the Brothertown, Nanticoke, and Tutelo remain and are identifiable today among the Iroquois, at least at the Six Nations Reserve in Ontario and at the Oneida Reservation in Wisconsin. Thus as the medical literature on stress suggests,[47] stress, as manifested in a refugee experience, may not altogether be destructive but may lead to adaptation and in some instances strength (e.g., the survival and adaptation of Jews as refugees for nearly two thousand years).

By focusing on the Indian towns of the Upper Susquehanna, one can clearly see some of the similarities that all forcibly displaced peoples face. Native Americans in the sweeping history of Indian-white relations must be seen as refugees, frequently dispersed and consolidated, often at the whims of policy-makers. Only in a refugee context can the Indian side of the New World drama of colonization and expansion be fully understood.

▶▶▶▶▶▶▶▶▶▶   7   ◀◀◀◀◀◀◀◀◀◀

VICTIM VERSUS VICTIM
The Irony of the New York Indians' Removal to Wisconsin

ROBERT W. VENABLES

AFTER THE WAR OF 1812, the United States federal government and the governments of the various states coordinated a policy of removing Indian peoples from their homelands in the northern and southern states and territories and placing them west of the frontier. East of the Mississippi River, with the exception of Maine, New York, Michigan, and Wisconsin, the Indian population was reduced by 92 percent between 1830 and 1860. The major political vehicle for Indian removal was the Removal Act passed by Congress and approved by President Andrew Jackson in 1830. Even assuming imprecise census figures and the decline of Indian populations through disease, a comparison of certain state Indian populations in 1830 and 1860 indicates the impact of removal in both the North and the South. With some notable exceptions—one of which is the subject of this chapter—New York's attempts to remove Indians was largely a failure: in 1830, New York had 4,820 Indians; in 1860, 3,925. Other states, however, were far more thorough in their imposition of removal upon Indian people. Georgia's population in 1830 included 5,000 Indians; in 1860, only 415. Alabama counted 19,200 Indians in 1830; in 1860, only 160. Mississippi in 1830 had 23,400 Indians in 1830; in 1860, 902. Ohio in 1830 had 1,877 Indians; in 1860, 30. Indiana reported 4,050 Indians in 1830; in 1860 only 674. Illinois included 5,900 Indians in 1830; in 1860, 32. Most had been removed to what is now Oklahoma, Kansas, and Wisconsin.[1]

During much of the removal era, Wisconsin was still regarded as wilderness, the west bank of Lake Michigan being perceived by Americans as a frontier like the west bank of the Mississippi. It was to

Wisconsin that hundreds of Oneida Iroquois, together with their Algonquin neighbors the Stockbridge, Munsee, and Brothertown Indians, were removed between 1821 and 1848. Joining them were a few
St. Regis Mohawks and individuals from other Iroquois nations. During the same period, some of the Oneidas chose to remove to Canada
while a few remained in New York.

The movement of the Oneidas, Stockbridges, Munsees, and
Brothertowns from New York to Wisconsin is part of Indian migration
history. As refugees of oppression, however, these Indian nations
provide insights into a regrettable theme in human history, the constant presence somewhere on the globe of streams of refugee populations. The British removal of 6,000 French Acadians from Nova Scotia
in 1755[2] demonstrates that the colonial precedents for removal could
be political as well as ethnic or racial, and the Acadian experience was
certainly as traumatic for the French refugees as removal was for
Indians. The arrival in America of tens of thousands of Indochinese
and Caribbean "boat people" is a reminder that refugee history continues as a main current in human events.

Refugee history often presents the wrenching apposition not
just of oppressor versus victim, but of victim versus victim. The refugee Jews seeking a post–World War II sanctuary in Israel, for example, caused another refugee problem when they displaced indigenous
Palestinians. Such a situation may be to the advantage of greater
political powers (in the case of the Middle East, for example, Western nations, the nations of Islam, and the Soviets too often find the
Israeli-Palestinian tension to their advantage). That the apposition of
victim versus victim is hardly new in the history of American international affairs is demonstrated by the Oneidas, Stockbridges, Munsees,
and Brothertowns in their quest for sanctuary in Wisconsin among the
Menominees.

The Stockbridges, Munsees, and Brothertowns were already
refugees from white expansion when in 1774 they began moving from
their New England and New York homes to lands granted to them by
the Oneidas in an area southwest of the Mohawk Valley, New York.
The outbreak of the American Revolution delayed the completion of
this move until the years following the war. The Stockbridges, Munsees, and Brothertowns spoke Algonquian languages. Their hosts, the
Oneidas, spoke an Iroquoian language and made up one of the Six
Nations of the Iroquois Confederacy. The relationship between these
three Algonquin groups and the Oneidas was never stabilized because
of the turmoil of the Revolutionary, post-Revolutionary, and removal
crises. However, the relationship can perhaps best be described briefly
as one of subject-ally to patron-protector.[3]

On their lands in New York, the Oneidas, Stockbridges, Munsees, and Brothertowns were beset by the settlement pressures of unfriendly whites: "we are pushed out of our own country," they told the Menominees of Wisconsin in 1822.[4] Furthermore, these New York Indians were stricken by poverty. They had yet to recover fully from the devastation wrought during the American Revolution, when the Iroquois Confederacy and its allied nations were rent by civil war. In that war most of the Iroquois Oneidas together with their Algonquin subject-allies the Stockbridges, Munsees, and Brothertowns had favored or actually aided the Patriot cause, while the rest of the Iroquois — Mohawks, Onondagas, Cayugas, and Senecas, with their Algonquin subject-allies, had aided the British or had attempted, unsuccessfully, to maintain neutrality. The Iroquois civil war during the American Revolution had left most Iroquois towns ruined.[5] Attack and counterattack by both white and Indian armies had especially weakened the traditional economic and political power of the Iroquois women, whose once-extensive political influence had been based in part on their control of the very domestic agricultural economy destroyed during the war.

The leaders of the New York Indians who were willing to remove to Wisconsin were partially assimilated, with white education and values, as were many of their followers. However, the economic depression among many of the Indians was regularly reported by white observers. "An Act relating to the purchase of lands from the Stockbridge Indians," passed by the New York State legislature in 1825, refers to "such of the poor and indigent Indians as belong to the Stockbridge tribe," while an 1827 New York State act refers to "such of the poor" among the Brothertown Indians.[6] In 1828 the Oneidas, Stockbridges, and Brothertowns — as well as other eastern Indians such as the Senecas — were specifically listed by the Reverend Isaac McCoy as "positively perishing, and perishing rapidly." McCoy noted that a few individuals "have acquired some knowledge of letters and of labor. ... But let none imagine, that these tribes ... are, as tribes, improving their conditions generally." McCoy felt that there was "not one of those bands on small reservations in New York ... of whom we can indulge any better hope than that of their total extermination"—an extermination caused by poverty and disease, not by the direct actions of the United States settlers or military units.[7] According to Oneida oral tradition, some of their people were so desperately hungry during the 1820s that they were reduced to scraping up flour which had been spilled on the loading docks along the Erie Canal.[8] Yet as soon as the New York Indians arrived in Wisconsin, the resident Menominees perceived them as exploitive interlopers. It is that irony which is explored in this chapter.

One reason the United States government gave in removing the Oneidas and their Indian neighbors to Wisconsin was to bring white-styled civilization and Christianity to the Menominees. This objective was acknowledged by the eastern Indians as well as by the intended recipients, the Menominees.[9] The Oneidas, Stockbridges, Munsees, and Brothertowns had been missionized for more than a century before removal, and during the era of the American Revolution were living on the frontier of New York in settlements of log cabins similar to the frontier settlements of their white neighbors. Historians Grant Foreman and Angie Debo have noted how after 1815 assimilative eastern Indians such as the Cherokees provided a vanguard of white-styled civilization in Oklahoma, and to a lesser extent, in Kansas. Foreman and Debo also detailed how the eastern Indians removed to Oklahoma and Kansas clashed with the indigenous Plains Indians.[10] Because such an apposition of refugee and indigenous Indians had its most widespread and notorious impact in Oklahoma, this clash of Indian versus Indian — victim versus victim — might be termed the Oklahoma Syndrome. The Oklahoma Syndrome occurred when the Oneidas, Stockbridges, Munsees, and Brothertowns confronted the Wisconsin Menominees, although unlike the situation in Oklahoma and Kansas, the apposition in Wisconsin never reached the point of armed conflict.

How well the Oneidas, Stockbridges, Munsees, and Brothertowns represented the vanguard of white civilization is in part demonstrated by the Menominees' contention that the eastern invasion was exploitive. Ironically, the Oklahoma Syndrome in general, and the confrontation between the New York Indian refugees and the Wisconsin Menominees in particular, include some of the major themes found in the broader clash between non-Indians and Indians, with the removed Indians fulfilling the attributes usually ascribed to whites. On the Wisconsin frontier the Menominees played out the traditional role of the exploited Indians, while the New York Indians acted the part usually reserved for the whites. In Wisconsin the Oklahoma Syndrome evolved into the tragedy of Indian versus Indian, rather than white versus Indian, in all of the following:

1. Treaties were often made with Indians who were not chiefs and were therefore not authorized by their tribes to represent them.

2. During negotiations, translation of treaty details into the language of the other tribe was often inadequate.

3. If the white government reacted to an illegal treaty, it usually worked for a compromise treaty rather than nullifying the illegal treaty or punishing the negotiators.

4. A justification for taking land from Indians by treaty was that the result would bring them the benefits of white civilization.

5. Land speculators often made immediate profits after treaties were signed.

6. Non-Indians often played major roles of influence among the Indians during treaty negotiations.

7. After a treaty, Indians often complained that settlers were not satisfied to remain on land ceded to them, and that the settlers intruded onto unceded lands, especially to hunt.

8. Following an illegal treaty, the white government often threatened to use military force to insure the treaty terms.

9. The argument was frequently put forward that the Indians did not need all the land they possessed.

10. Non-Indian laws, such as various trade and intercourse acts, did not insure a protection of the Indians during or after treaty negotiations.

11. White policies were forced on Indians who had been the whites' allies, just as they were forced on Indians who had been the whites' opponents.

In Wisconsin the apposition of Indian versus Indian, of victim versus victim, began in 1821. On August 18, 1821, at Green Bay, representatives of the eastern Indians, under the mixed-blood Mohawk missionary Eleazar Williams, purchased from some Menominees and some Winnebagoes 860,000 acres of land for $2,000 in goods. The sale was supervised and approved by a federal representative, as required under the Trade and Intercourse Act of 1802, and was approved by President James Madison on February 9, 1822. The New York Indians soon decided that the lands were too far from Green Bay, however, and on September 23, 1822, a second treaty was held with the Menominees, again under the supervision of a federal representative. This purchase extended the eastern Indians' Wisconsin land holdings in a grand fashion: 6.72 million acres for $3,000 in goods, to be distributed in three annual installments. One reason the acreage was so vast—140 miles long and 75 miles wide—was because politicians and land speculators back in New York were encouraging the entire Iroquois Confederacy to move to Wisconsin. While the Six Nations regarded such a move with suspicion, many Iroquois were considering the possibility that Wisconsin's wilderness might be preferable to being crowded and surrounded by white settlers in New York. An unusual provision was that the Menominees were to be allowed to occupy these lands in common with the eastern refugee Indians. In 1824 the first of the eastern Indians began to settle on these lands—and the Menominees launched their first protest because the easterners were claiming the treaties gave them ownership of the lands.

Joined by French inhabitants who were their friends, the

Menominees contended that none of their chiefs had been present at the 1821 treaty negotiations. They said that the interpreter had told them the treaty only gave the eastern Indians permission to hunt on Menominee lands and to settle in a small area. Furthermore, the Menominees complained that at the 1822 treaty the interpreter did not speak Menominee, but only "the Chippewa, which they understood imperfectly."[12] The Menominees summed up their grievances to a federal official: "They say that the deputies from these tribes only asked permission 'to come and sit down with them, (the Menominees;) [sic] that they would teach them how to cultivate the soil, and live together like brothers.'"[13] In 1827 the Menominee chief Great Wave scornfully reported the results of the New York Indians' promise: "They ploughed three little fields and a half!"[14] Menominee protests would continue until 1832, maintaining that since the lands were to be held in common, it was unjust for the New York Indians to claim exclusive ownership. Yet the New York Indians claimed exactly that, and they referred to the wording of the treaties to support their contention.

A government report in 1831 concluded that the Menominees "have apparently been entirely overreached; uneducated, poor and ignorant in business transactions, they were no match for their shrewd brethren from New York."[15] Part of this shrewdness was no doubt due to the Indians' missionary education. But the New York Indians had also learned first hand when they themselves had lost vast amounts of land in treaties with the whites. In 1832 the Menominee chief Grizzly Bear told territorial governor George B. Porter, through a translator:

> These New York Indians are hard to be satisfied. They are made like you are. They have education, and pride themselves upon it. But, father, they have no ears; they are like dogs; when we give them a piece, they want more. They have no hearts or souls, and I told you before they behave so badly that we hate them.[16]

One reasons that the Menominees hated the eastern refugees was that they hunted deer on Menominee land beyond the boundaries established by the treaty. But what angered the Menominees most was that some of the eastern Indians were involved in what the Menominees maintained was illegal land speculation — selling land which the Menominees believed the easterners had no right to sell. On January 8, 1825, the Brothertown Indians sold some of the lands they claimed they had acquired from the Menominees to the Oneidas, other Iroquois, Stockbridges, and Munsees. The Menominees protested that the Brothertowns were selling land "at a speculation to other tribes."[17]

During the rancorous eight-year debate over the validity and terms of the 1821 and 1822 treaties, it was clear to United States officials that both the eastern Indians and the Menominees were influenced by interested white parties. The Menominees' support came from French inhabitants who had a stake in continuing their rights to live among the Menominees. Many of the French had intermarried with the Menominees and still others were descendants of previous generations of French intermarriage. The New York Indians had their missionaries, but they also had, working back East, a powerful land speculator eager to see them out of New York. This speculator was Thomas Ogden, who kept the eastern Indians' mixed-blood missionary, Eleazar Williams, on his payroll throughout the altercation. The Indians who favored removal were in their exploitive negotiations with the Menominees playing a role usually acted out by the whites; but because removal to Wisconsin would benefit Thomas Ogden's Ogden Land Company, the proremoval Indians were acting *for* white interests.[18]

The official United States government response to the Menominees' initial 1824 protest was an order to the commanding officer of the army post at Green Bay by the commissioner of Indian affairs, Thomas L. McKenney. With the authorization of the secretary of war, McKenney instructed the commander to use his military power to enforce the eastern Indians' land rights among the Menominees, and to insure that neither the French inhabitants nor the Menominees committed hostile acts toward the New York Indians in the occupation of lands "made with the sanction of Government."[19]

In 1827 Commissioner McKenney and territorial governor Lewis Cass met with the disputing Indians at Butte des Morts, Wisconsin. McKenney was impressed by the Christian hymn-singing of the Oneidas, Stockbridges, Munsees, and Brothertowns. He wrote that

> They sang in three parts, base [sic], tenor, and treble, and with a time so true, and with voices so sweet, as to add harmony even to nature itself. . . . and as I listened to their songs of praise, and their prayers, I felt humbled, and ashamed of my country, in view of the wrongs it had inflicted, *and yet continues to inflict*, upon these desolate and destitute children of the forest. There were flowers and gems there which needed only to be cultivated and polished. . . . And yet they were, and are, neglected, trodden down, and treated as outcasts![20]

After what McKenney thought was a successful council, he observed how the New York Indians sang one evening:

their hymns being made more strikingly sweet by the yelling and whooping of the wild Indians by whom they were surrounded. What a contrast! The woods made vocal on the one hand by Christian music, and startled on the other by the wild yells of the uncivilized! And yet both proceeding from the same race.[21]

With such empathy toward the eastern Indians and such a racist attitude in general, it is not surprising that McKenney believed that the land issued would soon be solved—despite the fact that the Menominees continued to maintain that they had never sold any of their land to the New York Indians.[22]

Negotiations dragged on even after another special council in Green Bay in August 1830. In 1831 a desire to resolve the issue prompted Colonel Samuel C. Stambaugh, a federal Indian agent at Green Bay, to shift federal favor away from the New York Indians and toward the Menominees. His letter of August 4, 1831, to Lewis Cass, once territorial governor but now the secretary of war whose department was responsible for Indian affairs, details an argument in favor of the Menominees. It appears as though it was written today as part of a legal brief for one of the many Indian land cases before the modern federal courts, because like many of the modern cases it is based on a violation of the latest Trade and Intercourse Acts which the Congress had passed (in 1790, 1793, and 1802) to protect Indians from fraudulent land deals. However, in this circumstance the Oneidas and other eastern Indians are playing the role of the white lawbreakers.

> The New York Indians have undertaken to argue the *legality* of their purchases of 1821 and '22. Now, what is the law which can be made to operate on this case? The act of 1802, March 30th, entitled "An act to regulate Trade and Intercourse with Indian Tribes, &c," contains all the law to be found on the subject of Indian treaties. The 12th section enacts as follows: "That no purchase, grant, lease, or other conveyance of lands, or of any title or claim thereto, from any Indian or nation, or tribe of Indians within the bounds of the United States, shall be of any validity, in law or equity, unless the same be made by treaty or convention, entered into pursuant to the *Constitution*. . . .

> Now, as neither Mr. [Charles C.] Trowbridge nor Mr. [John] Sergeant [Jr. — Trowbridge and Sergeant were whites present at the negotiations], were appointed commissioners to negotiate for the purchase of Indian lands [on this point, Stambaugh erred, for the men were present in official capacities]; and as neither of the treaties made,

in their presence, were sent to the Senate for approval, they can have "no validity in law or equity," and their provisions are neither binding upon the United States, nor upon either of the tribes who may have become parties to them.

The New York Indians, however, contend that, inasmuch as the Government permitted their negotiations with the Menominees, and approved of their subsequent removal upon the lands thus acquired, that therefore it is bound to sustain their claim at every hazard, and at any expense. These arguments, besides being entirely fallacious, are ... extremely illiberal. ... The ready acquiescence of the Government ... only go[es] to show the kind feeling of the Government towards them; its great desire to indulge all their wishes.[23]

Stambaugh also believed it was ludicrous to turn over six million acres of land to the eastern Indians, that they didn't need that much. Moreover, he wrote, the land "contains all the valuable water power on the Fox river."[24] These two arguments would not have been made if the easterners involved in the treaties had been white.

Some of the Menominee resentment was linked to the fact that they were being simultaneously defrauded by their immediate, indigenous neighbors, the Potawatomies. After nations such as the Potawatomies and the Winnebagoes ceded much of their land in other treaties with the United States, they moved onto Menominee land.[25] The tension caused by this was increased when the Potawatomies were accused of selling some of the Menominee land. In 1832 the Menominee Grizzly Bear protested to a federal official that "the Pottawatamies had already sold a part of our [Menominee] land...and got a heap of money and annuities, and we got none of it."[26]

A major legal issue was whether or not the Menominees who signed the treaties of 1821 and 1822 were chiefs who had the authority to act on behalf of their people. In 1824 seven Menominee "chiefs and principal men" declared that during 1821 "some of their men, who had no right to dispose of the land, held the treaty."[27] The Menominee chiefs further stated that this applied to the 1822 treaty as well. Rejecting both the 1821 and 1822 treaties, the Menominee chiefs had made a firm point in 1824 of refusing to accept any of the goods the United States Indian agent tried to distribute to them as a partial payment for the two land cessions. By 1827, however, the Menominees had altered their version of the treaties. They admitted that in 1821 one of the six signers of the treaty was in fact a chief, and that three of the nine signers of the treaty of 1822 were chiefs. However, the final defense of the Menominees was that no matter who signed the treaties they did so "without knowing the contents" — the Menominees believed that ownership of the lands had not been purchased because the lands were to be held in common.[28]

In 1831 the United States arranged a compromise treaty between the federal government and the Menominees which stated that the Menominees, "although always protesting that they are under no obligation to recognize any claim of the New York Indians to any portion of their country; that they neither sold nor received any value, for the land claimed by these tribes; yet, at the solicitation of their Great Father, the President of the United States . . . they agree that . . . part of the land . . . may be set apart as a home to the several tribes of the New York Indians."[29] This land amounted to half a million acres, far less extensive than the more than seven million acres claimed by the 1821 and 1822 treaties. However, the Senate amended the definition of the 500,000-acre cession, substituting 200,000 acres not included in exchange for 200,000 acres the Senate amendment returned to Menominee control. The Menominees rejected this alteration and the treaty, and it was another year before the Menominees would negotiate another settlement. In the meantime the Menominees sought favor with the United States—and continued an old intertribal rivalry—by serving against the Winnebagoes and Sauk-Foxes involved in Black Hawk's War.[30]

As for the New York Indians, President Andrew Jackson met with a delegation of them on January 9, 1832, in the capital. Jackson told them he could not give them the lands the Menominees refused to cede. Jackson emphasized his point by saying that he could not lie to Indians — a hypocritical contention, given his consistent denial of Indian treaty rights throughout the removal era.

> I never told a red man a lie in my life, nor do I speak to you with a forked tongue. If I were to promise to give you this land, I would tell you a lie; I could not do it, I cannot deceive you.[31]

In 1832 eager to receive goods promised them by the United States, the Menominees signed another compromise treaty. In this cession of 500,000 acres, they gave up some of the controversial lands stipulated in the Senate amendment of the previous year.[32] Although Oneida Iroquois continued to remove to these lands where they joined Stockbridges, Munsees, Brothertowns, and Oneidas already there, the other Iroquois nations now gave clear signs to the United States government that the antiremoval forces within the Confederacy had effectively mobilized to block the influence of the proremoval Indians within their nations. The non-Christian, traditional Iroquois resented the proremoval leadership of the Christian Oneidas, and perhaps found it all the more galling that removal was also being promoted by Christian Indians who were not even Iroquois: Algonquin subject-allies — Stockbridges, Munsees, and Brothertowns. In addition to the powerful attachment to their New York homelands, some Iroquois who opposed removal to Wisconsin believed that after they settled there the United States would very shortly ask them to remove again to make room for white settlers. Among those who felt this skepticism were some who were white educated, according to a Seneca, George Jamison. In 1833 Jamison gave the federal government his analysis of the Senecas' various positions regarding removal. Jamison's testimony is succinct and compelling evidence of a society rent by factions, and it is also undoubtedly representative of the plight of the New York Indians in general.

The reasons for our indifference to the paternal scheme of Government, familiarly known as the Green Bay measure, are numerous and conflicting, as might be expected from a community made up of hunters, scholars, and farmers, into which three classes we may at this day properly be ranked.

The first class is composed of hunters, old men principally, who have outlived the age for enterprise, whose inborn love of woods and the chase is nearly equipoised by a superstitious faith in the dying words of Red Jacket [Seneca chief, d. 1830], well known to have been hostile to this scheme.

The second class is inconsiderable in numbers, but yet numbering in it our [white-] educated men, chiefly young men more given to theory than action. These pretend to see nothing attractive in the Green Bay plan, foretell the period (should we adopt it) when we should once more be invited to "make room," and regarding our race as foredoomed to insignificance within the borders of a territory no less than where we now are, qualify themselves for civilized employments rather than for the task of civilizing us.

The third class comprehends the bulk of the nation, not easily aroused by benefits purely prospective, or by considerations of thrift to result from their own future labors upon new land; the love of gain is not yet sufficiently developed to overcome the native love of ease, characteristic of all classes. Large portions of our present possessions are suffered to lie waste [i.e. uncultivated]. . . .

From a happy and united people we have become so broken and divided that there remains scarcely a common sentiment amongst us to be appealed to; a desire to perpetuate the Seneca name and nation, is perhaps the only and abiding one.[33]

The Iroquois acknowledged that the removal issue was tearing apart a confederacy council of chiefs which was meeting at Buffalo Creek, New York, in 1833. Nine traditional, non-Christian Iroquois chiefs representing the Oneidas, Onondagas, and Senecas noted that year that in debating removal the Iroquois chiefs "have separated from each other that formerly acted together, and one party has taken steps to depose the other from authority."[34] Ten Seneca chiefs[35] who favored removal explained that the traditionals, "by the help of a few designing and violent young men ... attempted to depose some of us from office."[36]

Ultimately, most of the Six Nations of the Iroquois Confederacy still living in New York in 1833 did not choose to remove to Wisconsin, nor did they agree to proposals that they remove west of the Mississippi to Kansas. Some fled to Canada, but most remained in their New York homeland. As for those who were already in Wisconsin and for those who would soon arrive — primarily Oneidas — white pressures set in immediately, just as some Iroquois who had opposed removal had predicted. The Oneidas and many of the Stockbridges, Munsees, and Brothertowns resisted these pressures and held onto their lands. But in 1839 some of the Stockbridges and Munsees in Wisconsin agreed to move to Kansas; in 1867 they removed again to Oklahoma.[37] For these Indians, the Oklahoma Syndrome was literally complete. The United States had successfully played off victim against victim, and from New York to Wisconsin and west of the Mississippi, the only victors were the whites.

▶▶▶▶▶▶▶▶ 8 ◀◀◀◀◀◀◀◀◀

A REPORT TO THE PEOPLE OF GRASSY NARROWS

KAI T. ERIKSON and CHRISTOPHER VECSEY

WE VISITED THE ONTARIO GRASSY NARROWS RESERVE in January 1979, to help assess the impact of several recent events on the people of the community, the most important of these being the relocation of the Grassy Narrows band to a new reserve in the early 1960s and the discovery of large quantities of methyl mercury in the English and Wabigoon river systems in the early 1970s.

The following is our report. We wish to begin by expressing our thanks to several persons for their cooperation and hospitality—to Chief Simon Fobister; to John Beaver, Andy Keewatin, Pat Loon, Steve Loon, Isaac Pahpassay, and Tom Payash; to Hiroyuki Miyamatsu and Anastasia Shkilnyk.

The Grassy Narrows band is involved in a mediation process that will be concerned with the "adverse effects" of those recent events on the "well-being" of the community. In order to fully understand those effects, however, it is important to appreciate that the impact of a disruption can only be judged properly by looking at two matters. The first, clearly, is the destructive force of the event itself. The second is the vulnerability of the people who are exposed to it, for a weakened and fragile community, or one that is ill prepared for the disruption culturally and socially, can suffer greatly from impacts that might cause less harm elsewhere. In this report, then, we deal first with the relative susceptibility of the people of Grassy Narrows to the events of recent years and then turn to the nature of those events themselves.

When the first European fur traders moved into the region around Grassy Narrows in the early eighteenth century, the Ojibway people had been living there for years. Their economic and spiritual existence depended on a close communion with the environment around them. Their totemic names, their myths and legends, their ceremonies, their religious world view, all reflected the unity of the Ojibway people with the natural world. The ways of nature were their ways; the rhythms of nature were their rhythms. They did not regard themselves as living *off* the land but as absorbed into it, nourished by it, a part of it; and to this day that sense of communion with nature remains an important part of the Ojibway heritage.

The ancestors of the people of Grassy Narrows had been hunters, fishermen, gatherers, and harvesters, and when the North-West and Hudson's Bay companies first moved into the region, the Ojibway people found that their native skills were very well suited to the new economy. Throughout the nineteenth and into the twentieth century, they became expert trappers, guides, harvesters of wild rice, and commercial fishermen. To that extent, at least, contact with white culture did not serve to undermine the traditional ways of the Ojibway people. They continued to live within the shelter of their own ancestral lands and their own clan ties even as they accepted an active part in the white economy, and in this way they were able to preserve much of their old culture, much of their self-sufficiency, and much of their autonomy.

In the last sixty years, however, the people of Grassy Narrows have experienced a number of shock waves that have weakened the cultural fiber of Ojibway life and left the community in a very vulnerable condition. Each of these shock waves can be traced directly or indirectly to white contacts, and each of them can be justly described as a disaster from the point of view of the people who were exposed to it.

The influenza epidemic of 1919 killed almost 75 percent of the population of Grassy Narrows, but even that awesome total does not entirely describe the extent of the damage it inflicted. The disaster created an economic crisis from which the people of the band were a long time in recovering, but it also created a spiritual crisis from which it has not recovered yet. Traditional healers proved powerless to explain or to cure the disease, which placed an enormous strain on the Ojibway system of belief, and the arrival on the scene of white medical personnel helped corrode that faith even further. There is a profound irony in this development, for at the very moment modern medicine was being called upon to control the strains of virus infecting the Ojibway people, another and more subtle kind of disease was infecting the tissues of Ojibway culture itself, and the name of this malady was doubt.

Traditional religion might have recovered from the immense shock of the epidemic had it not been for other developments in the continuing effort of the government to instruct the Ojibway people in its own special brand of civilization. There is considerable anthropological evidence to the effect that other people have experienced similar crises, gone through a period of intense doubt and confusion, and then found ways to revitalize the religious faith that had been in question. But circumstances here did not allow this natural sequence to occur.

To begin with, the 1873 Treaty #3 charged the Canadian government with the obligation of providing education for the people of Grassy Narrows, and the government elected to meet this obligation by building residential schools, often run by missionaries, at some distance from the Indian reserves. Whatever their intent, the effect of these schools was to separate children from their families for long stretches of time and to help strip them of their language, their religion, their native skills, and their very identity as Indians. Old men on the reserve still speak of their schooling with a kind of bitterness: they remember it not only as an assault on themselves as persons but as an assault on their traditional way of life as well; and even now, years later, they tell of the confusion they felt in returning to the reserve after a compulsory period in school—estranged from the Ojibway religion but not converted to the faith of the missionaries, lacking the native skills of their people but not introduced to useful new trades, and, in many other ways, strangers to both cultures at once.

The introduction of Western medicine and Western education into Ojibway culture had an indirect impact on the integrity of native religion, and those who take comfort from the fact are welcome to assume that white personnel in charge of the public health programs and the Indian schools did not intend that result. But in the 1930s and 1940s missionaries who did intend exactly that result secured the help of the Royal Canadian Mounted Police in discouraging Ojibway religious activities. Mounties raided Midewiwin ceremonies, forbade shaking tent rites, arrested and otherwise harrassed members of the Grassy Narrows band for engaging in religious ceremonies, and generally forced the old faith underground. Some religions thrive under persecution, gathering strength from the power of the opposition they attract, but the Ojibway religion — already weakened by spasms of doubt and the systematic efforts of the missionaries—can truly be said to have collapsed. And the people of Grassy Narrows lost a great deal more in that collapse than a scattering of specific beliefs that did not accord well with Christianity. They lost the sense that they were a coherent part of the ecology of nature, and they lost the spiritual insulation, as it were, that had been one of their major sources of protection against disaster and disruption.

The hope of the missionaries, of course, and of the well-meaning persons who joined them in their efforts to convert the Ojibway people, was that the Indians would embrace Christianity as a new system of meaning and explanation. But it is fair to conclude that this fond hope has not been realized, in part because the people of Grassy Narrows feel, like Indians everywhere on this continent, that they have been rejected by those very Christians who want to bring them into a fellowship of faith, and in part because Christianity, for whatever reason, has not provided them with a worldview consonant with the realities of their existence. Spiritually, then, they are caught between a past that no longer provides them with a sense of their place in the order of things and a future that must be faced without the kind of promise that a shared faith can offer. They are neither traditionalists nor Christians in anything but name. Chief Simon Fobister has said of his community, "we are a people with a broken culture," and that remark strikes us as wholly correct.

This is the background against which one must view the disruptive events of recent years. A generation ago the people of Grassy Narrows had a precarious hold on the conditions of their own existence and were deeply vulnerable to further misfortune. On the one hand, their clan structure was more or less intact, many of their traditional skills had been more or less preserved, and their independence as a people was generally respected. But, on the other hand, the religion that had given meaning and coherence to the Ojibway cycle of life was receding into memory — a private preoccupation of the aging rather than an integrative force for the young — and the old ways were disappearing without new ones to provide a relevant alternative.

In 1962 the government encouraged the people of Grassy Narrows to abandon their old reserve and to settle into a new one, and in the next few years the entire band did so. The advantages of the move seemed obvious at the time to some, since the new location offered easier access to electrical power, schools, medical help, roads, and the other benefits of modern life. But in every other respect relocation has to be classed as a true disaster to the lives of those involved. Whatever the motives of the white officials who planned the move, whatever the expectations of the Indians who accepted it, the new reserve is viewed by most of the people who now occupy it as a "cage" or a "concentration camp" that suppresses the true spirit of Ojibway life.

One key problem is that dwellings in the new reserve are tightly bunched together in the manner of a modern suburb, and this arrangement has a number of subtle but important consequences. In the old reserve people were strung out along the edges of the bay by clans. Each family household was separated from the next by open stretches of land or water and each had access to the waterways themselves. The new village, however, is of a type traditionally suited to the needs of an agricultural people, and it serves to violate the sense of space customary to the Ojibway and to other hunting and gathering peoples. It compresses space in such a way that traditional ways of relating to others no longer work. Anthropologists know that every people, every culture, has its own sense of how much distance should be reserved between neighbors, how wide a margin of privacy is necessary to protect individuality; and when that sense of space is disturbed, the result is that neighborliness itself can break down. People who are pressed too closely together by a change in circumstances can become more distant both emotionally and spiritually, for hostilities and aggressions that were once insulated by a cushion of space now fill the narrow gaps like charges of electricity.

This problem is aggravated by the fact that clan alignments, the traditional basis for Ojibway social relations, are difficult to maintain in the new reserve. Twenty years ago the clans occupied recognized territories within the community and generally respected one another's need for a measure of autonomy and privacy. Those were the conditions under which the clans could collaborate in the interests of the whole band. But today the clan members are scattered in an almost random fashion throughout the larger community, and the sense of spacing that once invited collaboration now invites a good deal of interclan tension. And in that sense Grassy Narrows has become not only a tight concentration of persons but a tight concentration of troubles. As one respected member of the band explained it:

> When we moved here, we were packed in. That was bad. But what was more bad was that the clans were pushed together. There was no sense of clan area. It isn't so much that we were pushed together, as that our clans were mixed up. It is too late now. The damage is done.

To add to the problems created by relocation, the new reserve is laid out in such a way as to disturb the traditional relationship between the Ojibway people and the rest of the natural environment. The residents of Grassy Narrows feel removed from their "source of life," separated from the land and the water and the creatures of the forest with whom they had alway felt a certain kinship.

For one thing, the Ojibways have generally moved from one place to another with special care. It was the duty of the spiritual leaders to ascertain the "healthfulness" of the new site, and this they normally did by consulting the spirits who resided there — conferring with the forces of nature, as it were — to learn whether the land was ready to welcome them, whether the new site was blessed for their use. The relocation did not take this tradition into consideration, and the people of the band, in varying degrees, often feel that they were never intended to settle in the place they now occupy. The older men on the reserve can be quite specific about the matter.

> This is a diseased place to live. Maybe the spirits here aren't good. Anyway, they were never consulted. We could see it right away. This place is no good for us.

And many of the younger people, too—although they are far less likely to speak of "spirits"—share the feeling that the new reserve has never been and can never become a home.

It may be more important to note, however, that the layout of the new reserve contributes in a number of ways to the sense of alienation the residents feel from the natural world. They live on small parcels of land, most of them stripped of foliage and most of them at some distance from the water. Deer and other game have been driven from the area by white sportsmen. What land there is has proven to be stubborn and inhospitable, unable to support the potatoes and corn that grew in the old reserve, and even the fish, as we shall see in a moment, are poisoned. The environment no longer serves as a source of life in the old way. A band of people who once lived scattered throughout the forest and along the edges of the water now find themselves clumped together on a bare stretch of land, and in that respect, at least, they have been removed from their natural habitat.

The new reserve, then, is like a no-man's-land. It has separated the people who live there from their traditional ways, but it has not yet served, and perhaps never will, to introduce them to newer ways. They have been drawn further and further away from Ojibway culture but have scarcely begun the process of becoming absorbed into the economic and cultural life of modern Canada. As a result, the new reserve has been a place of tension and even violence, a place of demoralization and extreme apathy. Even the most casual visitor to Grassy Narrows can sense that something is seriously wrong there. A people who once depended upon and respected the wisdom of their leaders are suspicious of them now. A people who once exerted their energies to preparing and storing food for the future now live as if there could be no tomorrows. A people who once enjoyed a reputation for devotion to children now neglect them.

In almost every way, the people of Grassy Narrows are vulnerable to misfortune. A human community uses its cultural and spiritual resources to resist an invasion of troubles in much the same way as a living organism uses its chemical resources to resist an invasion of germs, and it is clear that the people who now occupy the reserve had to face the most recent wave of trouble with a limited supply of such resources.

"Pijibowin" is an Ojibway term for poison, and it is used in the reserve to describe the enormous quantities of mercury that now contaminate the English and Wabigoon river systems. Some 20,000 pounds of the poison were dumped into the Wabigoon River between 1962 and 1970, and its effects are felt in a variety of ways.

In the first place, of course, the contamination poses a medical problem, for mercury poisoning leaves its marks on the tissues of the human body in the form of the degeneration of cerebellar cortices and the simple destruction of brain cells, resulting in symptoms that may not surface for years and even generations. We are not medical experts, but the evidence of mercury poisoning at Grassy Narrows seems a cause for real alarm. Not only have the classical symptoms of mercury poisoning begun to appear among the people of the reserve—tunnel vision, loss of balance, numbness in the extremities—but there is good reason to worry that the hidden effects of the malady are present as well. Such typical side effects as susceptibility to alcohol and extremes of temperature, irritability and aggressiveness, are difficult to identify clincially because they can result from any number of causes, but the symptoms themselves are found in abundance throughout Grassy Narrows.

In the second place, the contamination of the rivers has created a very serious economic problem. In 1970 the government closed virtually all of the waterways within easy reach of Grassy Narrows to commercial fishing, and a short time later the Ball Lake Lodge went out of business. These two developments, for all practical purposes, spelled the end of useful employment at the reserve. Ninety-five percent of men of Grassy Narrows were employed at the beginning of that moment of trouble and 95 percent unemployed at its end. The government responded to the crisis by providing food, welfare, and make-work projects of one kind or another, so the most immediate hardships of the loss were alleviated. But while the people of the reserve have not gone without food or shelter, they have gone without meaningful work; and that can create a kind of depression that long outlasts the economic crisis itself. Welfare is degrading to any people who pride themselves on their mastery of a craft or trade, and the Ojibways—expert hunters and trappers, fishermen and guides—feel that a good part of their dignity and humanity is denied when they are no longer needed in their traditional callings and can find little else of value to do.

In the third place, the discovery of mercury in the local waters has presented a psychological and perhaps even a spiritual problem, for the apprehensions and uncertainties that follow such a discovery can affect the mind as surely as the poison itself can affect the body. This process is a subtle one and difficult to document, but it takes the form of a pervasive fear that the world of nature and the world of men are now contaminated and can no longer be trusted in the old way. The fish are full of poison, the waters are polluted, the land is diseased, the game has retreated, and the social world, too, is becoming insecure and unreliable. When this happens, as sociologists have demonstrated in other settings, the community is quite likely to experience a striking rise in alcoholism, delinquency, vandalism, child neglect, drug abuse, theft, crimes of violence, and similar forms of deviation. We did not have time during our visit to collect very much data on this point, but we are convinced—and so is everyone else we know who has some acquaintance with life on the reserve — that these rates have now reached epidemic proportions. A statistical profile of the Grassy Narrows band would almost certainly show that the residents are addicted to alcohol in great numbers, that the traditional Ojibway respect for property has declined markedly, that a substantial number of children are being neglected, and that the death rate has taken some disastrous turns. We have seen the results of a household survey on alcohol use conducted by the Band Office, and those data emphatically confirm the impression that heavy drinking has become a critical problem on the reserve. We were also able to obtain some fairly hard data on causes of death among the people of Grassy Narrows by examining coroner reports and Band Office records as well as consulting a family of Mennonite missionaries who have lived in the region for years and know, both literally and figuratively, where the bodies are buried. These data presented in Table 1 indicate clearly that the odds of dying a natural death at Grassy Narrows have declined dramatically over the past twenty years, while the odds of dying by accident or homicide —almost surely a result of alcohol abuse—have passed the 50 percent mark.

This is as grim a statistical picture as one can imagine, and when one adds to that picture whatever information is available on child neglect and the other classical indications of disorganization, it is

Table 1
CAUSES OF DEATH, GRASSY NARROWS BAND
1957–1977

	1957–1963	1964–1970	1971–1977
Infant death	14 (38)	16 (38)	11 (17)
Old age	12 (32)	6 (14)	3 (5)
Illness	3 (8)	1 (2)	8 (12)
Accident	5 (14)	9 (21)	17 (26)
Drowning	3	2	6
Gunshot	0	1	1
House fire	0	0	2
Exposure	1	3	6
Other/unknown	1	3	2
Alcohol poisoning	0 (0)	0 (0)	6 (9)
Suicide	0 (0)	0 (0)	2 (3)
Homicide	2 (5)	6 (14)	16 (24)
Stabbing	0	1	2
Shooting	1	1	3
Other/unknown	1	4	11
Unknown	1 (3)	3 (10)	3 (5)
Total	37 (100)	42 (99)	66 (101)

(percentage in parentheses)

very likely to show that the people of Grassy Narrows are in serious trouble.

We have no way of knowing, of course, how many of these troubles can be attributed to mercury pollution, how many to relocation, how many to all of the other disruptions that have interrupted the flow of Ojibway life over the past sixty years. But it is only reasonable to conclude that these events, together, have helped create a situation that calls for relief. One of the present authors can testify that conditions at Grassy Narrows are as bad as those found in the wake of the most severe disasters, and the other author can testify that conditions in the reserve are a good deal worse than those found among other Ojibway bands or among other Indian peoples throughout the continent generally. In the absence of more complete data, which a poor community is in no position to obtain, the weight of evidence strongly points to the relocation of the early 1960s and the mercury contamination of the late 1960s as the leading causes of the distress found at Grassy Narrows. No other conclusion is responsible to the facts; no other conclusion is responsible to the needs of a damaged community.

We are convinced that the people of Grassy Narrows need and deserve compensation for the disruptions they have experienced, whether or not blame is assigned to the various groups that have contributed in one way or another to the present situation.

We feel, however, that a cash settlement is likely to aggravate the problems described in this report rather than to alleviate them, because the people of Grassy Narrows need something to regain their sense of independence and their traditional communion with the environment. Money can buy goods in the white economy but not the kind of integrity and wholeness of spirit that is now missing.

The most appropriate form of compensation we can imagine would be a very substantial grant of land, hopefully within range of the present reserve. The people of Grassy Narrows constitute a minority community within the boundaries of Canada, but they also constitute a kind of nation in the cultural sense; and what they need is a home territory, a true reserve, in which they can restore the security of their old ways. The lands in question ought to contain sufficient resources to provide an economic base for people who know the ways of nature, so that they can employ their native skills in such meaningful activities as timbering, fishing, trapping, harvesting wild rice, and serving as guides to tourists and sportsmen. The economic benefits of this arrangement are obvious. But the psychological and social benefits would be considerable too, for this tract of land could provide a sheltered territory in which the people of Grassy Narrows recover some of the strengths of their Ojibway past, and, at the same time, provide a base camp, a place to regroup, for those preparing to take their place in the economic structure of modern Canada. Sociologists have long known that the paths of mobility are easiest for people who know their roots and know how to draw nourishment from them.

There is one further advantage to this arrangement. In a world that has begun to recognize the fragility of nature and the scarcity of natural resources, anything the government can do to help the Ojibway people preserve their understanding of and respect for the ecology of the natural world may, in the long run, be a service to all the Canadian people. For the question may not simply be what the country can contribute to the welfare of its native inhabitants but what those native inhabitants can contribute to the country and to the rest of the world.

NAVAJO NATURAL RESOURCES

PETER MacDONALD

As I prepared this chapter, I received word from the tribal lawyer that the state of Arizona just passed a law that would put all water litigation into state courts rather than federal courts. The Navajo position is that we have a better chance fighting for our water rights in federal courts than state courts because states really have their own self-interest in mind when you go into state court. State people being what they are, they decided to pass a law. But the governor has not yet signed it, so what we want to do is file our suit for water rights in Colorado before the governor signs it and file it in federal court so that at least we may beat them to the punch before their act becomes law. It's that sort of a battle all the time.

There is a story about an easterner who went down west and got to Muskogee, Oklahoma, which always likes to pride itself as the Indian capital of the world. The man got to the train station and got out of the train, looking around wanting to see Indians and saw a big giant of a man standing right there. A fellow tourist nudged him in the side and said, "Say, where are the Indians?" And this big man standing there dressed in a three-piece suit looked down at the tourist and said, "I'm an Indian." The tourist looked up and said, "You're an Indian? Where's your feathers?" And the Indian said, "It's molting season."

So it is, I guess, molting season for some of us.

I went to school in Muskogee—Bacome Junior College. And from there I went to the University of Oklahoma, not because it's a great institution of higher learning but because the years I went there Bud Wilkinson was the football coach, and they had the number one football team in the nation. I just love football, and I thought that would be a good way to see football for at least three or four years. I graduated there as an electrical engineer and went to work for Howard

Hughes in Culver City, California. I worked for him for six and a half years and then returned to the Navajo reservation and eventually became chairman of the nation.

I am an engineer by trade—an electrical engineer. Now I'm a human engineer. When I first took office in 1971 on the Navajo nation, I received a call from NASA from Houston, and they asked if they could bring their astronauts to the reservation to practice the moon mission that was scheduled for them the next month. It was an Apollo 15 mission, Jim Urwin and David Scott. The reason they wanted to do this is that the southwestern portion of the Navajo reservation resembled very much the terrain and the location where the astronauts were going to land. So I said yes; they came up, the invited, myself, and a few of the tribal leaders, and we watched them.

They actually set up a mock space capsule, a landing craft, right on the reservation. They had full communication equipment, communicating with Houston all the time, and the two astronauts had their space suits and helmets on. They actually went through the motions as they would on the moon, getting off the landing craft down on the ground and getting on the moon buggy and riding around. And while they were doing this, an old Navajo medicine man showed up, and he asked me, "What are these two funny looking fellows doing here on the reservation?" They had the space suits on, and I said these two fellows are going to the moon next month and the medicine man said, "Is that right?" I said yes.

He said, "You know in our legend, Navajo legend, the Navajos were on the moon once on their way to the sun." He said, if there two guys are going to the moon next month, he'd like to send a message, maybe there are some Navajos still there on the moon. So I didn't say very much until the astronauts came back, and they were very pleased to see the medicine man, and then I told the astronauts what the medicine man wanted to do. And, of course, Jim Urwin said, yes, have him write it on a piece of paper and if we run into some Navajos we'll deliver the message. I said Navajo is not a written language. "Well," he said, "that's all right, here's a tape recorder, have him put it on tape, and if we run into some Navajos on the moon we'll play the tape for them." So I told this to the medicine man and he said OK. So the astronauts went back out to do some more work, and I turned the tape recorder on and the medicine man taped his message and stuck around a little bit and then went home.

Later on in the day the astronauts came in, and we had some refreshments and Jim Urwin said, "Did the medicine man tape a message?" I said yes, well let's listen to it. So I turned it on, but of course the message was in Navajo. Urwin asked, "What is he saying?"

And I said, "He says, beware of these two fellows, they will want to make a treaty with you."

The Navajo nation represents about 160,000 individuals, and we are growing at 2 percent net each year. The Navajo reservation is in three states, New Mexico, Arizona, and Utah. It's a large land area representing about 18 million acres, or twenty-four thousand square miles. It's about the size of the state of West Virginia or the size of Connecticut, Massachusetts, Rhode Island, Delaware, and Vermont all put together. That's the size of the Navajo nation. We have a treaty with the United States. The treaty was executed back in 1868 after Colonel Kit Carson was successful in rounding up the Navajos. We were marched 300 miles east into New Mexico, to Bosque Redondo and Fort Sumner where we were imprisoned for four and a half years after they couldn't handle the Navajos in terms of civilizing us or making us farmers or whatever they wanted to do with us. They decided to make a treaty with us. So the treaty of 1868 is the treaty between the Navajo nation and the United States government, and to date that is the basis of our relationship with the federal government.

Often easterners, sociologists, and politicians have a great deal of difficulty in understanding what the United States' or a state's relationship is with the Indians. A lot of them feel that the United States' relationship with Indians is more like the United States' relationship with the blacks, Chicanos, or other minorities. This is not so. Sovereignty no doubt is something that really no one agrees upon as to what it means or how it should be applied with respect to the government's relationship with the Indian tribes. We the Indians feel that sovereignty implies dealings with other nations. We fought the Germans, the Japanese. We conquered them, but we left them their sovereignty. By treaty we only took away what we thought would be appropriate for their existence and survival. The same applies with Indians who have treaties with the United States. We maintain that we had sovereignty; we were nations before we were conquered, and treaty provisions took away a certain degree of our sovereignty but not all of our sovereignty. And some of the provisions of the treaty state that in return for giving up the land, the United States would do this, this, this, and this forever. So in that sense, the United States' obligation, and the obligation of future generations is not based upon the fact that Indians are poor. Yes, indeed, we are poor. As a matter of fact we share in everything that the United States has—we have our share of poverty. But the thing that I want to come to is the issue of all the assistance going to the Indians. I'd like to make it as simple as possible. It probably isn't that simple. But suppose your grandmother had something that was very valuable and I wanted it. By whatever method I made an agreement with your grandmother and I want that something that she had. And I say, if you would give me that thing that you have I'll agree that I'll take care of you, your children, and their children forever regarding their educational needs, their health needs, and their economic needs. And your grandma and grandpa got rid of whatever they had that I wanted. They gave it to me, and I put my thumb print on and they signed it. And now my obligation to your father and your grandfather and to you and your children, their children from here on out would be that I'll always provide them with adequate education and see to their health needs and their economic well-being. It doesn't matter whether everyone of you have become millionaires or not. A deal is a deal. That's the way you would look at. Well, treaties with Indians are the same way.

The treaties exist. For instance, the Navajo had more than 50 million acres of land that they ceded in exchange for a small portion. In return there were certain guarantees that were made forever. That's what the treaty says, not ninety days, but forever. So on that basis, we have this relationship with the federal government.

Now, regarding the natural resources that the Indian tribes have and how we look at these resources and also the impact they have on our environment: let me talk about the Navajo first. The Navajo nation has more than 5 billion tons of coal on the reservation, and we produce on an annual basis more than 13 million tons a year and most of it is being strip mined. We also produce 12 million barrels of oil per year. We produce 30 million cubic feet of natural gas a year and about a million pounds of uranium ore per year now, and that's projected to go as high as 15 million pounds of uranium ore. That's not johnny cake. We have about 500 thousand acres of timber on the Navajo reservation, and we have now in production about 50 million board feet of lumber each year. We have rights to the Colorado River and Little Colorado River, San Juan River. I already told you that our land base has shrunk from 50 million to 18 million acres.

There are other tribes who have these energy resources. In 1975 I formed an organization called Council of Energy Resource Tribes, CERT. There are twenty-five tribes represented in this organization. Most all of them are west of Mississippi. They all have one thing in common. They all have energy resources in production on their reservations, coal, uranium, oil, and gas. These twenty-five tribes together have on their reservations better than 50 percent of all known uranium reserves in the United States, more than 30 percent of the selfstrippable coal west of the Mississippi, 10 percent of all coal reserves in America, and 3 percent of oil and gas production in the United States. These are substantial holdings. Since there was a national energy crunch, since the United States wants to become energy independent, and since we have a substantial amount of the energy reserves, we wanted to become a part of their nation's goal to become energy independent. I have written to the federal agencies and the president. I said that we, the twenty-five tribes who have these energy resources, want to be involved at the highest level with respect to energy policy making, regulations, and programs on the short and long-range basis that will affect America and certainly will affect those of us who have these energy resources.

Since I was not getting any response at all, I then approached whomever I felt would give us some assistance, because with all these resources in our hands we did not have the necessary technical expertise to program what we would do with these resources. Certainly we don't want to repeat what has happened in the past when our trustee, the federal government, through the Department of Interior and Bureau of Indian Affairs negotiated for many of these mineral resources on our behalf at such ridiculous and unconscionable prices in returns to the Navajo nation.

To give an example, on the Black Mesa Peabody Coal mining operation, the Bureau of Indian Affairs of the federal government negotiated back in the early 1960s on the Navajo nation's behalf. For the exploration and mining of that coal which belonged to the Navajo, the Navajo would get fifteen cents per ton for the coal mined on the Navajo reservation forever as long as the coal shall last. At the same time, the United Mine Workers negotiated a union contract with Peabody for the operation on Black Mesa and received in their contract sixty cents per ton for the coal mined on the Navajo reservation on an escalating basis depending on the cost of living. Yet the Navajo, the owners, were receiving 15 cents a ton forever no matter what the inflation rate was. Those were the kinds of contracts that we had in our hands, and we didn't want it repeated. There were hardly any reclamation provisions. There were hardly any provisions for people who would be relocated because of the project. There was absolutely nothing regarding air pollution and water pollution, depletion of water. So the twenty-five tribes that I have organized decided to go out somewhere and get some help.

The first thing that came to my mind was the OPEC nations because they and the Indian tribes have similar situations. They were dealing with the same companies that we were dealing with: Exxon, Texaco, Philips Petroleum, Standard Oil. So I made contact with the

OPEC nations to see what they knew about the companies and to see if we could exchange some ideas as to how together we might deal with these same outfits that were seemingly exploiting us. The OPEC nations were in similar positions some years back, and now they are appreciating their depleting resources, and we want to do the same thing. The minute I did that, news went across the nation that the Indians are going to join the OPEC nations and how terrible for Indians to do that; here we were nice to them and being gracious to them in every way, how ungrateful of them to go to the OPEC nations, our enemies. That's what the editorial pages across the country were saying. The Indians are unpatriotic, MacDonald is unpatriotic. Well, that's not the case. As I said, the reason we want some help with our resources is to make sure that we do not make the same mistake that was made on our behalf by our trustee.

What are some of the mistakes? One of the mistakes was this. The Navajo nation has had oil and gas in production for the last thirty years. Those early contracts were made on our behalf by the federal government, as I said. For example, last year we had to shut down several oil fields, simply because the oil companies were constantly going across our land as though they owned it. We had many women and children herding sheep and cattle out in those areas. Well, the oil companies disregarded this. Oil workers shot at the sheep and cattle. In some cases they just drove by, caught a goat, and butchered it right in front of the Navajo owners. They let oil they were pumping run down into our water. They ran after young Navajo women. The companies were Conoco, Texaco, Superior Oil, and Philips Petroleum. We stopped twenty-three thousand barrels a day until a new agreement could be reached to protect the people, the environment, and the land.

Another problem is two power plants which are on Navajo land and expel sulphur dioxide into the air: 120 million pounds of sulphur dioxide per year. The Navajo nation decided to require that the pollution be reduced to one million pounds per year. The utility company filed lawsuits in Arizona, New Mexico, and Utah saying the Navajo have no right to make such laws. They also said that it would bankrupt them to pay the fines we Navajo intended to impose if the pollution continued: ten cents per pound the first year, to seventy-five cents per pound at the end of five years. We wanted the company to put in scrubbers which have already been invented and already exist. We also have problems with the reclamation of lands that have been strip mined for their coal. Many of these issues are still in litigation.

Today radiation has been found in the tailings of the uranium mines on Navajo land. Several deaths have been attributed to this because the workers and local people were not protected. The mines let wash-off of yellowcake into the water of our people and our livestock. So this has brought in CERT for a better deal. Ten uranium producers will soon meet with me to resolve this problem.

I would like to explain a major problem regarding the economic development of the Navajo nation, for all Indian people. We have land and other resources. But we have never been given a fair market value for these resources. By fair market value I mean the highest price possible arrived at within a reasonable time, willingly agreed to by both buyer and seller. There has never been a fair market price set for Indians' resources. Your government says "sale." We say "condemnation." Condemnation is the alternative to a fair market value. I would like to make three propositions:

1. Indians have never received a fair market value for their resources.

2. Indians are not receiving fair market values now.

3. Indians *cannot* — ever — receive fair market value.

The reasons for these circumstances are many. First, the United States government has no understanding of Navajo values, values which to us would be part of determining what would be a fair market value. Furthermore, our resources are never put on the open market. We must deal with the supervision of the United States government. Indian resources can never be offered to all bidders, like the United Nations, or the Organization of American States, or the World Bank. American industries making airplanes are not in an open market either, but they get a better deal than Indians.

There is also the fact that in Indian dealings there is no absence of compulsion or duress. These are exerted upon us by the government and others. Finally, because Indians must deal through the United States government, Indians never know the buyers' needs. We don't have economic or social projections. We have one lawyer, the companies have thirty lawyers. That's not the white people's fault, though. These are facts of life, so we Indians must learn to understand this. We have done this in the past. In the early 1920s United States government officials came to one of our council meetings. After some time, an elder got up and spoke to the visitors: "You will forgive me if I tell you that we are not afraid of our trails."

To put the issue of fair market value in perspective, take my word, we are loyal Americans who care — in the past, however, we know that we had lax immigration laws and shaky border patrols! Now, all we want is to hold on to what was left to us. My people must go beyond subsistence and survival through economic development. In the future we must have self-sufficiency based on using our resources to serve future generations. This means we must be conser-

A WEST INDIES SCENE (also, "An Episode in the Conquest of America"), by Jan Mostaert, c. 1540–50. The first European engraving portraying the Western Hemisphere was made in 1493, but art historian Hugh Honour notes of Mostaert's work that "this is the earliest known painting [by a non-Indian] of the New World." The term West Indies originally meant the entire Western Hemisphere. The work portrays a vision of conflict in which innocent, noble savages defend their idyllic environment against a juggernaut of disciplined Spanish troops entering as a dark mass in the far right of the painting. It is possible that the painting portrays the attack by Coronado upon the Pueblos in 1540 or 1541, or it may be just a general comment on the Spanish incursion into the Southwest. In any case, it was meant in part to rally the Dutch who were themselves resisting the Spanish occupation of their homeland. It was also representative of the destructive forces of a materialistic world thrusting in upon a Garden of Eden. While the setting is meant to be the American Southwest, the people and animals appear European.

In the center of the painting is a natural "window rock," a feature common to the Southwest. Window Rock, Arizona, named after one of these prominent natural formations, is the present capital of the Navajo Nation. Five centuries after Mostaert's vision of conflict around a window rock, the struggle continues over control of the environment as the Navajo people confront the materialistic ambitions not of companies of invading soldiers but of twentieth century energy resource corporations. *Frans Hals Museum and the Government of the Netherlands* vationists and find a balance of all life. This we will do because of our religious concepts, our traditions — our nation's relationship to our land. It is holy land. Non-Indians do not understand our view of our sacred land. But you understand Jerusalem. Would you put a price on Israel? No. Our sacred land is watched over by our Sky Father and our Earth Mother. It is not subject to partition. Some things are not for sale.

While we ask you to respect our beliefs, we appreciate the American dream you have, and we are patriotic to the United States. During the wars of the twentieth century, including the recent Vietnam War, our youth served—and during Vietnam only non-Indian youth, not our youth, protested.

For better or worse, we are bound up in the same future. The United States can't win respect around the globe if it is not respected internally.

We Navajo understand your needs for energy resources. You should understand our needs. We should have a reciprocal agreement that national need is not biased. Our Navajo land is not the most expendable. Our land can provide solar and wind energy. But we also have a culture on that land which we want to preserve. We ask you to seek your own alternatives.

We are vulnerable. We may win a scrimmage with your government now and then, and some non-Indians panic. But we know what the stakes are. In 1864 after destroying our homes and crops, United States troops drove us off our lands — rounded us up and marched us from the Canyon de Chelly in Arizona, to the desolate Bosque Redondo of New Mexico — the Long Walk of the Navajo. In 1868 we were finally allowed to return. Exile and expropriation has been our fate in the past. We know we can be rounded up again.

AN IROQUOIS PERSPECTIVE

OREN LYONS

A LARGE PERSPECTIVE IS REQUIRED to understand the prospects of very real situations concerning the environment, of natural resources, of land claims, of interactions among nations, and of the welfare of not only mankind but the welfare of the natural world and all life. I will give you our perspective and you may agree or disagree.

There exists just to the south of Syracuse, New York, the central council of the chiefs of the Onondaga nation, part of the Six Nations of the Iroquois Confederacy. Onondaga is also the capital of the Six Nations. Meetings there of the Onondaga nation, and of the Six Nations, are an uninterrupted continuation of a government that's perhaps a thousand years old. The basis of our nation is that the sovereignty of the individual is supreme. We hear the word sovereignty bandied about and discussed and interpreted, but it is essential a very simple and a very direct application of reality as we see it. Sovereignty is the act thereof. You are as sovereign as you are. An example of sovereignty was Idi Amin in Uganda. Regardless of the position that you may take about Amin, very recently in Uganda, Amin carried out sovereignty in a horrendous manner which destroyed thousands and thousands of lives. It was not a just sovereignty, but it was a very absolute form of sovereignty. And that is the point.

The action of a people in a territory, the ability and willingness of a people to defend that territory, and the recognition of that ability by other nations: that's a definition of the practical application of sovereignty. It's very simple. It has to deal with government, power and people, and force. The history of my people, of the Ho-de-no-sau-ne, is a long history which deals in the principles of peace: basically peace and the power to keep the peace. Peace, equality, and justice for people is given over into the hands of the chiefs, the welfare

of all living things. In our perception all life is equal, and that includes the birds, animals, things that grow, things that swim. All life is equal in our perception. It is the Creator who presents the reality, and as you read this singularly, by yourself in your sovereignty and in your being and in your completeness, you are a manifestation of the creation. You are sovereign by the fact that you exist. And in this, the relationship demands respect for the equality of life. These are the principles through which the council governs in their sense of duty. We are a government that is intertwined with spiritual guidance. The first duty of the chiefs is to see that we conduct ceremonies precisely. That is the first duty. Only after that do we sit in council for the welfare of our people. So you can see the separation of spiritual, religious ways from political ways does not exist within the structure of the Ho-de-no-sau-ne, and also I might add, to most of all the other Indian nations as they had previously existed. There has been a great change in the affairs of our people, the manners of government.

We have sat through, as one of our elders said, five days of invasion, five days that our white brothers have been here, and in those five days, there has been tremendous change. We are looking ahead, as is one of the first mandates given to us as chiefs, to make sure and to make every decision that we make relate to the welfare and well-being of the seventh generation to come, and that is the basis by which we make decisions in council. We consider: will this be to the benefit of the seventh generation? That is a guideline. We have watched various forms of governments, we have watched internationally the development of industry. We have watched within our own nations and territories the exploitation of not only the people but the resources without regard to the seventh generation to come. We are facing together, you and I, your people and my people, your children and my children, we are facing together a very bleak future. There seems to be at this point very little consideration, minimum consideration, for what is to occur, the exploitation of wealth, blood, and the guts of our mother, the earth. Without the earth, without your mother, you could not be sitting here; without the sun, you would not be here. Over

THE IROQUOIS TREE OF PEACE, by Oren Lyons, contemporary Onondaga Iroquois. The Great Law of the Houdenosaunee (Iroquois) is symbolized by the pine tree and was established by the young lawgiver Deganawidah and his older associate Hiawatha. Human life on the turtle's back—Earth—is literally and figuratively related to all life, especially apparent in the Iroquois clans represented by the Creator's various creatures seen in and around the tree. *Courtesy of Onondaga Savings Bank* a time, a period, I've seen people become more and more distant and unrelated. Nevertheless, these very basic elements vitally concern you. The reality that you sit in, you're surrounded with at this point, this room that separates you from the true reality, the true power, the true understanding, the manifestation of these walls can also be likened to the manifestation of books, encyclopedias, interpretations as when you heard laws. In one rationalization upon another, you continue the exploitation for wealth and power. But you must consider in the process and in choosing the direction of your life: how will this affect the seventh generation? The system that we have observed not only here but internationally demands exploitation; industrialization demands a power base. It demands work forces for the gods of profit. It is our observation that the cathedrals that you worship in are not the ones that ring your bells on Sunday. The cathedrals that you worship in are the shopping malls that are found in this country.

Respect the proper manner so that the seventh generation will have a place to live in. Let us look at the large issues. We are concerned with all the children of this earth. We are concerned with the four colors of Man. Natural Law is very simple. You cannot change it: it prevails over all. There is not a tight rule, there is not a court, there is not a group of nations in this world that can change this Natural Law. You are subject and born to those Natural Laws. The Indians understood the Natural Laws. They built their laws to coincide with the Natural Laws. And that's how we survived.

Will people of all races learn? Will they observe? Will they reach beyond feelings of racism and antagonism to see what is good for the welfare of all people? And not only people, but all things that live. The water is shallow. There is less of it. There are four billion people in the world today. In the year 2009 there are going to be eight billion people on this earth. In thirty years time, well within your lifetime, you are going to be faced with double the population — and double the problems. What about that seventh generation? Where are you taking them? What will they have?

You may not agree with what I said, but in the course of freedom — and recognizing the sovereignty of the individual and his ability to be free — that's your choice. Define for yourselves your directions. Think about it. Today belongs to us, tomorrow we'll give it to the children, but today is ours. You have the mandate, you have the responsibility. Take care of your people—not yourselves, your people.

▶▶▶▶▶▶▶▶▶ ◀◀◀◀◀◀◀◀◀

NOTES

Chapter 1—AMERICAN INDIAN ENVIRONMENTAL RELIGIONS

1. Joseph Epes Brown, *The Spiritual Legacy of the American Indian* (Lebanon, Pa.: Pendle Hill, 1964), p. 16.

2. Howard F. Gregor, *Geography of Agriculture. Themes in Research* (Englewood Cliffs, N.J.: Prentice-Hall, 1970), p. 9.

3. Christopher Vecsey, "Traditional Ojibwa Religion and Its Historical Changes," (Ph.D. diss., Northwestern University, 1977), pp. vi–viii.

4. Edward Burnett Tylor, *Religion in Primitive Culture* (New York: Harper & Brothers, 1958; originally published as Chapters 11–19 of *Primitive Culture*, 1871), pp. 290–392, 315.

5. For example, see N. S. Shaler, *Nature and Man in America* (New York: Scribner's, 1891); and A. J. Fynn, *The American Indian as a Product of Environment with Special Reference to the Pueblos* (Boston: Little, Brown, 1907).

6. Andrew Lang, *Myth, Ritual, and Religion*, 2 vols. (London: Longmans, 1887), p. 41; James George Frazer, *The New Golden Bough*, ed. and abr. Theodore H. Gaster (New York: New American Library, 1964; originally published in 1890), pp. 339–587. Hartley Alexander, *The Religious Spirit of the American Indian as Shown in the Development of His Religious Rites and Customs* (Chicago: Open Court, 1910), pp. 1–4.

7. Harold Hickerson, "Fur Trade Colonialism and the North American Indians," *Journal of Ethnic Studies* 1 (Summer 1973):16.

8. Henry Benjamin Whipple, *Lights and Shadows of a Long Episcopate* (New York: Macmillan, 1899), p. 34.

9. Robert Berkhofer, Jr., *The White Man's Indian: Images of the American Indians from Columbus to the Present* (New York: Knopf, 1978), pp. 38–44.

10. Bernard W. Sheehan, "Paradise and the Noble Savage in Jeffersonian Thought," *William and Mary Quarterly* 26, 3 (1969):337–39; Richard Slotkin, *Regeneration through Violence: The Mythology of the American Frontier, 1600–1860* (Middletown, Conn.: Wesleyan University Press, 1973), pp. 59–60. Clark Wissler, *Indians of the United States* (Garden City, N.Y.: Doubleday, 1967; originally published in 1940), pp. 276–82.

11. For example, W. H. Hutchinson, "The Remaking of the Amerind," *Westways* (October 1972), pp. 18–21, 94.

12. George P. Marsh, *The Earth as Modified by Human Action: A New Edition of Man and Nature* (New York: Scribner, Armstrong, 1874; originally published in 1864), pp. 34–40.

13. A. L. Kroeber, *Cultural and Natural Areas of Native North America* (Berkeley and Los Angeles: University of California Press, 1953); Otis Tufton Mason, "Influence of Environment upon Human Industries or Arts," *Smithsonian Institution Annual Report*

(Washington, D.C.: Government Printing Office, 1896), pp. 639–65; W. J. McGee, "The Relation of Institutions to Environment," *Smithsonian Institution Annual Report* (Washington, D.C.: Government Printing Office, 1896), pp. 701–11; J. W. Powell, "Relation of Primitive Peoples to Environment, Illustrated by American Examples," *Smithsonian Institution Annual Report* (Washington, D.C.: Government Printing Office, 1896), pp. 625–37; Clark Wissler, *The Relation of Nature to Man in Aboriginal America* (New York: Oxford University Press, 1926).

14. Albert Ernest Jenks, "Faith as a Factor in the Economic Life of the Amcrind," *American Anthropologists*, n.s., 2, 4 (1900):676–77. William Christie MacLeod, "Conservation among Primitive Hunting Peoples," *Scientific Monthly* 43 (December 1936):562–66.

15. Frank G. Speck, "Utilization of Animals and Plants by the Micmac Indians of New Brunswick," *Journal of the Washington Academy of Sciences* 41, 8 (1951):250.

16. John Collier, *Indians of the Americas: The Long Hope* (New York: New American Library, 1947), p. 11; see Collier, *On the Gleaming Way* (Chicago: Sage Books, 1962).

17. Sue Whalen, "The Nez Perces' Relationship to Their Land," *The Indian Historian* 4, 3 (1971):30–32.

18. Frank Waters, *Masked Gods: Navaho and Pueblo Ceremonialism* (New York: Ballantine, 1970; originally published in 1950).

19. Gayle L. Dukelow and Rosalyn S. Zakheim, "Recovering Indian Lands: The Land Patent Annulment Suit," *Ecology Law Quarterly* 2 (Winter 1972):197; cf. 195–205.

20. Wilcomb Washburn, *The Indian in America* (New York: Harper & Row, 1975), p. 11.

21. Wilbur R. Jacobs, *Dispossessing the American Indian: Indians and Whites on the Colonial Frontier* (New York: Scribner's, 1972), p. 30.

22. Ed McGaa, "Dilemma of the Non-Indian World," *The Indian Historian* 5, 1 (1972):15–16.

23. Harvey A. Feit, "Twilight of the Cree Hunting Nation," *Natural History* 82, 7 (1973):54–56, 72.

24. Buffalo Child Long Lance, *Long Lance* (New York: Cosmopolitan Book Corp., 1928); Charles Alexander Eastman, *The Soul of the Indian* (Boston: Houghton Mifflin, 1911); Eastman, *From the Deep Woods to Civilization* (Boston: Little, Brown, 1917); Eastman, *Indian Boyhood* (New York: Dover, 1971; originally published in 1902); N. Scott Momaday, *The Names: A Memoir* (New York: Harper & Row, 1976); John G. Neihardt, *Black Elk Speaks: Being the Life Story of a Holy Man of the Ogalala Sioux* (New York: William Morrow, 1932); Peter Nabokov, *Two Leggings: The Making of a Crow Warrior* (New York: Thomas Y. Crowell, 1970); Luther Standing Bear, *Land of Spotted Eagle* (Boston: Houghton Mifflin, 1933); Stands in Timber, John Liberty, and Margot Liberty, *Cheyenne Memories*, with Robert M. Utley (Lincoln: University of Nebraska Press, 1972); Jim Whitewolf, *Jim Whitewolf: The life of a Kiowa Apache Indian*, ed. Charles S. Brant (New York: Dover, 1969).

25. Vine Deloria, Jr., *God is Red* (New York: Grosset & Dunlop, 1973); N. Scott Momaday, "An American Land Ethic," *Ecostatics: The Sierra Club Handbook for Environmental Activists*, ed. John G. Mitchell and Constance L. Stallings (New York: Trident, 1970), pp. 97–105; Momaday, "Native American Attitudes to the Environment," *Seeing with a Native Eye: Essays on Native American Religion*, ed. Walter Holden Capps (New York: Harper & Row, 1976), pp. 79–85.

26. Daniel Day Williams, "Changing Concepts of Nature," *Earth Might Be Fair: Reflections on Ethics, Religion, and Ecology*, ed. Ian G. Barbour (Englewood Cliffs, N.J.: Prentice-Hall, 1972), pp. 52–58.

27. Lynn White, Jr., "The Historical Roots of Our Ecologic Crisis," *Ecology and Religion in History*, ed. David Spring and Eileen Spring (New York: Harper & Row, 1974),

pp. 15–31; Arnold J. Toynbee, "The Genesis of Pollution," *New York Times*, September 16, 1973; Toynbee, "The Religious Background of the Present Environmental Crisis," *Ecology and Religion in History*, pp. 137–49; Edward B. Fiske, "Christianity Linked to Pollution," *New York Times*, May 1, 1970.

28. Huston Smith, "Tao Now: An Ecological Testament," *Earth Might Be Fair*, pp. 77–81; but see Yi-Fu Tuan, "Discrepancies between Environmental Attitude and Behavior: Examples from Europe and China," *Ecology and Religion in History*, pp. 91–113.

29. Stuart L. Udall, *The Quiet Crisis* (New York: Avon, 1963), pp. 16–21.

30. Joe Holland, *The American Journey: A Theology in the Americas Working Paper* (New York: IDOC/North America, 1976), p. 91.

31. T. C. McLuhan, *Touch the Earth: A Self-Portrait of Indian Existence* (New York: Outerbridge & Dienstfrey, 1972).

32. Cleo Crawford, "The First Ecologists," *Science and Children* 9, 6 (1972):21; Fred Fertig, "Child of Nature. The American Indian as an Ecologist," *Sierra Club Bulletin* 55 (1970):4–7; Albert J. Snow, "The American Indian Knew a Better Way," *The American Biology Teacher* 35, 1 (1973):20–22, 34.

33. Jean Paul Sartre, *Search for a Method*, trans. Hazel E. Barnes (New York: Random House Vintage Books, 1968, originally published in 1960), pp. xvii–xviii. Mason, "Influence of Environment upon Human Industries or Arts," pp. 643–45, 662–63.

34. Henry Nash Smith, *Virgin Land: The American West as Symbol and Myth* (New York: Random House, 1950).

35. Daniel A. Guthrie, "Primitive Man's Relationship to Nature," *BioScience* 21 (July 1971):721–23; N. B. Johnson, "The American Indian as Conservationist," *Chronicles of Oklahoma* 30 (Autumn 1952):33–40; D. R. McDonald, "Food Taboos: A Primitive Environmental Protection Agency," *Anthropos* 72 (1977):734–48; Jack Norton, "To Walk the Earth," *The Indian Historian* 7, 4 (1974):27–30; Frank G. Speck, "Aboriginal Conservators," *Bird Lore* 40 (1938):258–61; Douglas Hillman Strong, "The Indian and the Environment," *The Journal of Environmental Education* 5, 2 (1973):49–51.

36. Richard B. Lee and Irven De Vore, "Problems in the Study of Hunters and Gatherers," *Man the Hunter*, ed. Richard B. Lee and Irven De Vore (Chicago: Aldine, 1968), pp. 5–6.

37. Robert F. Heizer, "Primitive Man as an Ecologic Factor," *Kroeber Anthropological Society Papers* 8 (Fall 1955), p. 15.

38. Otis Tufton Mason, "Traps of the Amerinds —A Study in Psychology and Invention," *American Anthropologist*, n.s., 2, 4 (1900):659; John A. Eddy, "Probing the Mystery of the Medicine Wheels," *National Geographic* 151, 1 (1977):140–46; Boyce Rensberger, "Prehistoric Astronomy Was Pretty Good Science," *New York Times*, February 19, 1978; Ray Williamson, "Native Americans Were Continent's First Astronomers," *Smithsonian* 9, 7 (1977):78–85.

39. Jesse D. Jennings, *Prehistory of North America* (New York: McGraw-Hill, 1974, pp. 129–32; Douglas S. Byers, "The Environment of the Northeast," *Man in Northeastern North America*, ed. Frederick Johnson (Andover, Mass.: Robert S. Peabody Foundation for Archaeology, 1946), pp. 23–27; Willis H. Bell and Edward Castetter, *The Utilization of Mesquite and Screwbean by the Aborigines in the American Southwest* (Albuquerque: University of New Mexico Press, 1937); Willis H. Bell and Edward F. Castetter, *The Utilization of Yucca, Sotol, and Beargrass by the Aborigines in the American Southwest* (Albuquerque: University of New Mexico Press, 1941); Edward F. Castetter, *Uncultivated Native Plants Used as Sources of Food* (Albuquerque: University of New Mexico Press, 1935); Edward F. Castetter and Willis H. Bell, *The Aboriginal Utilization of the Tall Cacti in the American Southwest* (Albuquerque: University of New Mexico Press, 1937); Edward F. Castetter, Willis H. Bell, and Alvin R. Grove, *The Early Utilization and the Distribution of Agave in the American Southwest* (Albuquerque: University of New Mexico Press, 1938);

Edward F. Castetter and M. E. Opler, *The Ethnobiology of the Chiricahua and Mescalero Apache*. A. *The Use of Plants for Foods, Beverages and Narcotics* (Albuquerque: University of New Mexico Press, 1936); Edward F. Castetter and Ruth M. Underhill, *The Ethnobiology of the Papago Indians* (Albuquerque: University of New Mexico Press, 1935). Virgil J. Vogel, *American Indian Medicine* (New York: Ballantine, 1973), pp. 3–4 ff.; Richard Asa Yarnell, *Aboriginal Relationships between Culture and Plant Life in the Upper Great Lakes Region* (Ann Arbor: University of Michigan, 1964).

40. Heizer, "Primitive Man as an Ecologic Factor," p. 15; Edgar Anderson, *Plants, Man and Life* (Boston: Little, Brown, 1952); George F. Carter, *Plant Geography and Culture History in the American Southwest* (New York: Viking Fund, 1945).

41. George W. Beadle, "The Ancestry of Corn," *Scientific American* 242, 1 (January 1980):112–19; Richard S. MacNeish, "The Origins of New World Civilization," *New World Archaeology: Theoretical and Cultural Transformations*, ed. Ezra B. W. Zubrow, Margaret C. Fritz, and John M. Fritz (San Francisco: W. H. Freeman, 1974:155–63; Paul C. Mangelsdorf, *Corn: Its Origin and Improvement* (Cambridge, Mass.: Belknap Press of Harvard University Press, 1974); Paul C. Mangelsdorf, Richard S. MacNeish, and Walton C. Galinart, "Domestication of Corn," *Science* 143, 3606 (1964):538–45; Henry A. Wallace and William L. Brown, *Corn and Its Early Fathers* (n.p.: Michigan State University Press, 1956), pp. 3–43; Paul Weatherwax, *Indian Corn in Old America* (New York: Macmillan, 1954); Allan G. Harper, Andrew R. Cordova, and Kalervo Oberg, *Man and Resources in the Middle Rio Grande Valley* (Albuquerque: University of New Mexico Press, 1943, pp. 28–31, 36, 73.

42. Charles Hartsborne, "The Environmental Results of Technology," *Philosophy & Environmental Crisis*, ed. William T. Blackstone (Athens: University of Georgia Press, 1974), p. 70.

43. Herman Karl Haeberlin, "The Idea of Fertilization in the Culture of the Pueblo Indians," *Memoirs of the American Anthropological Association* 3, 1 (1916):1–55; John Witthoft, *Green Corn Ceremonialism in the Eastern Woodlands* (Ann Arbor: University of Michigan Press, 1949); see also Witthoft Press, *The American Indian as Hunter* (Harrisburg: Pennsylvania Historical and Museum Commission, 1967), for primary hunting integration. W. W. Hill, "Navajo Salt Gathering," *The University of New Mexico Bulletin*, Anthropological Series 3, 4 (1940):5–25; Ruth M. Underhill, "The Salt Pilgrimage," *Teachings from the American Earth*, pp. 42–74. Richard I. Ford, "An Ecological Perspective on the Eastern Pueblos," *New Perspectives on the Pueblos*, ed. Alfonso Ortiz (Albuquerque: University of New Mexico Press, 1972), pp. 1–17; Erna Gunther, "A Further Analysis of the First Salmon Ceremony," *University of Washington Publications in Anthropology* 2, 5 (1928):129–73; Stuart Piddocko, "The Potlatch System of the Southern Kwakiutl: A New Perspective," *Environment and Cultural Behavior*, ed. Andrew P. Vayda (Garden City, N.Y.: Natural History Press, 1969), pp. 130–56; Wayne Suttles, "Coping with Abundance: Subsistence on the Northwest Coast," *Man the Hunter*, pp. 56–68.

44. Ruth M. Underhill, *Ceremonial Patterns in the Greater Southwest*, monographs of the American Ethnological Society, no. 13 (New York: J. J. Augustin, 1948).

45. Ralph T. Coe, *Sacred Circles: Two Thousand Years of North American Indian Art* (Kansas City: Nelson Gallery of Art—Atkins Museum of Fine Arts, 1977), p. 11; Ralph Linton, *Use of Tobacco among North American Indians* (Chicago: Field Museum of Natural History, 1924); George A. West, *Tobacco, Pipes and Smoking Customs of the American Indians*, 2 parts (Milwaukee: Public Museum of the City of Milwaukee, 1934); Peter T. Furst, "To Find Our Life: Peyote among the Huichol Indians of Mexico," *Flesh of the Gods: The Ritual Use of Hallucinogens*, ed. Peter T. Furst (New York: Praeger, 1972), pp. 136–84; Barbara G. Myerhoff, *Peyote Hunt: The Sacred Journey of the Huichol Indians* (Ithaca, N.Y.: Cornell University Press, 1974); Hartley Burr Alexander, *The World's Rim: Great Mysteries of the North American Indians* (Lincoln: University of Nebraska Press, 1953); Joseph Epes

Brown, *The Sacred Pipe* (Norman: University of Oklahoma Press, 1953); See Mircea Eliade, *Patterns in Comparative Religion*, trans. Rosemary Sheed (Cleveland: World, 1970).

46. These are categories formulated by Åke Hultkrantz, the world's foremost scholarly authority on American Indian religious traditions. He has published more than three hundred articles and a half dozen books on Indian religions; his works demand the attention of any serious student of American Indian life. See his "An Ecological Approach to Religion," *Ethnos* 31 (1966):131–50; "Ecology of Religion: Its Scope and Methodology," paper presented at the Annual Meeting of the International Association for the History of Religions, Turku, Finland, 1973; "Religion and Ecology among the Great Basin Indians," *The Realm of the Extra-Human: Ideas and Actions*, ed. Agehananda Bharati (The Hague: Mouton, 1976), pp. 137–50.

47. Robert N. Redfield, "The Primitive World View," *Proceedings of the American Philosophical Society* 96 (1952):30–36.

48. Whalen, "The Nez Perces' Relationship to Their Land," p. 30.

49. Dorothy Lee, "Linguistic Reflection of Wintu Thought," *Teachings from the American Earth*, p. 133; Clara Sue Kidwell, "Science and Ethnoscience," *The Indian Historian* 6, 4 (1973):44.

50. Baron de Lahontan, *New Voyages to North-America*, ed. Reuben Gold Thwaites, 2 vols. (Chicago: A. C. McClurg, 1905; originally published in 1703), p. 446.

51. Alfred Irving Hallowell, "Ojibwa Ontology, Behavior, and World View," *Culture in History: Essays in Honor of Paul Radin*, ed. Stanley Diamond (New York: Columbia University Press, 1960), pp. 19–52.

52. Vecsey, "Traditional Ojibwa Religion and Its Historical Changes," pp. 79–86; Paul Radin, "Religion of the North American Indians," *Anthropology in North America*, Franz Boas et al. (New York: G. E. Stechert, 1919), pp. 283–85.

53. Ruth Fulton Benedict, *The Concept of the Guardian Spirit in North America*, memoirs of the American Anthropological Association, no. 29 (Menasha, Wis.: American Anthropological Association, 1923); Åke Hultkrantz, *Conceptions of the Soul among North American Indians: A Study in Religious Ethnology* (Stockholm: Ethnographical Museum of Sweden, 1953) pp. 497–510; Åke Hultkrantz, "The Masters of the Animals among the Wind River Shoshoni," *Ethnos* 4 (1961):198–218; Åke Hultkrantz, "Attitudes to Animals in Shoshoni Religion," *Studies in Comparative Religion* 4, 2 (1970):70–79, Roland B. Dixon, "Some Aspects of the American Shaman," *Journal of American Folklore* 21 (1908):3.

54. Åke Hultkrantz, "The Owner of the Animals in the Religion of the North American Indians," *The Supernatural Owners of Nature*, ed. Åke Hultkrantz (Stockholm: Almqvist & Wiksell, 1961), pp. 53–64; Åke Hultkrantz, *Les Religions des Indiens Primitifs de l'Amérique: Essai d'une Synthese Typologique et Historique* (Stockholm: Almqvist & Wiksell, 1963), pp. 47–83; Åke Hultkrantz, "The Elusive Totemism," *Ex Orbe Religionum—Studies in the History of Religions*, 22 (1972):218–27.

55. Lucien Lévy-Bruhl, *La Mentalité Primitive* (Paris: Presses universitaires de France, 1960); Géza Róheim, "Primitive Man and Environment," *International Journal of Psycho-Analysis* 2, pt. 2 (1921):157–78.

56. Bronislaw Malinowski, *Magic, Science and Religion* (Garden City, N.Y.: Doubleday, 1954).

57. W. W. Hill, *The Agricultural and Hunting Methods of the Navaho Indians* (New Haven: Yale University Press, 1938), pp. 52–55; George F. Will and George E. Hyde, *Corn among the Indians of the Upper Missouri* (Lincoln: University of Nebraska Press, 1964, originally published in 1917).

58. Kidwell, "Science and Ethnoscience," p. 44.

59. Frances Densmore, "Notes on the Indians' Belief in the Friendliness of Nature," *Southwestern Journal of Anthropology* 4, 1 (1948):94–97; Werner Müller, "North

America," *Pre-Columbian American Religions*, Walter Krickeberg et al., trans. Stanley Davis (New York: Holt, Rinehart, 1969), pp. 180–93; E. G. Squier, *The Serpent Symbol, and the Worship of the Reciprocal Principles of Nature in America* (New York: Putnam, 1851).

60. W. Vernon Kinietz, *Chippewa Village, the Story of Katikitegon* (Bloomfield Hills, Mich.: Cranbook Institute of Science, 1947), p. 161.

61. Hartley Burr Alexander, *The Mythology of All Races*, 10 North American, ed. Louis Herbert Gray (New York: Cooper Square, 1964); John Bierhorst, ed., *The Red Swan: Myths and Tales of the American Indians* (New York: Farrar, Straus, 1976); Daniel G. Brinton, *The Myths of the New World* (New York: Laypoldt & Holt, 1868); Tristram P. Coffin, *Indian Tales of North America: An Anthology for the Adult Reader* (Philadelphia: American Folklore Society, 1961); James Athearn Jones, *Traditions of the North American Indians: Being a Second Revised Edition of "Tales of an Indian Camp,"* 3 vols. (London: Henry Colburn and Richard Beatley, 1830); Alice Marriott and Carol K. Rachlin, *American Indian Mythology* (New York: New American Library, 1972); Lewis Spence, *Myths and Legends of the North American Indians* (Blauvelt, N. Y.: Multimedia, 1975); Stith Thompson, ed., *Tales of the North American Indians* (Bloomington: Indiana University Press, 1968; originally published in 1929).

62. Coe, *Sacred Circles*, pp. 10–14.

63. Émile Durkheim and Marcel Mauss, *Primitive Classification*, trans. and ed. Rodney Needham (Chicago: University of Chicago Press, 1975; originally published in 1903), pp. 3–9, 42–66, 81–88; Claude Lévi-Strauss, *La Pensée Sauvage* (Paris: Plon, 1962), pp. 4–13, 48–86, 120.

64. Róheim, "Primitive Man and Environment," pp. 157–58.

65. Benjamin S. Williams, "Hopi Classification System as Evidenced through Myth and Text" (unpublished paper, Hobart & William Smith Colleges, 1978), pp. 12, 32.

66. Diamond Jenness, *The Ojibwa Indians of Parry Island, Their Social and Religious Life* (Ottawa: J. O. Patenaude, ISO, 1935), p. 21.

67. Ruth M. Underhill, *Red Man's Religion: Beliefs and Practices of the Indians North of Mexico* (Chicago: University of Chicago Press, 1965), p. 40.

68. J. N. B. Hewitt, "Orenda and a Definition of Religion," *American Anthropologist*, n.s., 4, 1 (1902):33–37.

69. Tylor, *Religion in Primitive Culture*, pp. 290–392; Hultkrantz, *Conceptions of the Soul among North American Indians*, pp. 483–97.

70. Pierre de Charlevoix, *Journal of a Voyage to North-America*, 2 vols. (London: R. and J. Dodsley, 1761; originally published in 1744), 2:155.

71. William H. Keating, *Narrative of an Expedition to the Source of St. Peter's River, Lake Winnepeek, Lake of the Woods, &c. &c. Performed in the Year 1823*, 2 vols. (Philadelphia: H. C. Carey & I. Lea, 1824), 1:158–59; Henry Rowe Schoolcraft, *Algic Researches, Comprising Inquiries Respecting the Mental Characteristics of the North American Indians*, 2 vols. (New York: Harper, 1839), 1:42; Henry Rowe Schoolcraft, *Information, Respecting the History, Condition and Prospects of the Indian Tribes of the United States: Collected and Prepared under the Direction of the Bureau of Indian Affairs, per Act of Congress of March 3d, 1847*, 6 vols. (Philadelphia: Lippincott, Grambo & Company, 1853–1857), 3:520.

72. Mary B. Black, "Ojibwa Taxonomy and Percept Ambiguity," *Ethos* 5 (1977):90–118; Alfred Irving Hallowell, "Bear Ceremonialism in the Northern Hemisphere," *American Anthropologist*, n.s., 28, 1 (1926):45–46; Alfred Irving Hallowell, "Some Empirical Aspects of Northern Saulteaux Religion," *American Anthropologist*, n.s., 36, 3 (1934):390–91; Hallowell, "Ojibwa Ontology, Behavior, and World View," pp. 23–26, 38, 43–48.

73. Jenness, *The Ojibwa Indians of Parry Island*, pp. 22–27.

74. Lee, "Linguistic Reflection of Wintu Thought," p. 139.

75. Rosalie Wax and Murray Wax, "The Magical World View," *Journal for the Scientific Study of Religion* 1, 2 (1962):181.

76. June McCormick Collins, "The Mythological Basis for Attitudes toward Animals among Salish-Speaking Indians," *Journal of American Folklore* 65 (1952):353–59; Homer Huntington Kidder, "Ojibwa Myths & Halfbreed Tales Related by Charles and Charlotte Kobawgam and Jacques le Pique 1893–1895," American Philosophical Society Library Archives, 1918, pp.69–70.

77. Regina Flannery, "The Cultural Position of the Spanish River Indians," *Primitive Man* 13, 1 (January, 1940):6–7; Jenness, *The Ojibwa Indians of Parry Island*, pp. 80–81; Louise Phelps Kellogg, ed., *Early Narratives of the Northwest 1634–1699* (New York: Scribner's 1917), p. 112; Chase S. Osborn and Stellanova Osborn, *Schoolcraft — Longfellow — Hiawatha* (Lancaster, Pa.: Jaques Cattell, 1942), p. 57.

78. Joseph B. Casagrande, "Ojibwa Bear Ceremonialism: The Persistence of a Ritual Attitude," *Acculturation in the Americas*, ed. Sol Tax (Chicago: University of Chicago Press, 1952), pp. 113–15; Charlevoix, *Journal of a Voyage to North-America* 1:184; Hallowell, "Bear Ceremonialism in the Northern Hemisphere," pp. 69–73, 135–39, 144–46; Louis Hennepin, *A Description of Louisiana*, trans. John Gilmary Shea (New York: John G. Shea, 1880; originally published in 1683), pp. 333–34; Alexander Henry, *Travels and Adventures in Canada and the Indian Territories between the Years 1760 and 1776* (New York: I. Riley, 1809), pp. 143–45.

79. Andrew J. Blackbird, *History of the Ottawa and Chippewa Indians of Michigan, and Grammar of Their Language* (Ypsilanti, Mich.: Ypsilantian Job Printing, 1887), pp. 103–104; Hallowell, "Bear Ceremonialism in the North Hemisphere," p. 34; Momaday, "Native American Attitudes to the Environment," pp. 80–81; McDonald, "Food Taboos: A Primitive Environmental Protection Agency," pp. 734–48.

80. Raymond D. Fogelson, "Change, Persistence, and Accommodation in Cherokee Medico-Magical Beliefs," *Symposium on Cherokee and Iroquois Culture*, ed. William N. Fenton and John Gulick, Smithsonian Institution, Bureau of American Ethnology Bulletin 180, no. 21, pp. 216 –17 (Washington, D.C.: USGPO, 1961); Dorothy M. Reid, *Tales of Nanabozho* (New York: Henry Z. Walck, 1963), pp. 85–88.

81. Christopher Vecsey, "The Impact of Western Civilization on American Indian Medicine: The Ojibwa Case," paper presented at the Sixth Eastern Regional Conference on the Native American, New Paltz, 1977.

82. Yi-Fu Tuan, "Geopiety: A Theme in Man's Attachment to Nature and to Place," *Geographies of the Mind: Essays in Historical Geosophy in Honor of John Kirtland Wright*, ed. David Lowenthal and Martyn J. Bowden (New York: Oxford University Press, 1976), pp. 11–12.

83. Peter Heinegg, "Apologizing to the Bear: Notes on Ecological Ethics," paper presented at the American Academy of Religion Annual Meeting, New Orleans, 1978. Since completing this chapter I have heard cogent arguments, particularly from Marvin Bram, Rupert Costo, and Charles Ricehill, refuting this concept of environmental guilt. Ricehill, a Lakota, has indicated that his people regard the killing of animals as a natural act, if performed properly, an interpretation supported by other Lakotas with whom I have discussed this matter.

84. Peggy V. Beck and A. L. Walters, *The Sacred: Ways of Knowledge, Sources of Life* (Tsaile, Ariz.: Navajo Community College, 1977), p. 108, following Karl W. Luckert's quirky, but perceptive *The Navajo Hunter Tradition* (Tucson: University of Arizona Press, 1975), p. 134, which I read only after writing this chapter.

85. Sherwood L. Washburn and C. S. Lancaster, "The Evolution of Hunting," *Man the Hunter*, p. 299.

86. Frederick R. Burton, *American Primitive Music with Especial Attention to the Songs of the Ojibways* (New York: Moffat, Yard, 1909), pp. 243–45.

87. Works Progress Administration, "The Legend of the Birch and Maple Trees," in Chippewa Indian Historical Project Records, The State Historical Society of Wisconsin, Manuscripts, 1936–1940, 1942, p. 1; see also Vecsey, "Traditional Ojibwa Religion and Its Historical Changes," pp. 103–105.

88. John Fisher and Christopher Vecsey, "Two Approaches to an Understanding of the Ojibwa Creation Myth," paper presented at the American Academy of Religion Annual Meeting, Chicago, 1975; Vecsey, "Traditional Ojibwa Religion and Its Historical Changes," pp. 105–108.

89. Calvin Martin, *Keepers of the Game: Indian-Animal Relationships and the Fur Trade* (Berkeley: University of California Press, 1978) p. 129.

90. Robert N. Bellah, "Religious Systems," *People of Rimrock: A Study of Values in Five Cultures*, ed. Evon Z. Vogt and Ethel M. Albert (New York: Atheneum, 1970), pp. 229–30.

91. Claude Lévi-Strauss, *Mythologiques* 4 vols. (Paris: Plon, 1964, 1966, 1968, 1971).

92. William James, *The Varieties of Religious Experience; A Study in Human Nature* (New York: New American Library Mentor Books; originally published in 1902), p. 383.

93. Yi-Fu Tuan, *Topophilia: A Study of Environmental Perception, Attitude, and Values* (Englewood Cliffs, N.J.: Prentice-Hall, 1974); Tuan, "Geopiety: A Theme in Man's Attachment to Nature and to Place," pp. 11–39.

94. Mircea Eliade, *The Sacred and the Profane: The Nature of Religion*, trans. Rosemary Sheed (Cleveland: World, 1959), pp. 20–65; Imre Sutton, *Indian Land Tenure: Bibliographical Essays and a Guide to the Literature* (New York: Clearwater, 1975), p. 2.

95. Åke Hultkrantz, "The Indians and the Wonders of Yellowstone. A Study of the Interrelationships of Religion, Nature and Culture," *Ethos* 19 (1954):34–68.

96. Frederick W. Turner III in Virginia Irving Armstrong, ed., *I Have Spoken: American History through the Voices of the Indian* (New York: Pocket Books, 1972), p. xv.

97. Holland, *The American Journey*, p. 23.

98. Udall, *The Quiet Crisis*, p. 21.

99. McLuhan, *Touch the Earth*, p. 53.

100. Ibid., p. 56.

101. Beck and Walters, *The Sacred*, pp. 171–93.

102. American Friends Service Committee, *Uncommon Controversy: Fishing Rights of the Muckleshoot, Puyallup, and Nisqually Indians* (Seattle: University of Washington Press, 1970), p. xxvi.

103. Tuan, "Discrepancies between Environmental Attitude and Behavior: Examples from Europe and China," pp. 91–113.

104. Guthrie, "Primitive Man's Relationship to Nature," pp. 721–23.

105. Grover S. Krantz, "Human Activities and Megafaunal Extinctions," *American Scientist* 58, 2 (1970):164–70; Paul S. Martin and H. E. Wright, Jr., eds., *Pleistocene Extinctions: The Search for a Cause* (New Haven: Yale University Press, 1967); Martin, *Keepers of the Game*, pp. 166–72.

106. Williams, "Hopi Classification System as Evidenced through Myth and Text," p. 40.

107. Martin, *Keepers of the Game*, pp. 8–11. See also George T. Hunt, *The Wars of the Iroquois* (Madison: University of Wisconsin Press, 1940); Eleanor Leacock, *The Montagnais "Hunting Territory" and the Fur Trade*, American Anthropological Association Memoir no. 78 (Menasha, Wis.: American Anthropological Association, 1954), p. 3; E. E. Rich, "Trade Habits and Economic Motivation among the Indians of North America," *Canadian Journal of Economics and Political Science* 26, 1 (1960): 35–53; also Calvin Martin, "The European Impact on the Culture of a Northeastern Algonquian Tribe: An Ecological Interpretation," *William and Mary Quarterly* 31, 1 (1974):2–26.

108. Alfred Crosby, *The Columbian Exchange: Biological and Cultural Consequences of 1492* (Westport, Conn.: Greenwood, 1972), pp. 35–63; William H. McNeill, *Plagues and Peoples* (Garden City, N.Y.: Anchor Press/Doubleday, 1976), pp. 199–216; Vecsey, "Traditional Ojibwa Religion and Its Historical Changes."

109. Rich, "Trade Habits and Economic Motivation among the Indians of North America," pp. 35–53.

110. J. G. Kohl, *Kitchi-Gami: Wanderings Round Lake Superior* (London: Chapman and Hall, 1860), p. 38; Henry, *Travels and Adventures in Canada*, pp. 108, 127–28, 178.

111. Rich, "Trade Habits and Economic Motivation among the Indians of North America," pp. 43, 45, 46.

112. Arthur J. Ray, "Some Conservation Schemes of the Hudson's Bay Company, 1821–50: An Examination of the Problems of Resource Management in the Fur Trade," *Journal of Historical Geography* 1, 1 (1975):49–68; Rich, "Trade Habits and Economic Motivation among the Indians of North America," p. 46; Martin, *Keepers of the Game*, p. 165.

113. Guthrie, "Primitive Man's Relationship to Nature," p. 722.

114. Hu Maxwell, "The Use and Abuse of Forests by the Virginia Indians," *William and Mary Quarterly* 19, 2 (1910):86.

115. Hutchinson, "The Remaking of the Amerind," pp. 18, 20.

116. Rich, "Trade Habits and Economic Motivation among the Indians of North America," p. 46.

117. Frank Gilbert Roe, *The North American Buffalo: A Critical Study of the Species in Its Wild State* (Toronto: University of Toronto Press, 1951), pp. 367–484.

118. Hutchinson, "The Remaking of the Amerind," p. 94.

119. Donald W. Large, "This Land Is Whose Land? Changing Concepts of Land as Property," *Wisconsin Law Review* 1973, 4 (1974):1041–45. See also Beverly P. Smaby, "The Mormons and the Indians. Conflicting Ecological Systems in the Great Basin," *American Studies* 16, 1 (Spring 1975):35–36.

120. McLuhan, *Touch the Earth*, p. 15.

121. Michael Paul Rogin, *Fathers and Children: Andrew Jackson and the Subjugation of the American Indian* (New York: Random House Vintage Books, 1976), p. 6.

122. Roderick Nash, *Wilderness and the American Mind* (New Haven: Yale University Press, 1978), pp. 1–43; Peter N. Carroll, *Puritanism and the Wilderness: The Intellectual Significance of the New England Frontier 1629–1700* (New York: Columbia University Press, 1969), pp. 2–3, 8–10; Hans Huth, *Nature and the American: Three Centuries of Changing Attitudes* (Lincoln: University of Nebraska Press, 1972), pp. 2, 4–10.

123. See Fernand Braudel, *The Mediterranean and the Mediterranean World in the Age of Philip II*, trans. Sian Reynolds, 2 vols. (New York: Harper & Row, 1972); Fernand Braudel, *Capitalism and Material Life 1400–1800*, trans. Miriam Kochan (New York: Harper & Row, 1973); Herbert Marcuse, *One-Dimensional Man: Studies in the Ideology of Advanced Industrial Society* (Boston: Beacon, 1966), pp. 94–95; Alexander Spoehr, "Cultural Differences in the Interpretation of Natural Resources," *Man's Role in Changing the Face of the Earth*, p. 93.

124. Rogin, *Fathers and Children*, pp. 78–79; Carroll, *Puritanism and the Wilderness*, pp. 114–26; Leo Marx, *The Machine in the Garden: Technology and the Pastoral Ideal in America* (New York: Oxford University Press, 1972); Charles L. Sanford, *The Quest for Paradise: Europe and the American Moral Imagination* (Urbana: University of Illinois Press, 1961), p. viii.

125. Tuan, "Geopiety: A Theme in Man's Attachment to Nature and to Place," p. 29.

126. Rogin, *Fathers and Children*, p. 103.

127. René Dubos, "Franciscan Conservation versus Benedictine Steward

ship," *Ecology and Religion in History*, pp. 114–36; Roger L. Shinn, "Science and Ethical Decision: Some New Issues," *Earth Might Be Fair*, pp. 142–45.

128. M.-D. Chenu, *Nature, Man, and Society in the Twelfth Century*, ed. and trans. Jerome Taylor and Lester K. Little (Chicago: University of Chicago Press, 1968), pp. 1–48; Paul Piehler, *The Visionary Landscape: A Study in Medieval Allegory* (Montreal: McGill-Queen's University Press, 1971), pp. 7, 75; see Arthur O. Lovejoy, *The Great Chain of Being: A Study of the History of an Idea* (Cambridge, Mass.: Harvard University Press, 1976).

129. Peter Singer, *Animal Liberation* (New York: Avon, 1975), pp. 201–203.

130. See an interesting work, Carolyn Merchant, *The Death of Nature: Women, Ecology, and the Scientific Revolution* (San Francisco: Harper & Row, 1980), published after this chapter was written.

131. John Passmore, *Man's Responsibility for Nature: Ecological Problems and Western Traditions* (New York: Scribner's, 1974), pp. 18–21; Singer, *Animal Liberation*, pp. 9–10.

132. Karl Marx, "Economic and Philosophic Manuscripts of 1844," *The Marx-Engels Reader*, ed. Robert C. Tucker (New York: Norton, 1972), p. 61. See also *Marx and Engels on Ecology*, ed. and comp. Howard L. Parsons (Westport, Conn.: Greenwood Press, 1977).

133. Karl Marx, "Economic and Philosophic Manuscripts of 1844," *The Marx-Engels Reader*, ed. Robert C. Tucker (New York: Norton, 1972), pp. 52–103.

134. E.g., Braudel, *The Mediterranean*; Claude Lévi-Strauss, *Structural Anthropology*, trans. Claire Jacobson and Brooke Grundfest Schoepf (New York: Basic Books, 1963).

135. Sheehan, "Paradise and the Noble Savage in Jeffersonian Thought," pp. 330–36.

136. Peter J. Schmitt, *Back to Nature: The Arcadian Myth in Urban America* (New York: Oxford University Press, 1969).

137. Aldo Leopold, *A Sand County Almanac and Sketches Here and There* (New York: Oxford University Press, 1949).

138. S. P. Hays, *Conservation and the Gospel of Efficiency* (Cambridge, Mass.: Harvard University Press, 1959); Eugene P. Odun, "Environmental Ethic and the Attitude Revolution," *Philosophy & Environmental Crisis*, pp. 13–14.

139. Sigmund Freud, *Civilization and Its Discontents*, trans. James Strachey (New York: Norton, 1961; originally published in 1930), p. 39.

140. Thomas Sieger Derr, *Ecology and Human Need* (Philadelphia: Westminster, 1975), p. 75.

141. Kenneth Clark, "Animals and Men: Love, Admiration and Outright War," *Smithsonian* 8,6 (1977):53–61.

142. Martin Buber, *I and Thou*, trans. Ronald Gregor Smith (New York: Schribner's, 1958; originally published in 1923), for example.

143. Patrician Curtis, "New Debate over Experimenting with Animals," *New York Times Magazine*, December 31, 1978, pp. 18–23; Singer, *Animal Liberation*, pp. 27–162.

144. Marcuse, *One-Dimensional Man*, p. 158. See Marcuse's use of Carl Friedrich von Weizsäcker, *The History of Nature*, trans. Fred D. Wieck (Chicago, University of Chicago Press, 1949).

145. See Paulo Freire, *Pedagogy of the Oppressed*, trans. Myra Bergman Ramos (New York: Seabury, 1968), p. 45.

146. Lewis Hanke, *Aristotle and the American Indians: A Study of Race Prejudice in the Modern World* (Bloomington: Indiana University Press, 1970), p. 17.

147. Nash, *Wilderness and the American Mind*, p. 7; Carroll, *Puritanism and the Wilderness*, pp. 10–12.

148. Roe, *The North American Buffalo*, pp. 367–515, 804–816.

Chapter 2—SUBARCTIC INDIANS AND WILDLIFE

1. Frederica de Laguna, "The Atna of the Copper River, Alaska: The World of Man and Animals," *Folk* (Dansk Etnografisk Tidsskrift) 11/12 (1969/1970):19; Robert J. Sullivan, S. J., *The Ten'a Food Quest*, Anthropological Series, no. 11 (Washington, D.C.: Catholic University of America Press, 1942), p. 97; James W. VanStone, *Athapaskan Adaptations: Hunters and Fishermen of the Subarctic Forests* (Chicago: Aldine, 1974), p. 61; Frank G. Speck, *Naskapi: The Savage Hunters of the Labrador Peninsula* (Norman, Okla.: University of Oklahoma Press, 1935), p. 76.

2. Speck, *Naskapi*, p. 55.

3. See, for example, A. Irving Hallowell, "Ojibwa World View and Disease," *Man's Image in Medicine and Anthropology*, ed. Iago Galdston, monograph 4 of the Institute of Social and Historical Medicine, New York Academy of Medicine (New York: International Universities Press, 1963), pp. 271–72.

4. de Laguna, "The Atna of the Copper River, Alaska," p. 19.

5. Rosalie Wax and Murray Wax, "The Magical World View," *Journal for the Scientific Study of Religion* 1 (Spring 1962):181; Diamond Jenness, *The Ojibwa Indians of Parry Island: Their Social and Religious Life*, National Museum of Canada Bulletin no. 78, Anthropological Series, no. 17 (Ottawa: Department of Mines, 1935), pp. 18–20; Julius E. Lips, "Notes on Montagnais-Naskapi Economy," *Ethnos* 12 (January-June 1947):6; Alanson Buck Skinner, "Notes on the Eastern Cree and Northern Saulteaux," *Anthropological Papers of the American Museum of Natural History* 9, pt. 1 (1911):73, 76; Ruth Landes, *Ojibwa Religion and the Midewiwin* (Madison: University of Wisconsin Press, 1968), p. 27.

6. Selwyn Dewdney, *The Sacred Scrolls of the Southern Ojibway* (Toronto: University of Toronto Press for the Glenbow-Alberta Institute, 1975), p. 37; de Laguna, "The Atna of the Copper River, Alaska," pp. 22, 26.

7. Dewdney, *Sacred Scrolls*, p. 37.

8. Sullivan, *Ten'a Food Quest*, pp. 75, 79, 121; David Merrill Smith, *Inkonze: Magico-Religious Beliefs of Contact-Traditional Chipewyan Trading at Fort Resolution, NWT, Canada*, Ethnology Division paper no. 6, Mercury Series (Ottawa: National Museum of Man, 1973), pp. 12, 20.

9. A. Irving Hallowell, *Culture and Experience* (Philadelphia: University of Pennsylvania Press, 1955), p. 361; A. Irving Hallowell, "Ojibwa Ontology, Behavior, and World View," *Culture in History: Essays in Honor of Paul Radin*, ed. Stanley Diamond (New York: Columbia University Press, 1960), pp. 45–47; Hallowell, "Ojibwa World View and Disease," pp. 273–74, 283; Speck, *Naskapi*, pp. 48, 41, 22–23.

10. Speck, *Naskapi*, pp. 20, 139.

11. Ibid., pp. 112–13.

12. Adrian Tanner, "Bringing Home Animals: Religious Ideology and Mode of Production of the Mistassini Cree Hunters" (Ph.D. diss., University of Toronto, 1976), pp. 246, 265–66, 272, 343; Lips, "Notes on Montagnais-Naskapi Economy," pp. 5–6; de Laguna, "The Atna of the Copper River, Alaska," p. 18; Smith, *Inkonze*, p. 12; VanStone, *Athapaskan Adaptations*, p. 59; Calvin Martin, *Keepers of the Game: Indian-Animal Relationships and the Fur Trade* (Berkeley and Los Angeles: University of California Press, 1978).

13. Tanner, "Bringing Home Animals," pp. 110, 192, 248, 250, 316, 335–38, 370.

14. Ibid., pp. 230–31.

15. de Laguna, "The Atna of the Copper River, Alaska," pp. 20–21; Sullivan, *Ten'a Food Quest*, p. 123; Tanner, "Bringing Home Animals," pp. 154, 275–76, 319.

16. Speck, *Naskapi*, pp. 91–93, 112, 122–23; Tanner, "Bringing Home Animals," pp. 118–19, 230–31, 295–97, 306–307, 313–14, 324–25; Jenness, *Ojibwa Indians*, pp. 23–25.

17. Robin Ridington, "Beaver Dreaming and Singing," *Pilot Not Commander:*

Essays in Memory of Diamond Jenness, ed. Pat and Jim Lotz, *Anthropologica,* special issue, n.s., 13, 1–2 (1971):124–25.

18. Landes, *Ojibwa Religion,* p. 7; Ridington, "Beaver Dreaming and Singing," pp. 120–21; Tanner, "Bringing Home Animals," pp. 20, 110–11, 118–19, 142, 187, 204, 295, 307–308.

19. Hallowell, *Culture and Experience,* pp. 295–96, 299; Waldemar Bogoras, "Ideas of Space and Time in the Conception of Primitive Religion," *American Anthropologist,* n.s., 27 (April 1925):208–209.

20. Robert E. Ritzenthaler, "Chippewa Preoccupation with Health: Change in a Traditional Attitude Resulting from Modern Health Problems," *Bulletin of the Public Museum of the City of Milwaukee* 19 (December 1953):243; Hallowell, *Culture and Experience,* p. 268; Hallowell, "Ojibwa World View and Disease," p. 286; de Laguna, "The Atna of the Copper River, Alaska," pp. 23–24; Smith, *Inkonze,* p. 12.

21. Speck, *Naskapi,* p. 80; Tanner, "Bringing Home Animals," p. 39.

22. Speck, *Naskapi,* pp. 80–81.

23. Tanner, "Bringing Home Animals," pp. 125–26, 287–88, 319, 320–21, 324–25; Sullivan, *Ten'a Food Quest,* pp. 87–88.

24. Ridington, "Beaver Dreaming and Singing," pp. 122–24.

25. For a fuller discussion see Martin, *Keepers of the Game.*

Chapter 3—INDIANS AS ECOLOGISTS

1. Charles A. Lindbergh's perspectives on American environmental change within his lifetime are, in many respects, representative of many other concerned observers in past decades. Lindberg, his wife said in an interview, "flew over the country a great deal and was . . . terrified and horrified by the way civilization and big cities had spread over what was country before. . . . He just felt we were losing our country and our land and . . . the beauty of the land." Anne Morrow Lindbergh, "Conversations with Eric Sevaried," Los Angeles TV, Channel 2, May 27, 1977. John Schutz, Alexander DeConde, Roderick Nash, Calvin Martin, Lynn Donovan, and Robert Brunkow have read and improved this paper with their suggestions.

2. See Alfred W. Crosby's excellent, pathbreaking volume, *The Columbian Exchange: Biological and Cultural Consequences of 1492* (Westport, Conn.: Greenwood, 1972), especially his chapters on "Conquistador y Pestilencia" and "Old World Plants and Animals in the New World," pp. 35–121, and his bibliography covering a wide range of interdisciplinary data, pp. 222–60. This should be supplemented by the data and bibliographical notes in traditional Spanish sources in the article, "Antilles," *Enciclopedia Universal Illustrada Europeo-Americana* (Barcelona, 1905), 5:776–78. Henry F. Dobyns' unpublished paper, "Major Dynamics of the Historic Demography of Indo-Americans," presented at the April 1977 meeting of the Organization of American Historians, Atlanta, Georgia (copy in my possession), discusses the transmissions of pathogens evolved in the Old World as part of the Columbian exchange that caused a biological catastrophe among native people of the New World. This involved, Dobyns argues, the operation of William H. McNeill's "law of biological aggression" in which conquering societies transmitted their "domesticated" diseases to previously independent, isolated peoples, killing off key leaders and warriors in newly contacted societies. See also William H. McNeill, *Plagues and Peoples* (New York: Anchor Press/Doubleday, 1976), p. 55.

3. In his introductory address, "The Agency of Man on the Earth," Carol O. Sauer, opening a European environmental studies congress honoring George Perkins

Marsh, suggested several very useful definitions of environmental history. Sauer's address can be found in William L. Thomas, ed., *Man's Role in Changing the Face of the Earth* 2 vols., (Chicago: University of Chicago Press, 1956), 1:49–69.

4. Columbus' comments (on the first voyage) make his journal more than a seaman's logbook, as Samuel E. Morison has argued the preface, Samuel E. Morison, trans. and ed., *Journals and Other Documents on the Life and Voyages of Christopher Columbus*, (New York: Heritage, 1963), p. 42. The journal gives data on flora and fauna, Indians, and geography as well as information on the first contacts. In addition to observing the "very green trees, many streams, and fruits of different kinds," Columbus at once thought of enslaving these Indians, who, he wrote, "ought to be good servants." See pp. 64–65, for his comments of October 12, 1492. In his remarks of December 21, 1492, he is more explicit, stating that the Indians would "obey without opposition," pp. 128–30.

5. The best account of the destruction of the Bahamas and other Caribbean islands is Bartolomé de las Casas, *Brevíssima relacion de la destructión de las Indias* (Sevilla, 1552). This work translated by J[ohn] P[hilips] was printed in England under the title, *Tears of the Indians, Being An Historical and True Account of the Cruel Massacres and Slaughters of above Twenty Millions of Innocent People: Committed by the Spaniards in the Islands of Hispaniola, Cuba, Jamaica, & C., as also in the Continent of Mexico, Peru, & Other Places of the West-Indies, to the Total Destruction of Those Countries. Written in Spanish by Casaus, an Eye-Witness of Those Things—And Made English by J.P.* (London, 1656). This work has been made available in a facsimile printing from an original in the Huntington Library by Academic Reprints, P. O. Box 3003, Stanford, Calif. For specific references to the environmental impact of the Spaniards on the islands, see Philips, *Tears of the Indians*, pp. 1–26.

6. Philips, *Tears of the Indians*, p. 3. For a critical discussion of the impact of Las Casas' writings in helping to create a Black Legend of Spanish cruelty, see Philip Wayne Powell, *Tree of Hate: Propaganda and Prejudices Affecting United States Relations with the Hispanic World* (New York: Basic, 1971), pp. 30–36.

7. The reliability of Las Casas's estimates of Indian depopulation is also strengthened by the writings of Gonzalo Fernández Oviedo y Valdéz in his *Historia General y Natural de las Indias* (Madrid, Ediciones Atlas, 1959), 1:66–67, where Oviedo, one of the earliest historians of the Americas, states that of the million Indians on Santo Domingo, there "are not now believed to be at the present time in this year of 1548 five hundred persons, children and adults, who are natives and are the progeny or lineage of those first," in Crosby, *The Columbian Exchange*, p. 45. The key publication in the new Indian demography studies in Henry F. Dobyns, "Estimating Aboriginal American Population: An Appraisal of Techniques with a New Hemispheric Estimate," *Current Anthropology* 7 (1966):396–415. For further analysis of the new population estimates, see Wilbur R. Jacobs, "The Tip of the Iceberg: Pre-Columbian Indian Demography and Some Implications for Revisionism," *William and Mary Quarterly* 31 (1974):123–32; Francis Jennings, *The Invasion of America: Indians, Colonialism, and the Cant of Conquest* (Chapel Hill: University of North Carolina Press, 1975), pp. 16–31.

8. Las Casas judged the native population of Hispaniola to be three or four million, but Sherburne F. Cook and Woodrow Borah, in their *Essays in Population History: Mexico and the Caribbean* (Berkeley: University of California Press, 1972), 1:407, argue that the island's population was eight million and that the people of Hispaniola had perfected the production of food plants (maize, beans, cassava) to the extent that their fields had a greater yield per hectare than comparable fields harvested in Europe in 1492. This, along with protein from hunting and fishing, was, according to Cook and Borah, more than enough to feed eight million people. Carl Sauer, in *The Early Spanish Main* (Berkeley: University of California Press, 1966), p. 68, gives evidence to support Cook and Borah by pointing to the value of Yuca, or cassava bread, a a great staple among the Indians of the

Caribbean. According to Las Casas, who had been a commercial farmer, "twenty persons working six hours a day for one month will make a planting of such conucso that will provide bread for three hundred persons for two years." Sauer cites Las Casas, *Apologética Historia*, chap. 20, an unfinished work, probably written in the 1560s. For a complete list of Las Casas' writings, published and unpublished, much of which bears on Indian demography and early environmental history, see *Enciclopedia Universal Illustrada Europeo-Americana*, 29:913.

9. See Dobyns, "Estimating Aboriginal American Population," pp. 410–12; Dobyns, *Native American Historical Demography: A Critical Bibliography* (Bloomington: Indiana University Press, 1976), pp. 21–34.

10. The most vociferous of these is Angel Rosenblat, whose conservative estimates of aboriginal population rest on the earlier figures of James Mooney and A. L. Kroeber. For a discussion of Rosenblat's arguments, see Jacobs, "The Tip of the Iceberg," pp. 124–27.

11. For a discussion of Indian ecology (and significant ethnohistorical literature on the subject), see Calvin L. Martin's case study of the impact of Europeans on a northeastern American tribe: "The European Impact on the Culture of a Northeastern Algonquian Tribe: An Ecological Interpretation," *William and Mary Quarterly* 31 (1974):3–26.

12. See Conrad E. Heidenreich, "The Geography of Huronia in the First Half of the Seventeenth Century" (Ph.D. diss., McMaster University, 1970), pp.267–73, which contains a discussion of Iroquoian agricultural technology.

13. Victor Shelford, *The Ecology of North America* (Urbana: University of Illinois Press, 1963), pp. 1–3, 17–18, 23–24 ff.

14. Vine Deloria, Jr., *We Talk, You Listen: New Tribes, New Turf* (New York: Macmillan, 1970), p. 189.

15. Fairfield Osborn, *Our Plundered Planet* (Boston: Little, Brown, 1948), p. 64.

16. James C. Malin, *The Grassland of North America: Prolegomena to Its History* (Lawrence: University of Kansas Press, 1956), pp. 62 ff., 120–55; James C. Malin, *Winter Wheat in the Golden Belt of Kansas: A Study in Adaption to Subhumid Geographical Environment* (Lawrence: University of Kansas Press, 1944), pp. 34, 80–82, 84; James C. Malin, *Grassland Historical Studies: Natural Resources Utilization in a Background of Science and Technology* (Lawrence: University of Kansas Press, 1950), pp. 60 ff.

17. Malin's interest in environmental studies can be traced through his early books: *Indian Policy and Westward Expansion* (Lawrence: University of Kansas Press, 1921), a work that shows an awareness of Indian life styles and the impact that white advance had on Indian culture (see, for instance, pp. 7–85 ff.); and *The United States, 1865–1917: An Interpretation* (Lawrence: University of Kansas Press, 1924) which attacked wealthy, privileged interests (see p. 21). See also the personal copy of this volume owned by Frederick J. Turner, Huntington Library Rare Book No. 246464, with Turner's marginalia dealing with geographical expansionist themes (pp. 19, 21, 61). In Malin's *On the Nature of History: Essays about History and Dissidence* (Lawrence: University of Kansas Press, [1952]), written in the later part of his life, Malin attacked Frederick Jackson Turner and Walter Prescott Webb for their geographic space expansionism theories which tended to ignore the subtle relationships between ecology and history (see pp. 107 ff. where Malin cites his own articles on ecology in *Scientific Monthly* of 1950 and 1952 which had been ignored by historians). In one of his most provocative grassland ecology essays, Malin argued that heavy grassland duststorms were commonplace before the coming of the white man. Malin, "The Grassland of North America: Its Occupance and the Challenge of New Appraisals," in Thomas, *Man's Role in Changing the Face of the Earth*, 1:354–56.

18. Robert Beverly, *The History and Present State of Virginia*, ed. Louis B. Wright (Chapel Hill: University of North Carolina Press, 1947), p. 319. See also pp. 44, 49, 318, for above quotations.

19. Washington is cited in A. F. Gustafson et al., *Conservation in the United States* (Ithaca, N.Y.: Cornell University Press, 1961), p.109. See also John C. Fitzpatrick, ed., *Writings of George Washington* (Washington, D.C.: USGPO, 1931–44) for discussions of erosion and ditching, especially, 30:238; 36:240.

20. Patrick Henry is quoted in Gustafson, *Conservation*, p. 109.

21. See, for example, ibid., pp. 101–195; Eugene P. Odum, *Fundamentals of Ecology*, 3rd ed., (Philadelphia: Saunders, 1971), pp. 24 ff; Avery Odelle Craven, *Soil Exhaustion as a Factor in the Agricultural History of Virginia and Maryland, 1606–1680* (Urbana: University of Illinois Press, 1926), pp. 163 ff. On p. 163 are F. J. Turner's annotations (Huntington Library Rare Book 183897). Here Turner has marked Craven's point that one-crop agriculture which caused depletion of soil was "typical" of "all frontiers."

22. Julian Ursyn Niemcewicz, *Under their Vine and Fig Tree: Travels through America in 1797–1799, 1805 with Some Further Account of Life in New Jersey*, trans. and ed. Metchie J. Budka (Elizabeth, N.J.: Grassman, 1965), p. 230, cited in Curtis Solberg, "As Others Saw Us: Travelers in America during the Age of the American Revolution" (Ph.D. diss., University of California, Santa Barbara, 1963), p. 158.

23. William Priest, *Travels in the United States of America, Commencing in the Year 1793 and Ending in 1797, with the Author's Journals of His Two Voyages across the Atlantic* (London: printed for J. Johnson, 1802), p. 11, cited in Solberg, "As Others Saw Us," p. 157.

24. Cadwallader Colden, *The History of the Five Nations of Canada*, 2 vols. (New York: New Amsterdam, 1902), 1:69, 72, 166; W. R. Jacobs, *Dispossessing the American Indian* (New York: Scribner's, 1972), p. 10, 182.

25. These locations are not publicized because of the danger of renewed hunting and trapping. However, beaver families have been successfully relocated from areas in the Far West to rural parts of Arkansas, according to Arkansas state government reports.

26. I have traveled extensively through almost all of rural New England, including the northern woods of Maine. The great pine softwood forests disappeared long ago, sacrificed for housebuilding, shipbuilding, and other uses. Only a small part of the larger hardwood forests remain, and very recently a part of New England's woodlands have fallen to attacks by pests on birch and elms. In colonial times the extraordinary population invasion of settlers into New England resulted in the wars of conquest against the Indians and rapid occupation of inland areas, particularly river valleys. This phenomenon led go dispossession of Indians, destruction of wildlife, and the rapid depletion of the fragile topsoil cover in large parts of New England by the late 1700s. I have observed many stone fences marking out abandoned fields and pastures dating back to the eighteenth century. Although Indian farmers seem to have maintained the ecological balance in New England, the invasion of settlers who carelessly used the land and introduced herding—Indians had no domestic animals requiring pasture—began a sweeping ecological change. See also Jennings, *The Invasion of America*, pp. 19–20, 61–69, 146 ff., 202 ff.; and Calvin L. Martin, "Keepers of the Game: The Ecological Issue of Indian-White Relations" (Ph.D. diss., University of California, Santa Barbara, 1974), pp. 150–90.

27. A comment often made by the late John D. Hicks in his American history lectures at the University of California, Berkeley.

28. Robert Brunkow, "Environmental and Social Control in Colonial Rhode Island" (Ph.D. diss., University of California, Santa Barbara, 1978).

29. Ibid.

30. Jeremy Belknap, *The History of New Hampshire* (Boston: for the author, 1792), 3:333–34.

31. Thomas Jefferson, *Notes on the State of Virginia*, ed. William Peden (Chapel

Hill: University of North Carolina Press, 1955) pp. 53 ff., 82 ff.; Clarence J. Glacken, *Traces on the Rhodian Shore* (Berkeley: University of California Press, 1967), pp. 681–82; Jacobs, *Dispossessing the American Indian*, p. 158.

32. Jefferson, *Notes on the State of Virginia*, p. 83. Jefferson, however, did have reservations about the possible "spirit, warp, and bias" of foreign immigrants. See also quotations from Jefferson in Albert K. Weinberg, *Manifest Destiny* (Chicago: University of Chicago Press, 1963), pp. 120–21.

33. Henry R. Schoolcraft, *A View of the Lead Mines of Missouri* (New York: Charles Wiley, 1819, reprinted by the Arno Press, New York, 1972, facsimile edition), pp. 64–67, 249–50.

34. David Dale Owen, *Report of a Geological Survey of Wisconsin, Iowa, and Minnesota and Incidentally of a Portion of Nebraska Territory* (Philadelphia: Lippincott, Grambo, 1852), pp. 148–50.

35. Ibid.

36. Richard A. Bartlett, *Great Surveys of the American West* (Norman: University of Oklahoma Press, 1962), pp. 141 ff.; William H. Goetzmann, *Exploration and Empire* (New York: Knopf, 1966), pp. 327 ff., 430 ff., 478 ff. Goetzmann has an excellent descriptive account of the King, Hayden, and Wheeler surveys. I have made a preliminary examination of the huge mass of data left by these explorers and intend to probe further for information about environmental change.

37. Historiographical controversies concerning the "myth" of the "great American desert" are discussed in Ray A. Billington's excellent bibliographical commentary in Billington, *Westward Expansion, A History of the American Frontier*, 4th ed., (New York: Macmillan, 1974), p. 743. See also W. Eugene Hollon, *Lost Pathfinder: Zebulon Pike* (Norman: University of Oklahoma Press, 1949).

38. John Wesley Powell, *Report on the Lands of the Arid Region of the United States, with a More Detailed Account of the Lands of Utah*, ed. Wallace Stegner (Cambridge: Belknap Press of Harvard University Press, 1962).

39. Ibid., 32.

40. One of the popularizers of this kind of thinking, Powell complained, was a Professor Cyrus Thomas who served with the Hayden Survey and later with the Bureau of American Ethnology. Thomas went so far as to argue that farms, mines, towns, and roads led to increased moisture in arid regions: "that is, as the population increases the moisture will increase." Quoted in Powell in Arid Region, p. 85. Powell's persistent attempts to get his views before competent audiences are revealed in his correspondence, as for instance, in a letter written in the summer of 1878 (undated) to Professor O. C. Marsh of Yale (Marsh Papers, box 26, Sterling Memorial Library, Yale University), enclosing copies of his *Report on . . . the Arid Region* and requesting that his correspondent distribute copies to members of National Academy of Sciences. He hoped that he would be asked to appear before academy members and to deliver a "statement" providing a "clearer understanding" of the "physical character" of the arid country.

41. George Perkins Marsh, *Man and Nature, or Physical Geography as Modified by Human Action*, ed. David Lowenthal (Cambridge: Belknap Press of Harvard University Press, 1965), p. xvii.

42. Ibid., pp. 18–20, 33 ff., 259–60, 304–306, 311–25, 413–14, 447–53.

43. Ibid., p. 661. Among Marsh's many areas of investigation in connection with man's abuse of the land was the origin of national character and whether or not it was "influenced by physical causes." G. P. Marsh, letter, June 19, 1847, box 26, Marsh Papers.

44. Stuart Udall, *The Quiet Crisis* (New York: Avon, 1963), p. 82.

45. For an excellent analysis of Marsh's *Man and Nature*, see David Lowenthal, *George Perkins Marsh, Versatile Vermonter* (New York: Columbia University Press, 1958),

pp. 246–76. For further comment on Marsh's conservationist views and their impact upon the thinking of geographers, see Lowenthal, "George Perkins Marsh and the American Geographical Tradition," *Geographical Review* 42 (1953):207–213. For an appraisal of Marsh's role in awakening the public to urban sprawl and its environmental impact, see Lewis Mumford, "The Natural History of Urbanization," in Thomas, *Man's Role in Changing the Face of the Earth*, 1:388–89.

46. Walker's career is traced in an older and almost worshipful but essentially accurate biography by James Phinney Munroe, *A Life of Francis Amasa Walker* (New York: Holt, 1923); many of Walker's ideas on economic growth are set forth in Walker, *Discussion in Economics*, intro. Joseph Dorfman, 2 vols. (New York: A. M. Kelley, 1971). This work was first published in 1889.

47. "I must deem any man very shallow in his observation of the facts of life," Walker wrote, ". . . who fails to discern in competition the force to which it is mainly due that mankind have risen from stage to stage, in intellectual, moral, and physical power." Walker, "Mr. Bellamy and the New Nationalist Party," *Atlantic Monthly* 45 (1890):248.

48. For the above quotations, see a clipping (heavily annotated by F. J. Turner) of a Phi Beta Kappa address by Walker given on June 19, 1889, Frederick Jackson Turner Papers, File Drawer 15, Huntington Library. See also Turner's reference to Walker's statements about the census of 1890 in W. R. Jacobs, ed. *Frederick Jackson Turner's Legacy* (San Marino, Calif.: Huntington Library, 1965), p. 84.

49. Ibid., p. 19.

50. This argument is expanded in W. R. Jacobs, "Frontiersmen, Fur Traders, and Other Varmints: An Ecological Appraisal of the Frontier in American History," *American Historical Association Newsletter* 7 (1970):5–11.

51. Turner's Papers (in the Huntington Library) for the late 1920s and early 1930s show his great concern for the need to conserve nonrenewable resources through such population control measures as family planning. He reluctantly concluded that educated, middle-class, white families (members of his own class) would be the first to limit sizes of their families, but he believed the program should nevertheless be tested to see if wider population limitations could be obtained.

52. Joseph Dorfman, *Thorstein Veblen and His America* (New York: Viking, 1940), pp. 5–10.

53. These ideas are set forth in a number of Veblen's books and articles, but especially pinpointed in one of his last publications *Absentee Ownership and Business Enterprise in Recent Times: The Case of America* (New York: B. W. Huebsch, 1923), pp. 168–69. Veblen's concepts on general "land grabbing" are stated at more length the section, "The New Gold," pp. 165–86.

54. Ibid., pp. 168–69.

55. Ibid. John Kenneth Galbraith, in analyzing the impact of Thorstein Veblen's writings upon himself and others, concluded that Veblen was "the greatest voice from the frontier world of America," in Galbraith, *The Affluent Society* (Boston: Houghton Mifflin, 1969), p. 52. When Galbraith was president and program chairman of the American Economic Association, he arranged a program which reflected his own social concerns as well as those of younger, revisionist economists. The papers, in one sense, were reminiscent of chapter headings in Veblen's books and dealt with such subjects as "poor and rich," "contradictions of capitalism," "the women's place" (Veblen wrote at length on women's roles), "arts in the affluent society," and "the economics of full racial equality." See "Papers and Proceedings of the Eighty-fourth Annual Meeting of the American Economic Association," *American Economic Review* 42 (May 1971):ii–v.

56. John Muir, *The Story of My Boyhood* (Boston: Houghton Mifflin, 1913), pp. 168–69.

57. Muir's voluminous unpublished correspondence at the Huntington Li-

brary shows him to be one of the most energetic and widely traveled naturalists of his time. Moreover, though self-taught he easily communicated with professional scholars and scientists of his day in several areas of knowledge (geology, botany, history) where he was extraordinarily competent. This range of professional skills is also illustrated in the remarkable variety of Muir's publications. See "A Bibliography of John Muir," comp. Jennie Elliot Doran, *Sierra Club Bulletin* 10 (1916):41–59.

58. Muir is quoted in Roderick Nash, *Wilderness and the American Mind* (New Haven: Yale University Press, 1969), p. 130.

59. Muir, *Our National Parks* (1901; Boston: Houghton Mifflin, 1909), pp. 7 ff. Muir in the early 1900s was also concerned about the persistent war against wildlife in America by the human population. Writing to Henry Fairfield Osborn on July 16, 1906, he expressed concern about "the extinction" of animals. "I have written on the subject," he said, "but mostly with no effect. The murder business and sport by saint and sinner alike has been pushed ruthlessly, merrily on until at last protective measures are being called for, partly, I suppose, because the pleasure of killing is in danger of being lost from there being little or nothing left to kill, and partly, let us hope, from a dim glimmering recognition of the rights of animals and kinship to ourselves." William Frederick Badé, *The Life and Letters of John Muir*, 2 vols. (Boston: Houghton Mifflin, 1924), 2:350.

60. Bernard DeVoto, *The Easy Chair* (Boston: Houghton Mifflin, 1955), pp. 231–55; DeVoto, "The West: A Plundered Province," *Harper's* 149 (August, 1934):355–64; Gene M. Gressley, *The Twentieth-Century American West: A Potpourri* (Columbia: University of Missouri Press, 1977), pp. 39–40. See also Robert Edson Lee, "The Easy Chair Essays of Bernard DeVoto: A Finding List," *Bulletin of Bibliography* 23 (Sept.-Dec. 1960):64–69, which identifies all of DeVoto's Easy Chair essays.

61. DeVoto, "Western Paradox," container 74, DeVoto Papers, Stanford University Library. DeVoto in his lecture notes on "Public Domain and Conservation" (container 96, DeVoto Papers), also makes the argument that "gigantic waste & destruction of natural resources, esp. timber," were accompanied by "gigantic graft & corruption" in the period 1850–1870. He placed part of the blame on the land-grant railroads, which "whooped up" their land sales by propaganda. "Fraud, either deliberate or inadvertent, [was] perpetuated upon hundreds of thousands of people who, upon reaching the great plains in the expectation of bettering their estate, went bankrupt instead," ibid. See also Gilbert B. Workman, "Only Lovers Can Be Sound Critics: Bernard DeVoto and American Conservation" (M.A. thesis, San José State University, 1960), pp. 80 ff.

62. Carl O. Sauer, "Theme of Plant and Animal Destruction in Economic History," in *Land and Life: A Selection from the Writings of Carl Ortwin Sauer*, ed. John Leighly (Berkeley: University of California Press, 1969), pp. 148–49.

63. Ibid. Sauer's long and tenacious research on the history of the domestication of varieties of maize by Indian people is revealed in his correspondence with the botanist, Edgar Anderson. Their letters detail their discoveries of ancient types of maize. See, for instance, Sauer to Anderson, Oct. 10 and 27, 1941, Aug. 31 and Oct. 8, 1942; Anderson to Sauer, Nov. [?], 1941, Sauer Papers, Bancroft Library, University of California, Berkeley.

64. Sauer, *Land and Life*, 148.

65. Ibid., p. 154. Sauer was also convinced that modern man did not understand his historic role as "the dominant of ecology" by reason of his being "a fire bringer and then a fire maker." Today's "thermal technics," Sauer wrote, have become "a great hazard" to the world. Sauer to Jacobs, Feb. 21, 1972.

66. Leopold spent his early years in Iowa but became a Wisconsinite by adoption when he was in his thirties. He loved the sand and scrub country near Portage, Wisconsin, the boyhood hometown of Frederick Jackson Turner. Leopold's most produc-

tive writings were undertaken when he was a forester at the U.S. Forest Service's Laboratory at Madison. See Nash, *Wilderness and the American Mind*, pp. 182–87.

67. Aldo Leopold, "Wilderness as a Form of Land Use," *Journal of Land and Public Utility Economics* 1 (1925):401, quoted in Nash, *Wilderness and the American Mind*, p. 188.

68. Aldo Leopold, *A Sand County Almanac with Essays on Conservation from Round River* (New York: Oxford Unviersity Press, 1974), pp. 237–64.

69. Ibid., p. 140.

70. Ibid., p. 262.

71. Frank Graham, Jr., *Since Silent Spring* (Boston: Houghton Mifflin, 1970), p. 21.

72. Rachel Carson, *Silent Spring* (Boston: Houghton Mifflin, 1962), pp. 162 ff.

73. Although a mass of available evidence exists to show that Indian people should be recognized as our first ecologists (as I have stated earlier in this paper), there are instances of erosion and other types of environmental stress caused by Indian agricultural practices in ancient Mexico. See, for instance, Sherburne F. Cook, *Historical Demography and Ecology of Teotlalpan* (Berkeley: University of California Press, 1949), pp. 41 ff.

74. For an example of the Department of Agriculture's persistent and reckless support of the use of herbicides, see the report by Fred H. Tschirley, department specialist in physiological ecology, "Defoliation in Vietnam," originally published in *Science* 163 (1969):779–886, and reprinted in Thomas R. Detwyler, ed., *Man's Impact on the Environment* (New York: McGraw Hill, 1971), pp. 536 ff. Here Tschirley argues that, although large areas of vegetation "were not defoliated, but were killed," "the concept of defoliating in strips or in checkerboard pattern has great merit" (ibid., p. 544). For an excellent historical overview of the destructive impact of the U.S. Army Corps of Engineers in America, see Elizabeth B. Drew, "Dam Outrage: The Story of the Army Corps of Engineers," in George E. Frakes and Curtis B. Solberg, eds., *Pollution Papers* (New York: Appleton-Century-Crofts, 1971), pp. 189–214. For an example of the Dr. Strangelove attitude toward the environment that the Atomic Energy Commission often exhibited in the 1950s and 1960s, see Glen C. Werth, "Plowshare: Scientific Problems," in William R. Judd, ed., *State of Stress in the Earth's Crust: Proceedings of the International Conference, June 13 & 14, 1963 — The Amand Corporation* (New York: American Elsevier, 1964), pp. 83–97. Werth in this article is an enthusiastic advocate of the use of nuclear AEC "Plowshare" explosives by the government, industrialists, and ordinary businessmen. "We have a problem. Perhaps," Werth states, "it can be solved by use of nuclear explosive. Let's look into the problem and explore the feasibility." He does acknowledge that this kind of everyday use of nuclear explosives may have to await further developments in weapon technology. Atomic Energy Commission leaders of the "Plowshare" project at one time had plans to explode bombs for a new harbor at Perth, Australia, and a new canal through Central America. Such proposals were dropped because of possible dangerous radiation. Confidential interview, July 1977, Department of Geophysics, University of California, Berkeley.

75. E. F. Schumacher, *Small Is Beautiful: Economics as if People Mattered* (New York: Harper & Row, 1975), discusses pollution problems and growth, questions of size, proper use of the land, and the importance of re-examining "appropriate" of "intermediate" technologies—that is, technologies less offensive to the environment. See esp. pp. 102 ff. See also Barbara Ward, "Small Is Beautiful," *Los Angeles Times*, Sept. 20, 1977; and S. David Freeman et al., *A Time to Choose* (Cambridge, Mass.: Ballinger, 1974), pp. 19 ff; Garrison Wilkes, "Plant Germplasm Resources," *Environmental Review* 1, 1 (1976): 2–13.

76. Social losses, or costs as an economic concept are discussed in K. William

Kapp, *Social Costs of Business Enterprise* (New York: Asia, 1963), pp. 13 ff. See especially Kapp's analysis of the historic social costs of air pollution, water pollution, and loss of nonrenewable resources (ibid., pp. 47 ff.).

77. The history of Indians in North America in prehistory and in modern times should be distinguished from the history of Indian-white relations. This point was stressed by Francis Jennings and other scholars at sessions of the Annual Conference on Iroquois Research and the Annual Meeting of the American Society for Ethnohistory held simultaneously in Albany, New York, Oct. 11–14, 1979.

Chapter 4—JUSTIFYING DISPOSSESSION OF THE INDIAN

1. *The Texas Monthly*, January 1979, p. 83.

2. Quoted in Wilcomb E. Washburn, "The Moral and Legal Justifications for Dispossessing the Indians," *Seventeenth-Century America*, ed. James Morton Smith (Chapel Hill: University of North Carolina Press, 1959), p. 24.

3. Quoted in Monroe E. Price, *Law and the American Indian* (Indianapolis: Bobbs-Merrill, 1973), p. 369.

4. For an excellent discussion of the relative use of land by Indians and whites, see Peter A. Thomas, "Contrastive Subsistence Strategies and Land Use as Factors for Understanding Indian-White Relations in New England," *Ethnohistory* 23, 1 (Winter 1976):1–18.

5. Quoted in Roy Harvey Pearce, *The Savages of America*, rev. ed. (Baltimore: Johns Hopkins Press, 1965), p. 11.

6. Quoted in Randolph C. Downes, *Council Fires on the Upper Ohio* (Pittsburgh: University of Pittsburgh Press, 1940), p. 155.

7. Quoted in Albert K. Weinberg, *Manifest Destiny* (Baltimore: Johns Hopkins Press, 1935), p. 26.

8. Ibid., p. 76.

9. Ibid., p. 78.

10. Ibid., p. 80.

11. Ibid., p. 79.

12. Reginald Horsman, *Expansion and American Indian Policy, 1783–1812* (East Lansing: Michigan State University Press, 1967), pp. 130–31.

13. *Register of Debates*, 21st Congress, 1st Session, 16.

14. Quoted in Pearce, *Savages of America*, p. 57.

15. James M. Wayne in *Register of Debates*, May 24, 1830, pp. 1124–26.

16. Quoted in Price, *Law and the American Indian*, pp. 363–64.

17. As reproduced in Wilcomb E. Washburn, *The American Indians and the United States: A Documentary History*, 4 vols. (New York: Random House, 1973), 4:2560.

18. T. Hartley Crawford to Major Joshua Pilcher, March 1, 1841, Indian Office Letter Book, 30, pp. 146–47, Record Group 75, National Archives.

19. Quoted in Warren S. Tryon, ed. *A Mirror for Americans*, 3 vols. (Chicago: University of Chicago Press, 1952) 2:723.

20. James Clarke in 1846 *Annual Report of the Commissioner of Indian Affairs*, p. 241.

21. As advanced by Commissioner of Indian Affairs William Medill in his 1848 annual report, p. 396.

22. A. B. Greenwood in his 1859 annual report, p. 11.

23. Caleb B. Smith, extract from his annual report, in 1862 *Annual Report of the Commissioner of Indian Affairs*, p. 7.

24. 1848 *Annual Report of the Commissioner of Indian Affairs*, pp. 388–89.

25. Thomas S. Twiss in 1859 *Annual Report of the Commissioner of Indian Affairs*, p. 131.

26. O. H. Browning in his 1867 annual report, p. 8. See also, 1860 annual report, p. 249, and Secretary of the Interior James Harlan to Major General John Pope, July 6, 1865, Indian Division—Letters Sent, Record Group 48, National Archives.

27. Commissioner of Indian affairs to secretary of the interior, May 23, 1876, Indian Office Report Book No. 30, Record Group 75, National Archives.

28. Commission of Indian affairs to secretary of the interior, January 13, 1879, Indian Office Report Book No. 32, Record Group 75, National Archives.

29. 1878 *Annual Report of the Commissioner of Indian Affairs*, p. iv.

30. "Minutes of a Council Held at Lumni Reservation, Washington Territory, by Commissioner Felix R. Brunot," in 1871 *Annual Report of the Commissioner of Indian Affairs*, p. 142.

31. J. Q. Smith in his 1876 annual report, p. 386.

32. Carl Schurz in his 1879 annual report (Serial 1910, HED, 46th Congress, 2nd Session), p. 4.

33. Secretary Columbus Delano to Senator W. B. Allison, March 18, 1875, Indian Division—Letters Sent, Record Group 48, National Archives.

34. Welsh to R. T. Woods, February 3, 1890, in Papers of the Indian Rights Association, Microfilm Edition, Roll 103.

35. 1885 annual report of the association, p. 14, in ibid., Roll 103.

36. Welsh to John L. Gardiner, April 27, 1886, in ibid., Roll 68.

37. For a discussion of the George Cook case, see the 1890 *Annual Report of the Commissioner of Indian Affairs*, p. xxxiii, and Assistant Secretary of the Interior H. L. Muldrow to James Harlow, November 28, 1888, Indian Division—Letters Sent, Record Group 48, National Archives.

38. Act of February 16, 1889 (25 Stat. 673).

39. For such an interpretation on timber, see secretary of the interior to the president, March 2, 1889, Indian Division—Letters Sent, Record Group 48, National Archives. For mining, see acting commissioner of Indian affairs to James F. Randlett, Kiowa Agency Files, Oklahoma Historical Society.

40. *Minco Minstrel*, October 13, 1893.

41. Guthrie *Daily Leader*, November 2, 1893.

42. Reprinted in *Edmonson Democrat*, March 23, 1894.

43. W. F. Harn to land commissioner, March 7, 1892, in File 191, Record Group 75, National Archives.

44. Secretary of the interior to speaker of the house of representatives, May 8, 1878, Indian Division—Letters Sent, Record Group 48, National Archives.

45. Arthur Lazarus, Jr. to the editor, *New York Times*, August 31, 1976.

46. Barry Goldwater to the editor, ibid.

47. This problem was raised, as an example of the complexity of the issue, by Leo M. Krulitz, solicitor of the department of the interior. See *Indian Natural Resources*, Bulletin of the Association on American Indian Affairs, Inc., August 1977, p. 3.

48. Ibid., May 1977, p. 6.

49. *American Indian Journal*, December 1978, p. 43.

50. *Indian Natural Resources*, December 1977, p. 6.

51. Ibid., August 1977, p. 5.

52. The adage in its original form appears in an article on western water problems by Grace Lichtenstein in the *New York Times*, August 22, 1976, p. 49.

53. That the Indians can win some of these battles can be seen in the 1978 law guaranteeing water for the Papagos and Pimas of the Ak Chin Reservation in Arizona.

However, this is water to be drawn from nearby federal land and will not be immediately and directly at the expense of non-Indians.

54. For example, see secretary of the interior to the commissioner of Indian affairs, February 23, 1876, Indian Division — Letters Sent, Record Group 48, National Archives.

55. *New York Times*, February 18, 1979, p. 26.

Chapter 5 — IROQUOIS ENVIRONMENTS

1. Jeremy Bentham, *The Collected Works of Jeremy Bentham*, gen. ed. J. H. Burns; ed. H. L. A. Hart, *Of Laws in General* (London: University of London, Athlone Press, 1970), p. 18.

2. Ferdinand Tönnies, *Community and Society (Gemeinschaft und Gesellschaft)* trans. and ed., Charles P. Loomis (East Lansing: Michigan State University Press, 1957; New York: Harper & Row, 1963), pp. 64–65. It is ironic that Tönnies published this dualistic approach to human societies in 1887, the very year the United States government initiated a unilateral, ethnocentric policy toward Native American societies with the passage of the General Allotment Act (Dawes Act).

3. Ibid., p. 65. Emile Durkheim reviewed Tönnies' work in 1889, citing a portion of this passage as representative. See Werner J. Cahnman, "Tönnies and Durkheim: An Exchange of Reviews," in Werner J. Cahnman, ed., *Ferdinand Tönnies: A New Evaluation: Essays and Documents* (Leiden: E. J. Brill, 1973), p. 243.

4. Ferdinand Tönnies, "The Revision of the Medieval World View," from Tönnies' *Thomas Hobbes Leben und Lehre*, in E. G. Jacoby, ed. and trans., *Ferdinand Tönnies: On Social Ideas and Ideologies* (New York: Harper & Row, 1974), pp. 11–36.

5. Ferdinand Tönnies, review of Gabriel Tarde's *Les Lois de L'Imitation* in Cahnman, ed., *Tonnies*, p. 250.

6. *Choctaw Nation v. State of Oklahoma* 397 U.S. 620 (1970), 631. A concurring opinion by Justice William O. Douglas (642) notes "the classic rule that treaties or agreements with Indians are to be construed in their favor, not in favor of commercial interests that repeatedly in our history have sought to exploit them."

7. *Worcester v. Georgia* 6 Pet. (31 U.S.) 515 (1832), 552–553; "Treaty with the Cherokee, 1785," in Charles J. Kappler, ed., *Indian Treaties, 1778–1883* (originally *Indian Affairs: Laws and Treaties*, Vol. 2 *(Treaties)*, Washington, D.C.: 1904; New York: Interland Publishing, 1972), p.9. For Marshall's views on the revolutionary generation, see *Worcester v. Georgia*, pp. 549–51.

8. Special Committee to Investigate the Indian Problem of the State of New York, Appointed by the Assembly of 1888, *Report*, Doc. 51, 7 Ass. Docs., 112th Sess. (1889) [hereinafter cited as the *Whipple Report*], pp. 190, 237, 216.

9. *Worcester v. Georgia*, 582.

10. *Jones v. Meehan* 175 U.S. 1 (1899), 10–11.

11. *United States v. Winans* 198 U.S. 371 (1905), 380–81.

12. Ibid., 381.

13. *Cherokee Nation v. Georgia* 5 Pet. (30 U.S.) 1 (1831), 16.

14. Ibid., 17–18.

15. *United States v. Mazurie* 419 U.S. 544 (1975) 557, quoted in the American Indian Policy Review Commission, *Final Report* 2 vols. (Washington, D.C.: U.S. Government Printing Office, 1977), 1: 102.

16. For discussions of sovereignty, see Felix S. Cohen, *Handbook of Federal Indian Law* (Washington, D.C.: United States Government Printing Office, 1942; reprint

ed. New York: AMS Press, 1972), p. 122 [Chapter 7 is entitled "The Scope of Tribal Self-Government," pp. 122–50]; American Indian Policy Review Commission, *Final Report*, I: 99–103, 573–83 (pages 573–83 are part of a dissent by Congressman Lloyd Means who challenges the concepts on pages 99–103]; Charles F. Wilkinson and John M. Volkman, "Judicial Review of Indian Treaty Abrogation: 'As Long as Water Flows, or Grass Grows Upon the Earth'—How Long a Time is That?" *California Law Review* 63, 3 (May 1975):619; James W. Clute, "The New York Indians' Right to Self-Determination," *Buffalo Law Review* 22, 3 (Spring 1973):985–1019; Kirke Kickingbird, Lynn Kickingbird, Charles J. Chibitty, and Curtis Berkey, *Indian Sovereignty* (Washington, D.C.: Institute for the Development of Indian Law, 1977); Martin B. Wasser and Louis Grumet, "Indian Rights—The Reality of Symbolism," *New York State Bar Journal* 50 (October 1978):82–485, 514–18; Vine Deloria, Jr., "Self-Determination and the Concept of Sovereignty," in Native American Studies, University of New Mexico, Development Series No. 1, *Economic Development in American Indian Reservations* (Albuquerque: University of New Mexico Printing Plant, 1979), pp. 22–28; Robert Weil, *The Legal Status of the Indian* (New York: Columbia College, 1888; reprint ed., New York: AMS Press, 1975); Imre Sutton, *Indian Land Tenure: Bibliographical Essays and a Guide to the Literature* (New York: Clearwater, 1975), especially pages 150–56; Francis Paul Prucha, *A Bibliographical Guide to the History of Indian-White Relations in the United States* (Chicago: University of Chicago Press, 1977), pp. 229–39. I am grateful to my good friend Laurence M. Hauptman for sharing with me the draft of Hauptman and Jack Campisi, "Residual Sovereignty: The Iroquois Record," in one of the forthcoming volumes of the *Handbook of North American Indians* (Washington, D.C.: Smithsonian Institution).

17. An introduction to the Canadian involvement in the issue of sovereignty can be found in "Indian Government Conference," *Indian News* (June 1979), pp. 1–11. An Iroquois point of view is presented on pages 6 and 10 of this newspaper, published by the Canadian government's Department of Indian Affairs and Northern Development, and written and edited "by Indian people."

18. *Worcester v. Georgia*, 551–52, 556–57.

19. Ibid., 559–60.

20. While the concepts may have been "well understood," many of Marshall's contemporaries believed the concepts had ceased to be relevant in Indian affairs. See Francis Paul Prucha, *American Indian Policy in the Formative Years* (Boston: Harvard University Press, 1962; Lincoln: University of Nebraska Press, 1970), pp. 234–35, 242–45.

21. William A. Longacre, ed., *Reconstructing Prehistoric Pueblo Societies* (Albuquerque: University of New Mexico Press, 1970), passim; Erik K. Reed, "The Greater Southwest," in Jesse D. Jennings and Edward Norbeck, eds., *Prehistoric Man in the New World* (Chicago: University of Chicago Press, 1964), pp. 175–91; Edward P. Dozier, "The American Southwest," in Eleanor Burke Leacock and Nancy Oestreich Lurie, eds., *North American Indians in Historical Perspective* (New York: Random House, 1971), pp 228–32; Douglas Osborne, "Slow Exodus from Mesa Verde," *Natural History* (January 1976), pp. 38–44.

22. Robert L. Blakely, ed., *Biocultural Adaptation in Prehistoric America*, Southern Anthropological Society Proceedings, no. 11, Gwen Kennedy, series ed. (Athens: University of Georgia Press, 1977); David S. Brose and N'omi Greber, eds. *Hopewell Archaeology: The Chillicothe Conference* (Kent, Oh.: Kent State University Press, 1979); numerous articles in Bruce G. Trigger, ed., *Northeast*, volume 15 of the *Handbook of North American Indians*, William C. Sturtevant, gen. ed. (Washington, D.C.: Smithsonian Institution, 1978); Olaf H. Prufer, "The Hopewell Cult" in Ezra B. W. Zubrow et al., comps., *New World Archeology* (San Francisco: W. H. Freeman, 1974), pp. 222–30; James B. Griffin, "The Northeast Woodlands Area" and William H. Sears, "The Southeastern United States," in Jennings and Norbeck, eds., *Prehistoric Man*, pp. 223–58 and 259–87;

James Marshall, "Geometry of the Hopewell Earthworks," *Early Man* (Spring 1979), pp. 1–5; and Walter Sullivan, "Ancient Mounds Taken as Clues to Advanced Culture," *New York Times*, June 19, 1979, p. C3.

23. Christopher Vecsey's "American Indian Environmental Religions," Chapter 1 of this book, demonstrates this complex point. See also Walter Holden Capps, ed., *Seeing With A Native Eye* (New York: Harper & Row, 1976).

24. Jean Bodin, *The Six Bookes of a Commonweale*, ed. with intro. by Kenneth Douglas McRae (Cambridge, Mass.: Harvard University Press, 1962), pp. A13–A14; Julian H. Franklin, *Jean Bodin and the Rise of Absolute Theory* (Cambridge: Cambridge University Press, 1973), pp. vii, 1–22.

25. Bodin, *The Six Bookes of a Commonweale*, pp. 84–85.

26. Ibid., p. A14.

27. William N. Fenton, "The Iroquois in History," in Leacock and Lurie, eds., *North American Indians*, pp. 129–33, 148.

28. Regarding traditional Iroquois concepts of government, religion, the environment, and politics, past and present, I am grateful for the insights given to me by many Iroquois, all of whom wish to remain anonymous.

29. Fenton, "The Iroquois in History," in Leacock and Lurie, eds., *North American Indians*, p. 143; Allen W. Trelease, *Indian Affairs in Colonial New York: The Seventeenth Century* (Ithaca, N.Y.: Cornell University Press, 1960), pp. 326–27; William N. Fenton, "The Iroquois Confederacy in the Twentieth Century: A Case Study of the Theory of Lewis H. Morgan in Ancient Society," in Deward E. Walker, Jr., ed., *The Emergent Native Americans: A Reader in Cultural Contact* (Boston: Little, Brown, 1972), pp. 475, 477; M. J. Heale, *The Making of American Politics* (London and New York: Longman, 1977), pp. v, 17–19, and passim. In both the Iroquois and the European circumstances the political systems provided the initial cohesion.

30. Jean de Quen, Journal, 3 November 1656, in Reuben Gold Thwaites, ed., *The Jesuit Relations and Allied Documents*, 73 vols. (Cleveland: Burrows Brothers, 1899), 42:253.

31. Cadwallader Colden, in *The History of the Five Indian Nations* (1727, 1747; reissued Ithaca, N.Y.: Cornell University Press, 1964), noted that "The Indians always express a League by a Chain by which two or more things are kept fast together," (p. 30). See also Fenton, "The Iroquois in History," in Leacock and Lurie, eds., *North American Indians*, p. 134; and Arthur O. Lovejoy, *The Great Chain of Being: A Study of the History of an Idea* (Cambridge, Mass.: Harvard University Press, 1936; 1964). The Great Chain of Being is not completely analogous to Iroquois concepts, for while the Europeans "chain" stressed interdependence it also included a defined hierarchy which is at best vague in Iroquois thought. However, the medieval chain of being and the Iroquois' chain are both concepts in Gemeinschaft.

32. Requerimiento, in Charles Gibson, ed., *The Spanish Tradition in America* (New York: Harper & Row, 1968), p. 60.

33. David Beers Quinn, ed., *The Roanoke Voyages, 1584–1590*, 2 vols. (London: Hakluyt Society, 1955) 2:504, 531.

34. Lyon Gardiner Tyler, ed., *Narratives of Early Virginia*, in the series *Original Narratives of Early American History*, gen. ed. J. Franklin Jameson (New York: Scribner's, 1907), pp. 152–55. Francis Jennings, in his fine book *The Invasion of America: Indians, Colonialism, and Cant of Conquest* (Chapel Hill: University of North Carolina Press, 1975), pp. 115–19, uses the Powhatan coronation as an example in his discussion of feudal vassalage in colonial affairs.

35. *A Relation Or Journall of the beginning and proceedings of the English Plantation Setled at Plimoth* [1622] (n.p.: Readex Microprint, 1966), p. 45.

36. Thomas Church, *The History of the Great Indian War of 1675 and 1676*, Samuel

G. Drake, ed. (Hartford: Silus Andrus & Son, 1851), pp. 125–27; Alvin M. Josephy, Jr., *The Patriot Chiefs* (New York: Viking, 1969), p. 62.

37. Arnold Toynbee, intro.; Fred L. Israel, ed.; commentaries by Emmanuel Chill, *Major Peach Treaties of Modern History, 1648–1967*, 4 vols. (New York: Chelsea House and McGraw Hill, 1967), 1:210, 308–310, 346–47; Francis Parkman, *A Half-Century of Conflict* (1892; New York: Collier, 1962), p. 383; and also see Frances Gardiner Davenport, ed., *European Treaties bearing on the History of the United States and its Dependencies*, 4 vols. (Washington, D.C.: Carnegie Institution of Washington, 1917–1937; reprint Gloucester, Mass.: Peter Smith, 1967), 3:198, 213.

38. "Treaty with the Six Nations, 1784" in Kappler, ed., *Treaties*, p.5.

39. *Whipple Report*, pp. 190, 216, 237. The 1788 Onondaga treaty was not approved by the Onondagas until 1790. (Ibid., pp. 191–94).

40. "Abstract of the Proposalls of the Onoundagaes and Cayouges Sachims at New Yorke 2. August 1684," in John Romeyne Brodhead, E. B. O'Callaghan, and Berthold Fernow, comps. and eds., *Documents Relative to the Colonial History of the State of New York*, 15 vols. (Albany: Weed, Parsons, and others, 1853–1887), 3:347.

41. See the excellent study by Robert F. Berkhofer, Jr. *The White Man's Indian* (New York: Knopf, 1978).

42. General Thomas Gage, 7 October 1772, to Sir William Johnson, in James Sullivan et al., eds., *The Papers of Sir William Johnson*, 14 vols. (Albany: University of the State of New York, 1921–1965), 12:995; Johnson, 2 September 1772, to Gage, in Ibid., 8:586–88.

43. Aaron Hill, October 1784 speech, quoted in Barbara Graymont, *The Iroquois in the American Revolution* (Syracuse, N.Y.: Syracuse University Press, 1972), p. 280.

44. Ibid., p. 218; *Whipple Report*, pp. 37–40, 94–112; Gerald Gunther, "Governmental Power and New York Indian Lands—A Reassessment of a Persistent Problem of Federal-State Relations, *Buffalo Law Review* 8, 1 (Fall 1958):3; The Oneida Indian Nation . . . , *Plaintiffs' Post-Trial Memorandum on the Issue of Liability*, United States District Court, Northern District of New York (Syracuse, N.Y.: Bond Schoeneck & King, 1975), p. 11.

45. James Monroe, 15 November 1784, to James Madison, in Robert A. Rutland et al., eds., *The Papers of James Madison* (Chicago: University of Chicago Press, 1973), 8:140.

46. Madison, 27 November 1784, to Monroe, in Ibid., pp. 156–57.

47. "The New England Confederation," in Henry Steel Commager, ed., *Documents of American History*, 9th ed. (Englewood Cliffs, N.J.: Prentice-Hall, 1973), p. 28.

48. Michael G. Hall, Lawrence H. Leder, and Michael G. Kammen, eds., *The Glorious Revolution in America: Documents on the Colonial Crisis of 1689* (Chapel Hill: University of North Carolina Press, 1964; New York: Norton, 1972), pp. 3–4.

49. William Penn, "A briefe and plain scheme . . . ," in Commager, ed., *Documents*, pp. 39–40.

50. Benjamin Franklin, 20 March 1750/1, to James Parker, in Leonard W. Labaree, ed., *The Papers of Benjamin Franklin*, 15 vols. (New Haven: Yale University Press, 1959–1972), 4:118–19.

51. Verner W. Crane, *Benjamin Franklin and a Rising People* (Boston: Little, Brown, 1954), p. 71.

52. Edmund Cody Burnett, *The Continental Congress* (New York: Macmillan, 1941; New York: Norton, 1964), p. 97.

53. *Whipple Report*, p. 107.

54. Joseph Brant, 7 September 1784, address to New York Commissioners, Fort Stanwix [Fort Schuyler], in Franklin B. Hough, ed., *Proceedings of the Commissioners of Indian Affairs, Appointed by Law for the Extinguishment of Indian Titles in the State of New York* (Albany: Joel Munsell, 1861), p. 54.

55. Brant, [10 or 12] September 1784, address to New York Commissioners, Fort Stanwix, in ibid., p. 61.

56. The 1784 treaty did not include the Wyandot and other Indian nations who lived in the area claimed by the Iroquois "empire." These Indian nations were dealt with separately. To what degree the Iroquois actually possessed an "empire" west of their homelands is debatable. Nevertheless, the United States wished to establish a legal basis for its jurisdiction and expansion, just as the British had in 1768 in the first Treaty of Fort Stanwix to lands claimed by the Iroquois *south* of the Ohio. Certainly the Iroquois had established through conquest a better claim to the lands ceded in 1784 to the United States than had Britain, which ceded jurisdiction over them in the Treaty of Paris 1783 to the United States, or the United States, which claimed some military successes in the area during the Revolution. Furthermore, the Iroquois' claim was far stronger than that of Massachusetts, which ceded its claims to New York in 1786. Yet in law the British, the United States, and the Massachusetts claims were (and are) taken very seriously. The same standard applied to the Iroquois' claim would have to acknowledge the Iroquois' rights.

57. Two excellent maps of the cessions to the United States and to Pennsylvania made by the Iroquois in 1784 are in Lester J. Cappon, ed., *Atlas of Early American History: The Revolutionary Era, 1760–1790* (Princeton, N.J.: Princeton University Press, 1976), p. 61. These maps represent the claims and lines as perceived by the non-Indians of the era and in subsequent decades. An approximate line running north to Canada through the eastern Adirondacks is certainly one line which can be contested by the Six Nations today. See the 1788 map reprinted in Hough, ed., *Proceedings*.

58. Eugene Parker Chase, ed., *Our Revolutionary Forefathers: the Letters of François, Marquis de Barbé Marbois* (New York: Duffield, 1929), p. 205. From the internal evidence, it appears that the reconciliation took place sometime between October 2 and October 11. The confederacy tacitly accepted the 1784 treaty but never ratified it. See Anthony F. C. Wallace, *The Death and Rebirth of the Seneca* (New York: Random House, 1969), p. 152.

59. *Whipple Report*, pp. 190–94, 216–20, 237–41.

60. "Treaty with the Six Nations," 9 January 1789, in Kappler, ed., *Treaties*, p. 24.

61. "An Act to regulate Trade and Intercourse with the Indian Tribes," 22 July 1790, United States Statutes at Large, 1:138.

62. "An act to regulate Trade and Intercourse with the Indian Tribes," 1 March 1793, United States Statutes at Large, 1:331.

63. Brief of the United States, Appellant [Kent Frizzell, Assistant Attorney General], Appeal No. 13–71 In the United States Court of Claims, *The United States of America, Appellant, v. The Oneida Nation of New York, Et Al., Appellees.* On Appeal from the Indian Claims Commission, Docket No. 301 (Claims 3–8), (Washington, D.C.: April 1972), pp. 20, 79.

64. "Treaty with the Six Nations," 11 November 1794, in Kappler, ed., *Treaties*, pp. 35–36.

65. Arthur C. Parker, "The Code of Handsome Lake, the Seneca Prophet," in William N. Fenton, ed., *Parker on the Iroquois* (Syracuse, N.Y.: Syracuse University Press, 1968), pp. 9–13, 66. This passage, together with the entire code, is still a part of Iroquois religious life. For example, the passage quoted in the text was recited at Onondaga, in Onondaga, on June 12, 1980.

66. "Treaty with the Six Nations," 11 November 1794, in Kappler, ed., *Treaties*, p. 36.

67. Timothy Pickering, 29 June 1795, to Israel Chapin, Jr., quoted in Jack Campisi, "New York-Oneida Treaty of 1795: A Finding of Fact," *American Indian Law Review* 4, 1 (1976):76.

68. *The Oneida Indian Nation of New York State, et al.* v. *The County of Oneida, New York and The County of Madison,* heard in November 1975, in the federal court at Auburn, New York, was decided in the Oneidas' favor in July 1977, and is at this writing being appealed by the two counties involved. I had the privilege of testifying on behalf of the Oneidas at this trial. I would like to take this opportunity to note that the late Oscar Archiquette, an Oneida from Green Bay, Wisconsin, taught me a great deal of what I later used in my testimony. He had been working to have many Oneida claims tried since he was a young man in the 1920s. That he died on December 25, 1971, years before this case came to trial, is an example of the pace of American justice in Indian affairs.

69. [Richard H. Kohn, consultant,] *Petitioners' Proposed Findings of Fact and Brief . . . , The Oneida Nation of New York, The Oneida Tribe of Indians of Wisconsin, The Oneida Nation by Julius Danforth, Oscar Archiquette, Sherman Skenandore, Mamie Smith and Amanda Pierce, Petitioners,* v. *The United States of America, Defendant.* Before The Indian Claims Commission, Docket No. 301 (Claims 3–7) [Washington, D.C.: n.d.], p. 38.

70. *Whipple Report,* pp. 234, 363.

71. Ibid., pp. 63, 74, 84.

72. Andrew Jackson, 8 December 1829, First Annual Message, in James D. Richardson, ed., *A Compilation of The Messages and Papers of the Presidents,* 11 vols. ([Washington, D.C.:] Bureau of National Literature and Art, 1907), 2:457. Referring to a hypothetical effort by Indians to establish any independent republic within a state such as Ohio, Jackson asked rhetorically, "would it be the duty of this [federal] Government to protect them [the Indians] in the attempt?" The implied negative answer to this question seemed to Jackson to be "obvious." Ibid., pp. 457–58.

73. Gunther, "New York Indian Lands," *Buffalo Law Review* 8, 1 (Fall 1958):8–9, 9 n.43; *Brief of the United States,* Court of Claims, No. 301, pp. 49–51, 62.

74. "An act to provide for the allotment of lands," [General Allotment or Dawes Act], 8 February 1887, in Francis Paul Prucha, ed., *Documents of United States Indian Policy* (Lincoln: University of Nebraska Press, 1975), p. 174; *Whipple Report,* pp. 3, 22–37.

75. Ibid., title page.

76. *Worcester* v. *Georgia,* 593.

77. *Whipple Report,* pp. 413–14.

78. Ibid., pp. 415–16. In *Seneca Nation* v. *Christie* (162 U.S. 283) in 1896 the court affirmed New York's control over the Indians within its borders. Clute, "New York Indians' Rights to Self-Determination," *Buffalo Law Review* 22, 3 (Spring 1973):990–91.

79. *Lone Wolf* v. *Hitchcock* 187 U.S. Reports 553 (1903), 566.

80. Ibid., 567.

81. Hazel W. Hertzberg, *The Search for an American Indian Identity: Modern Pan-Indian Movements* (Syracuse, N.Y.: Syracuse University Press, 1971), p. 175.

82. *Report of the New York State Indian Commission to Investigate The Status of the American Indian Residing In the State of New York* [17 March 1922] (Albany, N.Y.: New York State Education Department, typewritten copy, 1972), pp. iv. 88. (Hereinafter cited as the *Everett Report;* the New York State Education copy stops at page 399; the Onondaga Nation has Everett Report material numbered through page 477, photocopied from Department of Interior records.); *State of New York Subcommittee on Governmental Operation, 1970,* 8 vols. *Proceedings,* 18 November 1970, Syracuse, N.Y., Public Hearings: Oneidas' Testimony, pp. 4, 39–40.

83. *Everett Report,* p. 399.

84. "An Act making Appropriations for . . . the Indian Department," 3 March 1871, in Prucha, ed., *Documents,* p. 136.

85. *Everett Report,* pp. 395–99.

86. The Oneida Indian Nation . . . , *Plaintiffs' Post-Trial Memorandum* (1975), pp. 32–33, 35.

87. Clinton Rickard, *Fighting Tuscarora: The Autobiography of Chief Clinton Rickard*, ed. Barbara Graymont (Syracuse, N.Y.: Syracuse University Press, 1973), pp. 95–96; Gunther, "New York Indian Lands," *Buffalo Law Review* 8, 1 (Fall 1958):13 n.74; C. C. Daniels, 21 November 1934, memorandum preceeding *Everett Report*, p. v; Clute, "New York Indians' Right to Self-Determination," *Buffalo Law Review* 22, 3 (Spring 1973):1019 n.211.

88. Gunther, "New York Indian Lands," *Buffalo Law Review* 8, 1 (Fall 1958):14.

89. Ibid., p. 16.

90. *Federal Power Commission* v. *Tuscarora Indian Nation* 362 U.S. 99 (1960); Rickard, *Fighting Tuscarora*, p. 151.

91. *Oneida Indian Nation of New York et al.* v. *County of Oneida, New York, et al.* 414 U.S. 661 (1974), 678–79. The author had the opportunity to work with the Oneidas of New York and of Wisconsin on this case beginning in 1970.

92. Edmund Port, *Memorandum-Decision and order*, 12 July 1977, *The Oneida Indian Nation of New York State, et al.* v. *The County of Oneida, New York, and The County of Madison, New York*, United States District Court, Northern District of New York, Auburn, New York; American Indian Policy Review Commission, *Final Report* 1:571–617; Rupert Costo and Jeannette Henry, *Indian Treaties: Two Centuries of Dishonor, The American Indian Reader* series, no. 5 (San Francisco: The Indian Historian Press, 1977), pp.46–56; "The New War Against Native Americans," *Wassaja*, January/February 1978, p. 20; "A Bill To provide for the settlement of the land claims of the Cayuga Indian Nation," H.R. 6631, 96th Cong., 2d sess., 1980.

93. Thomas Hobbes, *Leviathan, Or the Matter, Form and Power of A Commonwealth, Ecclesiastical and Civil*, intro. A. D. Lindsay (London: J. M. Dent & Sons, 1970), pp. 97, 106. Ferdinand Tönnies (see note 4) wrote *Thomas Hobbes Leben und Lehre* and co-founded the Societas Hobbesiana because Tönnies admired Hobbes's ability to discern the complex elements of society and order.

94. Hobbes, *Leviathan*, p. 107.

95. Thomas Jefferson, *The Declaration of Independence*, in Commager, ed., *Documents*, p. 100.

96. Sir Henry Sumner Maine, *Lectures on the Early History of Institutions* (New York: Henry Holt, 1875), pp. 370–400.

97. *Worcester* v. *Georgia*, 561.

98. Anthony F. C. Wallace, *King of the Delawares: Teedyuscung, 1700–1763* (Philadelphia, 1949; reprint ed. Freeport, N.Y.: Books for Libraries, 1970), pp. 203–207; Paul A. W. Wallace, *Indians in Pennsylvania* (Harrisburg, Pa.: Pennsylvania Historical and Museum Commission, 1968), p. 57; Randolph C. Downes, *Council Fires on the Upper Ohio* (Pittsburgh: University of Pittsburgh Press, 1940; 1969), pp. 170–78.

99. Ibid., pp. 177–78.

100. Ibid., pp. 10–11, 141–48.

101. Conference at Johnson Hall, 18–20 December 1766, in Sullivan, et al., eds. *Papers of Sir William Johnson*, 12:242.

102. Editors of the Oxford English Dictionary, *The Compact Edition of the Oxford English Dictionary: Complete Text Reproduced Micrographically*, 2 vols. (Oxford: Oxford University Press, 1971), 2:2094.

103. John Locke, *Two Treatises of Government*, ed. with intro. by Peter Laslett, 2nd ed. (Cambridge: Cambridge University Press, 1967),pp. 118–19, 168–71, 287–96, 343; Ramon H. Lemos, *Hobbes and Locke: Power and Consent* (Athens, Ga.: The University of Georgia Press, 1978), pp. 115–23, 167–72; Harold J. Laski, *Authority in the Modern State* (New Haven: Yale University Press, 1919), pp. 23–24.

104. *Cherokee Nation* v. *Georgia*, 17.

105. Conversations with various Iroquois leaders, March–April 1979.

106. *Whipple Report*, p. 413.
107. *Everett Report*, p. 67.
108. Ibid., pp. 67–68.
109. Ibid., p. 68.
110. Ibid., pp. 70–71.
111. Ibid., p. 95.
112. Maine, *Institutions*, p. 30.
113. Franklin, 20 March 1750/1, to Parker, in Labaree, ed., *Papers of Benjamin Franklin*, 4:118–19.
114. A survey, with documentation, of the wampum issue is in Jeannette Henry, ed., *The American Indian Reader: Education, The American Indian Reader* series no. 2 (San Francisco: The Indian Historian Press, 1972), pp. 198–232.
115. The concepts of Gemeinschaft and Gesellschaft could be applied to understand more completely the clash of Iroquois and non-Indian sovereignties which are detailed in a stimulating article (also cited in note 16 above) by Martin B. Wasser and Louis Grumet, "Indian Rights—The Reality of Symbolism," *New York State Bar Journal* 50 (October 1978):482–85, 514–18. Without evidently being aware of Tönnies' theoretical concepts, the authors have touched upon a few examples of what might be termed Gemeinschaft or Gesellschaft.
116. Hans Kelsen, *General Theory of Law and State*, trans. Anders Wedberg (Cambridge, Mass.: Harvard University Press, 1945), pp. 384–87, 442–46. Cf. George Wilhelm Friedrich Hegel, *Hegel's Philosophy of Right*, trans. T. M. Knox (Oxford: Oxford University Press, 1942), pp. 180–83.
117. An appreciation of the world's commercial interdependence can be seen in "Auto Industry: 'Single' truckers seeking partners," *The Financial Times of London World Business Weekly*, 4 June 1979, pp. 11–13. This article reviews world production of trucks. The integration of commercial sovereignties is exemplified in a deal struck between the epitome of American private enterprise, Mac Trucks — with its stalwart bulldog symbol—and the French government-owned Renault. The state-owned Renault now has a "20% stake" in Mack (Ibid., p. 13).

Chapter 6—REFUGEE HAVENS

1. See United Nations, High Commissioner for Refugees, *Refugee Report* (New York: United Nations, 1969).
2. Bayard Webster, "Studies Report Refugees Plagued by Persistent Stress," *New York Times*, September 11, 1979, sec. C, pp. 1, 4–6. See Keh-Ming Lin et al., "Adaptional Problems of Vietnamese Refugees," *Archives of General Psychiatry* 26 (August 1979):955–61. See also William Liu, *Transition to Nowhere* (Nashville, Tennessee: Charter House, 1979); H. P. David, "Involuntary International Migration: Adaptation of Refugees," in *Behavior in New Environments* (Beverly Hills, Calif., 1970), pp. 73–95.
3. Richard K. Harding and John G. Looney, "Problems of Southeast Asian Children in a Refugee Camp," *American Journal of Psychiatry* 134 (April 1977):407. Keh-Ming Lin has summarized these post–World War II studies of refugees: "Paranoid reaction, depression, anxiety, reaction psychosis, and conversion reaction have been observed as particulary prevalent. A marked tendency toward somatic over-concern and increased incidence of somatic complaints were also found to be present in several refugee groups," in "Adaptional Problems of Vietnamese Refugees," p. 955.
4. The exceptions include Arrell M. Gibson, ed., *America's Exiles: Indian Colonization in Oklahoma* (Oklahoma City: Oklahoma Historical Society, 1976); Virginia

Allen, "The White Man's Road: The Physical and Psychological Impact of Relocation on the Southern Plains Indians," *Journal of the History of Medicine* 30 (April 1975):148–63; R. Palmer Howard and Virginia Allen, "Stress and Death in the Settlement of Indian Territory," *The Chronicles of Oklahoma* 54 (Fall 1976):352–59.

5. See Jack O. Waddell and O. Michael Watson, eds., *The American Indian in Urban Society* (Boston: Little, Brown, 1971); B. M. Alfred, "Some Aspects of the Behavior of the Cornell Medical Index among Navajo Migrants to Denver, Colorado," *Transcultural Psychiatric Research Review* 6 (1969):82–83. According to John W. Olson, social casework director at Chicago's American Indian Center: "Not all Indians encounter severe problems in moving from country to city; probably the majority do not. It is not Indians alone who encounter problems — they merely represent a segment of the multitude of individuals who are more or less forced into urbanization without proper preparation," in "Epilogue: The Urban Indian as Viewed by an Indian Caseworker," *The American Indian in Urban Society*, p. 407. Consequently, it appears from Olson's description that governmental relocation policies produced among some Indians a parallel situation to some refugee groups' experience.

6. Oquaga is the present site of Colesville, New York. Otsiningo is present-day Binghamton, New York; Chugnut is the southern area opposite Binghamton; Chemung is present day Chemung, New York; Tioga is Athens, Pennsylvania; and New Stockbridge is the present locations of Stockbridge and Vernon, New York.

7. See Laurence M. Hauptman, "The Dispersal of the River Indians: Frontier Expansion and Indian Dispossession in the Hudson Valley," *Neighbors and Intruders: An Ethnohistorical Exploration of the Indians of Hudson's River*, ed. Laurence M. Hauptman and Jack Campisi (Ottawa: National Museums of Canada, 1978), pp. 242–57.

8. Ted J. C. Brasser, *Riding on the Frontier's Crest: Mahican Indian Culture and Culture Change* (Ottawa: National Museums of Canada, 1974), pp. 24–27.

9. Laurence M. Hauptman, "The Dispersal of the River Indians," pp. 251–52; C. A. Weslager, *The Delawares: A History* (New Brunswick, N.J.: Rutgers University Press, 1972), p. 182.

10. Edmund B. O'Callaghan, ed., *Documents Relative to the Colonial History of the State of New York* (Albany: Weed, Parsons, 1853–1887) 5:343, 376, 387 (hereafter cited as *NYCD*); Peter Wraxall, *An Abridgement of the Indian Affairs ... Transacted in the Colony of New York, from the Year 1678 to the Year 1751*, ed. Charles H. McIlwain (Cambridge: Harvard University Press, 1915), pp. 94, 96, 101; John W. Lydekker, *The Faithful Mohawks* (Port Washington, N.Y.: I. J. Friedman, 1938), p. 49.

11. E. M. Ruttenber, *The Indian Tribes of Hudson's River* (Albany: J. Munsell, 1872), pp. 200–201; Brasser, *Riding on the Frontier's Crest*, p. 68.

12. Weslager, *The Delawares*, p. 182. Weslager claims that the Nanticokes were being resettled by 1747 (p. 182). Also see his *The Nanticoke Indians* (Harrisburg: Pennsylvania Historical and Museum Commission, 1948).

13. *Pennsylvania Colonial Records (Minutes of the Provincial Council)*, 2:471.

14. James Sullivan et al., eds., *The Papers of Sir William Johnson* (Albany: State University of New York, 1921–1965), 9:113 (hereafter cited as *JP*).

15. *NYCD*, 7:582.

16. Ibid., p. 250. Mahicans were by 1756 at Oquaga, Tioga, and Otsiningo, Brasser *Riding the Frontier's Crest*, pp. 68–70.

17. Ruttenber, *Indian Tribes of Hudson's River*, pp. 230–31.

18. *JP*, 9:846.

19. *NYCD*, 12:94, 96, 99–100.

20. Ibid., 7:113, 152, 159.

21. *JP*, 9:424–25, 434–35, 440, 463–67, 470. Johnson elaborated on these removals to the Indians at Otsiningo: "You have lived in too dispersed a manner, which

must naturally weaken a people and make them of little consequence; whereas if you keep together in a body you may be strong and respectable."

22. Ruttenber, *Indian Tribes of Hudson's River*, p. 231. *JP*, 7:394–95; 11:62, 67, 188; 12:718–19, 734, 802.

23. *JP*, 8:1202; 12:1037–38, 1060, 1117–19; 13:683–84; James D. McCallum, ed., *Letters of Eleazar Wheelock's Indians* (Hanover, N.H.: Dartmouth College Publications, 1932), pp. 157–79.

24. See Barbara Graymont, *The Iroquois in the American Revolution* (Syracuse: Syracuse University Press, 1972), pp. 192–222; Francis W. Halsey, *The Old New York Frontier* (New York: Scribner's, 1902), pp. 235–37; Majory B. Hinman, *Onaquaga: The Hub of the Border Wars* (n.p., 1975); William M. Beauchamp, *A History of the New York Iroquois* (Albany: New York State Education Department, 1905), p. 364.

25. Brasser, *Riding on the Frontier's Crest*, p. 70.

26. Samuel Kirkland to James Bowdoin, March 10, 1784, Kirkland MSS., Letters, 1776–1784, Hamilton College, Clinton, N.Y.

27. Brasser, *Riding on the Frontier's Crest*, p. 38.

28. David Landy, "Tuscarora Tribalism and National Identity," *Ethnohistory* 5 (Winter 1958), pp. 250–51, 278.

29. Ibid., pp. 263–64. For a different view, see Douglas W. Boyce, "Did a Tuscarora Confederacy Exist," *Four Centuries of Southern Indians*, ed. Charles M. Hudson (Athens, Georgia: University of Georgia Press, 1975), pp. 28–45.

30. Quoted in Paul A. W. Wallace, *Conrad Weiser* (Philadelphia: University of Pennsylvania Press, 1945), p. 88.

31. Ibid., p. 118.

32. "Reverend Gideon Hawley's Journal to Oghquaga, 1753," *Documentary History of the State of New York*, ed. Edmund O'Callaghan (Albany, 1849–1851), 3:1043–44.

33. Ibid., 3:1045–46.

34. *JP*, 9:791.

35. *NYCD*, 7:111.

36. Quoted in Wallace, *Conrad Weiser*, p. 86.

37. Ibid., p. 88.

38. *JP*, 11:40; Kirkland Journal, March 16, April 4, 1765, Kirkland MSS., Kirkland Journal November 1764–June 1765, Hamilton College, Clinton, N.Y.

39. Samuel Kirkland to Jerusha Kirkland, September 10, 1785, Kirkland MSS., Letters, 1776–1786, Hamilton College, Clinton, N.Y.

40. Karen Ordahl Kupperman, "Apathy and Death in Early Jamestown," *Journal of American History* 66 (June 1979):40.

41. The Indians at Oquaga and Chugnuts appealed to Johnson for help in 1756: "We beg leave to lay our immediate danger and distress before you. We are now entirely exposed to the merciless power of the French and their Indians, and our and your common enemy their hatchet is ready to fall upon our heads, their Indians who live not far from us, threaten us for our attachment to you for they call and look upon us as English as we truly are. Now Brother our earnest request is that you would build us a small place of defense, wherein our old men, women and children may have shelter in this time of danger, and that you would also supply us with arms, ammunition, etc., wherewith to defend ourselves from any attempts the enemy may make upon us." *NYCD*, 7:50.

42. Lewis Moorman, "Tuberculosis on the Navajo Reservation," *American Review of Tuberculosis*, 61 (1950), p. 586.

43. *JP*, 7:394–95; 11:62, 67, 188; 12:718–19, 734, 802.

44. *NYCD*, 8:243.

45. Moreover, some individuals, and perhaps societies as a whole, may adapt

to stress more successfully than others. In addition, dispersals of people as well as violent revolution, natural catastrophes, and excessive strivings may be to some individuals or groups less stressful than more mundane matters of life. Harold G. Wolff, *Stress and Disease*, 2nd ed. (Springfield, Ill.: Thomas, 1968), p. 5.

46. Laurence M. Hauptman, *Iroquois Field Notes*, 1976–1979.

47. "Although stress is commonly thought of as destructive, it is not necessarily so. Frustration and misfortune may lead, and perhaps be essential to the growth and strengthening of a person, just as they may also lead to maladaptive reactions." Wolff, *Stress and Disease*, p. 5.

Chapter 7—VICTIM VERSUS VICTIM

1. [Lewis Cass], "Documents and Proceedings relating to the Formation and Progress of a Board in the City of New York, for the Emigration, Preservation, and Improvement of the Aborigines of America. July 22, 1829." in *The North American Review*, New Series 21, 30, 66 (January 1830):63; U.S., Congress, House, *Preliminary Report on the Eighth Census. 1860*, by Joseph C. G. Kennedy, Superintendent of the Census, 37th Cong., 2d sess., 1862, pp. 136, 245–94. The *Preliminary Census 1860* divided the Indians who were recorded into two categories: "Indian population in the States and Territories not enumerated in the Census and retaining their tribal character" (p. 136) and "Indians included in the white population" (e.g., p. 245).

State	Tribal	"Included in white population"	Total
New York	3,785	140	3,925
Georgia	377	38	415
Alabama	—	160	160
Mississippi	900	2	902
Ohio	—	30	30
Indiana	384	290	674
Illinois	—	32	32

2. Francis Parkman, *Montcalm and Wolfe*, intro. Samuel Eliot Morison (New York: Collier, 1962), pp. 174–206.

3. Studies of the Oneidas and these Algonquin neighbors include Jeremy Belknap and Jedidiah Morse, *Report on the Oneida, Stockbridge and Brotherton Indians: 1796*, Museum of the American Indian, Heye Foundation, Notes and Monographs no. 54 (New York: Museum of the American Indian, Heye Foundation, 1955); Commissioners of the Land Office in Answer to a Resolution Calling Upon Them for Information in Relation to the Stockbridge Indians, "Report," Doc. 30, *Documents of the Senate of the State of New York*, 89th Sess. (1866), 1:1–6; Special Committee to Investigate the Indian Problem of the State of New York, Appointed by the Assembly of 1888, *Report*, Doc. 51, 7 Ass. Docs., 112th Sess. (1889) [also known as the Whipple Report], pp. 8–9, 45–46, and passim; J. K. Bloomfield, *The Oneidas* (New York: Alden Brothers, 1907); Robert E. Ritzenthaler, "The Oneida Indians of Wisconsin," *Bulletin of the Public Museum of the City of Milwaukee* 19, 1 (November 1950):1–52; Richard H. Kohn, Report, Petitioners' Pro-

posed Findings, *The Oneida Nation of New York . . .* vs. *The United States of America,* Indian Claims Commission, Docket 301 (Claims 3–7), 1971; and Jack Campisi, "Ethnic Identity and Boundary Maintenance in Three Oneida Communities" (Ph.D. diss., State University of New York at Albany, 1974).

4. Great Wave, a Menominee chief, 9 August 1827, testimony (translated) before Lewis Cass and Thomas L. McKenney, in "Extracts from the Journal of a Treaty," in U.S., Congress, Senate, *Correspondence on the Subject of the Emigration of Indians,* furnished . . . by the Commissary General of Subsistence, 23d Congress, 1st sess., 5 vols. (Washington: Printed by Duff Green, 1835; reprint ed., New York: AMS Press, 1974) 2:541. Hereafter cited as *Correspondence.*

5. Anthony F. C. Wallace, *The Death and Rebirth of the Seneca* (New York: Vintage Books of Random House, 1969), pp. 141–44, 194–202; Barbara Graymont, *The Iroquois in the American Revolution* (Syracuse, N.Y.: Syracuse University Press, 1972), pp. 192–235.

6. "An Act relating to the purchase of lands from the Stockbridge Indians, and for the relief of settlers on the same," 1825, and "An Act to authorize the Brothertown Indians to sell and dispose of their lands in this state," 1827, in *Laws of the Colonial and State Governments, Relating to Indians and Indian Affairs, from 1633 to 1831, Inclusive* (Washington City: Thompson and Homans, 1832; reprint ed., Stanfordville, N.Y.: Earl M. Coleman Enterprises, 1979), pp. 117, 127.

7. [Cass], "Documents and proceedings," pp. 113–15.

8. This is an Oneida account passed from generation to generation and told to me by the prominent Oneida Oscar Archiquette 9 July 1970, at Shell Lake, Wisconsin. cf. [Cass], "Documents and Proceedings," pp. 113–15.

9. Great Wave, 9 August 1827, testimony (translated), in *Correspondence,* 2:541.

10. The following, all published in their latest editions by the University of Oklahoma Press, represent the research of Foreman and Debo. Grant Foreman, *Indians and Pioneers* (1930, 1936); *Indian Removal* (1932, 1953), and *Advancing the Frontier* (1933). Angie Debo, *The Rise and Fall of the Choctaw Republic* (1934, 1967); *The Road to Disappearance: A History of the Creek Indians* (1941); and *A History of the Indians of the United States* (1970).

11. Samuel Stambaugh, 4 August 1831, to John H. Eaton, secretary of war, in *Correspondence,* 2:524–28. Stambaugh refers to Eleazar Williams as "a half-breed of the St. Regis [Mohawk] tribe," (in ibid., p. 525). However, the United States commissioners negotiating at Butte des Morts in August 1827, refer to Williams as "a half-breed of the Oneida tribe," ("Extracts from the Journal of a Treaty," in ibid., p. 541). For a brief account of Williams and his involvement with the Oneidas, see Ritzenthaler, "The Oneida Indians," pp. 11–12.

12. Stambaugh, 4 August 1831, to Eaton, in *Correspondence,* 2;529; Pierre Grignon, deposition at Green Bay, Wisconsin, 17 June 1824, in ibid., p. 538.

13. Stambaugh, 4 August 1831, to Eaton, in ibid., p. 527.

14. Great Wave, 9 August 1827, testimony, in ibid., p 541.

15. Stambaugh, 4 August 1831, to Eaton, in ibid., p. 527.

16. George B. Porter, Journal, 1832, in ibid., 4:38.

17. Stambaugh, 4 August 1831, to Eaton, in ibid., 2:517; Porter, 3 February 1832, to Cass, in ibid., 3:185; Grizzly Bear, speech (translated) to Porter, 23 October 1832, in ibid., 4:32.

18. Kohn, Report, Indian Claims Commission, p. 46.

19. Thomas L. McKenney, March 1825, to Major Henry B. Brevoort, in *Correspondence,* 2:542.

20. Thomas L. McKenney, *Memoirs, Official and Personal,* intro. Herman J. Viola (Lincoln: University of Nebraska Press, 1973), p. 81.

21. Ibid., pp. 83–84.

22. Stambaugh, 4 August 1831, to Eaton, in *Correspondence*, 2:528.

23. Ibid., pp. 531–32.

24. Ibid., pp. 530.

25. Stambaugh, 18 July 1831, address to Menominees, in ibid., 2:547.

26. Grizzly Bear, 23 October 1832, speech (translated) to Porter, in ibid., 4:31.

27. Menominee Chiefs, 16 June 1824, Memorial and Petition (translated), in ibid., 2:536.

28. Great Wave, 9 August 1827, testimony (translated), in ibid., 2:541–42. cf. 526.

29. Treaty with the Menominee, 1831, in Charles J. Kappler, ed., *Indian Affairs, Laws and Treaties*, Vol. II, *Treaties* (Washington, D.C.: USGPO, 1904; reprint ed., New York: Interland Publishing Inc., 1972), pp. 319–20.

30. Grizzly Bear, 23 October 1832, speech (translated) to Porter, and Porter's response, in *Correspondence*, 4:36.

31. Andrew Jackson, 9 January 1832, speech to New York Indian delegation, quoted by Porter, 3 February 1832, to Lewis Cass, in ibid. 3:181. A careful if controversial discussion of how Jackson was guilty of breaking his word to Indians during the removal era is in Michael Paul Rogin, *Fathers and Children: Andrew Jackson and the Subjugation of the American Indian* (New York: Vintage Books, 1975), pp. 319–30. Cf. James C. Curtis, *Andrew Jackson and the Search for Vindication* (Boston: Little, Brown, 1976), p. 109.

32. Treaty with the Menominee, 1832, in Kappler, *Treaties*, pp. 379–80.

33. George Jamison [Seneca], 16 November 1833, report [probably dictated] to Elbert Herring, commissioner of Indian affairs, in *Correspondence*, 4:716.

34. "Chiefs of the Seneca, Onondaga, and Oneida nation [sic] of New York Indians," to Lewis Cass, 3 October 1833, in ibid., 4:714. Indian agent James Stryker refers to these chiefs and other Indians who opposed removal as "recusants." This term, meaning religious dissenters or those who resist authority, was especially applied in England during the sixteenth and seventeenth centuries to those English Roman Catholics who refused to convert to the Anglican faith. Furthermore, the term could be used to imply treason, as recusants are regarded as opposing a sovereign rather than a foreign power. The term as Stryker uses it seems to refer not only to these Iroquois' resistance to United States federal authority, but to their non-Christian beliefs which in 1833 would have been defined either under the code of the Iroquois prophet Handsome Lake (ca. 1735–1815) or under the pre–Handsome Lake religious traditions. Thus the word "recusant" indicates that Stryker perceived the antiremoval Iroquois as refusing to make way for the new wave of a white-imposed future which intended to reform the North American continent much as the Protestant Reformation had altered England and Europe. [Stryker to Herring, 18 November 1833, in ibid., 4:713; Editors of the Oxford English Dictionary, *The Compact Edition of the Oxford English Dictionary: Complete Text Reproduced Micrographically*, 2 vols. (Oxford: Oxford University pres, 1971), 2:2450.]

35. Traditionally there are only eight chiefs in the Seneca nation's council. The number ten may include other leaders, including Pine Tree and/or war chiefs. Or the word "Seneca" may be used as it was frequently during the colonial period by translators as synonymous with "Iroquois Six Nation Confederacy."

36. Seneca Chiefs, 3 October 1833, to Cass, in ibid., 4:714.

37. Muriel H. Wright, *A Guide to the Indian Tribes of Oklahoma* (Norman: University of Oklahoma Press, 1951), pp. 188, 246.

AMERICAN INDIAN ENVIRONMENTS

was composed in ten-point Mergenthaler VIP Palatino and leaded 2 points,
with display type in Report Open by Utica Typesetting Company, Inc.;
printed on 50-pound Warren acid-free Antique Cream paper,
Smyth-sewn and bound over 70-point binder's boards covered with Crown Linen,
and also adhesive bound with 10-point Carolina covers,
by Maple-Vail Book Manufacturing Group, Inc..;
and published by

SYRACUSE UNIVERSITY PRESS
SYRACUSE, NEW YORK 13210